HARMED
AND
DANGEROUS

RAY HILL

WITH MATT TROLLOPE

MT Ink

MT.Ink

Published by MT Ink, 2024
ISBN (Hardback) 978-1-8383883-2-4
ISBN (Paperback) 978-1-8383883-5-5

Cover artwork: Vaibhav Punia
Cover font: Bebas Neue

A catalogue record of this book is
available from the British Library.

Anecdotes and conversations in this book have been written and paraphrased based on the author's recollection of relevant events in his life, and in some cases fictionalised.

The views of the author, whether in this book or online, are not necessarily those of the publisher or the ghostwriter.

To explore film, TV and stage rights contact us at MT.Ink

Printed and bound in Great Britain by Bell & Bain Ltd, Glasgow

It's very easy to become a criminal without understanding the guidelines. I see everybody in jail as a victim one way or another.
— John Lydon

SOME OF THE NAMES HAVE BEEN CHANGED TO PROTECT THE GUILTY

Ray Hill

DEDICATION

To Mum...

CONTENTS

FOREWORD by Shaun Attwood

Within minutes of interviewing Ray Hill two years ago, my camera crew and I were mesmerised by his candid, hard-hitting and fast-paced delivery. It's a skill guaranteed to grip the readers of this book, which charts Ray's rise through the criminal ranks, after a traumatic childhood created a disruptive and violent robbery-minded teenager, hellbent on earning a living by any means necessary.

To have a story is one thing, to be able to tell it another. I would class Ray in the top ten raconteurs out of more than a thousand people I have interviewed.

Ray is lucky to be alive. His near death experiences are countless and started at a young age. They range from a deeply disturbed convict attempting to shank him to death to guards unleashing their fury on Ray's body which they had injected with an immobilisation drug. It's almost as if amid the darkest recesses of the UK's barbaric penal system of 50 years ago, Ray had a guardian angel that allowed his enemies to push him to the brink of death, only to intervene to save him just in time.

Or perhaps what saved him was the karmic credit from his moral code. Ray is an old-school villain with traditional values that include not harming innocent people, especially women and kids, whose safety he champions. Whenever he encountered a convict who had harmed females or children, especially if the crimes were of a sexual nature, Ray would, without a second thought, risk his life and freedom to dispense convict justice. Such stories are some of the most compelling in this book, which also discusses whether Ray's abusive childhood can be blamed for his life of crime, or could he have possibly 'inherited' the criminal leanings of a father he never knew.

A root cause of his vigilante violence against sex offenders and rapists lies in his own horrific experiences from five years of age, which rendered sickening injuries that required hospitalisation. Ray deserves credit for having the bravery to detail what happened to him, a subject that many survivors try, often with great difficulty, to bury in their past. It is a double tragedy that even after his abuser was apprehended, Ray's resultant wayward behaviour condemned him to an even more unimaginable fate.

Ray told me that he believes he became the black sheep of his family because of this childhood trauma. In my *Tedx Talk, Sex-Abuse Survivors and Heroin Users Transformed My Worldview,* I posit that childhood trauma is the primary root cause of crime, and Ray's incredible story backs this up. Sadly, for many of the survivors of the care homes from that era, their lives are cut short by self-medication using hard drugs and alcohol. But not Ray. It is a testament to his spirit that such a formidable character emerged from the hell that he endured as a child. The dark energy that would have consumed an average person was challenged by Ray's discipline for fitness, so that he emerged as a powerhouse of a human being — a rough yet appealing anti-hero.

Because Ray was in prison across five different decades, this book also looks at how both committing crime and serving time have changed dramatically in his lifetime, influenced by advances in technology and the rise of drug gangs.

Some of Ray's most compelling tales relate to battles with rivals while incarcerated or ex-military guards seeking retribution. He established himself as the hardest of hard men. He knew how to handle himself and how to make a weapon if need be. This skill set did not go unnoticed by organised crime, who are quick to recruit warriors of the prison system. With such a résumé, perhaps it was inevitable that Ray would become an enforcer, working with crime families and legendary faces. Yet throughout it all, Ray maintained his old school values.

Harmed And Dangerous has a fascinating cast of characters, ranging from associates of iconic London gangsters, the Krays, Ronnie and Reggie ...to warped sex offenders, notorious bank-robbers, drug-addled rock stars...and some of the most notorious and evil serial killers in the UK.

Having myself been involved in a life of crime for over a decade, I now look back at how absurd it all was. With Ray living a criminal existence most people couldn't even comprehend, I can only imagine how, in the heat of the action, it seemed perfectly normal to him too. Drug addiction made it even harder for Ray to grasp any sense of reality.

Fortunately, Ray was handed one last chance to rehabilitate and to try and finally go straight, more out of necessity than choice. As usual with Ray, there were more bumps in the road.

Ray now inspires young people through his *YouTube* channel: *'Bang Bang' Ray Hill*. He shines a light on the dark reality of prison in contrast to the glamorisation of crime prevalent in movies and music videos, and the tabloid-induced belief for young people that prison is all about PlayStations and gourmet food. With many from his generation deceased, Ray is one of the few remaining old-school villains qualified to tell stories about the consequences of the gangster lifestyle, and by looking at the comments on his *YouTube* channel, it seems as if people worldwide are listening and absorbing his life lessons.

PROLOGUE

My life has always been about survival. That's why I always had to come across as 'Charlie big potatoes' in prison. Why I had to quickly establish myself at the start of a stretch.

Inside, there are potential red flags on an hourly basis. I had to be on guard every minute of the 27 years in total that I spent inside. Always looking, always sensing. A process and structure that actually kept me busy.

My aim was to be quickly running my wing and letting anybody in my way know about it. Then when new people came in, if I'd had issues with them in the past, it didn't matter, because I already had a good rep and name. Now they needed me, more than I did them.

Each time I was away, the rug had literally been pulled from underneath my feet again, but it all came with the territory of being a career criminal and living a life of constant contrasts.

Like being couped up in a grubby prison cell on a ropey old mattress with years left on my sentence...or rolling around with a girlfriend on a bed of cash in a five star hotel after an armed robbery. One week earning thousands of pounds as a feared enforcer, the next banged up again, barely earning twenty quid a week working day-in-day-out in a prison kitchen.

Abuse, in many forms, has also been a constant in my life. A damaged and fractured childhood led to destructive adult years plagued by violence, villainy, poor choices and drugs.

Could one final crazy crackpot job possibly save my life?

It's so difficult to say how much my troubled start influenced my life of crime, but I hope this book helps explain where I came from and how the fuck, via a dozen or so stays at Her Majesty's pleasure, I ended up here...and somehow still in one piece!

WRONG SIDE OF THE TRACKS

Sitting in the coal bunker, shaking and sobbing, felt safer than indoors. With bath water a luxury, I was usually filthy dirty anyway. Constantly bashed up by my brother, or getting a hiding from Mum because of my violent temper, the bunker was my sanctuary. Barely seven years old, and so confused. Sexually abused for half of my young life.

Mum was a good woman, with four jobs — first thing in the morning at the laundrette, then cleaning rounds, including at the cinema following her shift there as an ice cream lady.

I was born at Park Royal Hospital, Raymond Roy Stephen John Rowlings, and I guess I craved a father figure ever since my dad, Patrick, died from pleurisy in 1952 when I was one. Just 32 years old, he worked as a paint sprayer, building coaches. I'm convinced every son needs a father, because in a mother's eyes, ultimately, that boy can do no wrong...but I have no recollection of my old man. Mum would tell me years later that he bashed her up loads. If he had lived a longer life, and kept that up, who knows what I would have done to him. I wouldn't have stood for that.

Home was a small flat in a house alongside the rail tracks, bang on the level crossing, opposite Acton Central station in East Churchfield Road. Just one bedroom for me and my older brother and sister, a front room our mum slept in, and a tiny kitchen.

Only a few years since the end of the Second World War, the house was partially derelict. The back side was smashed to pieces and unsafe. Many families still lived in prefabs. Poverty was everywhere. Our clothes, always a size smaller or larger, were either hand-me-downs or came from jumble sales. But Mum always did the best she could.

The only bath in our whole house was in the basement, shared with the other tenants in the building. Mum couldn't afford to feed the meter on the boiler with shillings or sixpences to get us hot water, so she came to an arrangement with others who lived there. When they'd finished their baths, she put us in their dirty lukewarm water for free. The smell was awful, disgusting. A big coal man lived in the top flat, so if we went after him you couldn't see the bottom of the tub.

On very, very rare occasions, Mum treated us to our own water, but I was still the last one in. She caught me and my brother scrapping in the bath one day and flipped, pushing both of us under. My brother grabbed on to a pipe but I had nothing to hold on to. When Mum pulled me out I was unconscious. Still only a toddler, I remember coming round in our bunk beds. I've never felt safe around water since.

Sure, I was the naughty younger brother a lot of the time, but fighting with Keith and Diana, four or five years older than me, was spiteful and caused me awful migraines. When I was about four or five, Mum gave birth to another sister, Jackie, from a brief relationship with another man. I was too young to understand.

I took my aggression to East Acton Infants School, and started beating up the other kids. My anger spilled out, but I felt like it wasn't my fault. Headmistress Miss Pengally couldn't handle me. She tried tying cloth plimsole bags around my hands to stop me grappling with my classmates, but I'd move the material in between my fingers and still be able to fight.

Asking Aunty Gladys and Uncle Don to babysit me after school at their house in Hammersmith seemed like a good idea to Mum. I'm not even sure she knew how much time I spent in the attic with Gladys' brother Eric. He'd take me up there to 'play' and soon made me do things to him, which I didn't understand, but seemed improper, even to a five year old. The sexual assaults continued for many weeks, and only fuelled my anger on the outside. I became more and more violent towards my brother, sisters and Mum.

The term paedophile wasn't widely used or known about then, but looking back now in the years directly after and since, I have a weird feeling that Gladys knew Eric was that way — maybe even Don did too — but they were somehow powerless to stop him.

Mum came to collect me from the house one day. Keith ran upstairs to the attic to get me, and found me laying on the bed naked, playing with some medals. Eric threatened Keith, so he was too scared to say anything, and ushered him downstairs while I got dressed. Because of the awkward atmosphere, Mum and us kids left quickly, and got the next trolley bus home. Mum sat me on her lap and out of nowhere, whacked me round the head and pushed me to the floor. I saw the blood all over her clothes, as she noticed unusual stains on mine. She was incensed. I was so frightened.

Blood was pouring down my legs as Mum marched us back to the house, bewildered. How could she imagine I had been penetrated anally at that house? Now she began asking questions, screaming, 'Who has done this to my son?' Aunty and Uncle looked helpless. Blank expressions. No explanations.

Mum took me home and tried to clean me up. It was only then that she realised I was bleeding behind my testicles, where Eric had literally split me open. I was taken to the Hammersmith (Charing Cross) Hospital and sewn back up. Growing up, I was told the scar was from a cyst.

Mum went to see her brother, my uncle Roy, a sergeant at Hammersmith police station, who sent a team of officers to deal with Eric. I'm told they nearly killed the geezer — smashed him to pieces. Thankfully, he was eventually charged and convicted and given a seven-year jail sentence. I wasn't told any of this until many years later. It's only in recent times that Keith has explained his side of the story, fearful that when old enough I would have found Eric and killed him, which is probably true.

To add to the trauma, I wrongly believed in later life that I was in fact abused by my uncle Roy's brother in-law, also a copper, in a local station house. As a child, I was just unable to process where and when these things happened. It certainly wouldn't help my attitude towards the police.

*****

At school, I became more and more disruptive. My vulnerable mind was unable to work out exactly what I'd experienced. I was now a serious risk to the other children. I smashed up the classroom, and other kids, on a regular basis.

Miss Pengally recommended that I was sent to a children's home. It was the last thing Mum wanted, but she reluctantly agreed. The papers were signed and I was sent to Wales, possibly with a view to being eventually fostered by another family, out of the glare of my twisted life in London and the toxic environment I'd grown up in.

The train tickets to Wales were paid for, and Mum travelled down with me from Paddington. As we sat with a couple of old suitcases in a 12-seater carriage, I really thought I was going to the seaside for a few days. Although, my brother and sister weren't with us, so that was strange.

Mum had been more affectionate to me since the abuse, and clearly wanted the best for me, but going to Wales was nothing other than catastrophic. Mum was so upset as she cuddled me goodbye, and then she was gone. I was surrounded by other kids, so it felt exciting. It was 1957. I was six.

I was assigned a bed in one of the dormitories at the home. Boys and girls mixed together, but mostly boys. There seemed to be more playtime during our daily classroom-based lessons, than at school.

I remember we were taken to the beach, only a few minutes away, quite regularly...maybe they treated us nicely at times to make the other things that happened seem better. We were taken in one of those old coaches, with the big noses. I caught a little eel one day with a lolly stick. I took it back and put it in the fish tank at the home. It might have been a fucking worm for all I knew.

After dinner, which was late afternoon, we'd be put to bed, chatting and mucking around together, until lights out, early evening.

On my first night, in and out of sleep, I noticed other kids were woken up and led away from their beds by members of staff at the home. Hand in hand, they were ushered through the door at the end of the dorm. They returned through the same door, maybe an hour or two later, sobbing.

Three or four days in, it was my turn. Finally, I would find out what happened behind that door. I knew it couldn't be nice.

I shuddered as a female and a male member of staff collected me, one taking me by the hand, both walking slowly towards the door. Down a steep staircase, then sat in a room on my own. Given fruit pastilles sweets and orange squash.

When the door opened again, a man, who I didn't recognise, came in the room. An outsider, who seemed 'well-to-do'. Posh. Not really Welsh. Although coming from Acton, most accents would have sounded posh to me. The man gave me more sweets, and then cuddled me for a while. Then he asked me to hold his hand. It all seemed quite innocent.

Sometimes, a man came in the room on his own. Other times it was a man with a woman. Never a woman on her own. Then after three or four times, it started getting sexual, although at that age, of course, I still had little idea of what that was exactly. The couples would touch each other, and then me. The men seemed to prefer to do things to themselves, while the women preferred to touch me.

I was now chosen regularly, like the other kids. Always different people coming into the rooms downstairs. Never the same people. It was so hard to understand what was happening, yet I still didn't see much wrong. Maybe because I was so used to it already? I was soon being anally abused again. I began to think that because it had happened to me before, I was easier to penetrate than other kids.

I've always wondered how the staff at the home let that happen to me. They must have known why I had been sent to their home, and probably what had happened to me in the attic. There must have been a report generated, even in those days. I must have had a file, and there would have been a record somewhere of what I had endured. Had the staff at that home purposely taken in kids who had been abused before? It certainly felt more organised, like some sick kind of business.

Each time, I could have been in that room for anything from ten minutes to an hour. As a child that young, it's hard to tell. Once they started messing around with me like that, it seemed like it would never end.

The cycle was continuing. Like getting dropped off at my Uncle and Aunty's a few years earlier, being at the home was meant to help and keep me safer. Of course, again, it had the opposite effect. Now the helpless victim of a paedophile ring, maybe my moral compass was already broken. Just so hard for a child to process. My mum had taken me to both of those places, so was it actually wrong? I still didn't know for sure.

Each day blurred into another. Screams regularly rang out from downstairs at the home. Us kids were always crying in that dorm, either because we'd already been downstairs, were on our way back up or were about to go.

I wondered what happened in the other rooms. I felt bad for the kids maybe experiencing it for the first time. Because I had been sewn up before, maybe I wasn't as tight down there as them so it didn't hurt as much. Such horrible thoughts for a child to have.

One day, my mum appeared and picked me up. Thank God! She couldn't put up with me being away any more. I told her what happened but I think, because she'd made such a fuss of me the last time I was abused, and I'd got lots of sweets and affection, she thought I was trying it on, to get more treats. While I sensed she didn't take it seriously, any disappointment was forgotten because I was so glad to be heading home, even though I was also worried about what I was going back to.

I don't know exactly how long I was at the home, because to a kid, going through what we went through, a day seems like a week. It was probably about six months.

*****

Now back from the horrors of my time in Wales, I became even more disruptive. In fact, I already felt out of control. Increasingly, I began to mess myself. Several times a week. One day, it happened so fast sitting on my mum's lap on the bus to Ruislip Lido, I was dragged to the nearest toilet and given another big hiding.

Aged about seven and now causing havoc at John Perryn Primary School, the coal bunker underneath our house became my refuge, my safe place. A traumatised kid, cold and grubby and covered in soot, his mother always at work. Hiding from his spiteful brother, dreading the cries of, 'Raymond, where are you?' when Mum came home.

I'd shout out, 'I'm downstairs having a wee.'

It was freezing in that outside lavvy…freezing! Our toilet roll was more like writing paper. It was so coarse. Useless. Mum would cut it into squares and put them on a nail on the wall. It felt like I was either covered in coal, dirt…or shit.

Like hot water, we couldn't afford coal either, so when the coal train pulled up at the level crossing yards from our house, Mum lifted me over a fence so I could throw any stray huge lumps of coal back to her. She'd rush home and smash them up for our fire. Occasionally, we'd get caught and had to give the coal men a sob story and plead with them not to call the police.

One afternoon, I heard some mice in the bunker. I went back down with a little cardboard box, and caught a mouse. I fed it small pieces of bread or spiders, collected from small indents in the granite stone walls, and it started to make a nest in the box out of straw and other bits and pieces I collected. One day a spider bit me — at least it felt like a bite. I wanted to kill any spider I could find after that, and did.

I was so relieved to have the coal bunker as an escape. The mouse seemed happy to see me each time, so this relationship gave me comfort, as opposed to the constant aggression upstairs.

Then I made the mistake of telling Keith about my mouse. The next day it wasn't there. My brother told me it had gone to heaven, which was his way of telling me he killed it. I was left wondering where the mouse's body was, so my brother took that closure away from me, as well as our companionship.

I also found a couple of tortoises in the shared garden at the back of our house. One I named Grandpa had a bad crack in its shell, so I tried to look after him the best I could, but it kept wandering off in the middle of the night. I'd be looking for him all the time.

I loved digging in that garden, which had a filled-in air-raid shelter underneath it. One day I found a hand grenade, a dummy one they used during the war. Mum took me to a police station to hand it in and they gave me some sweets. Soon after I found a silver coin from 1371. I couldn't believe it and went inside and washed it. Keith took it to school the next day, and I never saw it again. Said he'd lost it. I went mad and tried to fight him, but there was only ever one winner. The same happened with a gold casket I found. That vanished too.

Only back in Acton a matter of months, I was becoming angrier and angrier, especially at school. Thankfully, my mum refused to send me to another so-called 'care home', but she did speak to her sister, my aunty Nell, who lived nearby in Vale Flats in Vincent Road, and she agreed to look after me for a couple hours a day after school. Mum also cleaned Nell's house.

Mum met a man called Bob Hill, who became my step-father, and we moved to a four-bedroomed detached council house nearby in Mill Hill Road. Bob worked all his life as a security guard at car manufacturers Rootes Motors in Acton, who made the Hillman. Mum and Bob got married when I was six, and Mum asked Bob if the family could take his surname. One day, he announced that it was all sorted. We were now Hills.

*****

Nell Nelhams was a larger-than-life character, who loved me to bits. Everything was, 'fuck, fuck, fuck,' so that started me swearing.

Nell was mother to Terry Nelhams, who growing up pretended to play double bass with a piece of wire and a broom handle attached to huge tea chest at the house. At 19, he was eleven years older than me and had just become the lead singer of the skiffle band, the Worried Men, who had regular evening work at coffee bars in Soho and appeared on *BBC* live music TV show *Six-Five Special*. The producer was so taken by Terry, he pulled some strings and HMV Records signed him on a deal under the stage name Adam Faith.

To our shock, Terry (or Adam) went on to become a huge pop star. By the time I was ten, he'd had seven national Top 5 chart hits in a row, including his first two releases, *What Do You Want* and *Poor Me* going to No 1. It all felt so above us at the time, but you could sense the whole family was proud of him. I'd watch Terry in awe on Nell's small black and white TV — this older cousin of mine now famous. It was unbelievable. On the back of his success, Terry bought Nell a six-bedroomed house off Bromyard Avenue in east Acton, nearer to Shepherd's Bush, and also a confectionary shop in The Vale in Uxbridge Road, which she called Terry's. Mum got a job cleaning both.

Like my own brother, Terry's younger one, Roger, was four years old than me. He was aggro too, so we scrapped all the time as well. Still aggression everywhere I went, it seemed. I also felt, like me, that Roger Nelhams was the black sheep of his family. Nell couldn't really handle it when me and Roger were fighting so hard.

When I was about eight, the fair came to town twice a year in Acton Park. I blagged some work on a rifle range stall, picking corks up off the floor. I'd sneak out of the house through the coal bunker. Mum was furious when she found out. I reckon she thought I could get abused again. She worked so much, my idea was just to try and earn some money for the family, to help Mum out and give her some relief. I'd get dragged off home from the fair, but I'd always sneak out again.

Mum continued to work every hour God sent. She eventually got sacked from the Granada cinema in Acton for letting us kids in through the back doors.

By now, I was always outside headmaster Mr Hatfied's office at junior school, for fighting with both pupils and teachers. I was terrible at reading, and worse at writing. I now know I was dyslexic, but that wasn't a thing back then. I got the cane every week, usually a whack across my wrists, and often messed myself at the same time. Mum went mad one day when I came home in just my pants and shirt. One of my teachers, Mr Wholly, was always throwing chalk rubbers and books at me for being naughty in class, and pushed me too far one day. The next morning, I hid behind the classroom door and, as he walked in, smashed him around the head with a chair. He dropped to the floor and I ran out of class, out of school and straight home. The police came round an hour or so later and gave me a talking to. My mum told them that she couldn't control me.

The authorities wanted to put me back in a home, but thankfully Mum refused. I wasn't suspended or expelled from school, as such, but I was politely told to stay away as much as possible.

SHAKEN, NOT DETERRED

An old boy in a wheelchair began talking to me outside his house at the top of Perryn Road. One day he pulled me closer to him, and put his hand down my trousers. In my naivety, I still hadn't been completely sure whether this was right or wrong, but in this moment something must have clicked.

I was large for my age, and part of a little gang of kids now, all of us nine, ten years old...always up to no good. We had a chat about this geezer in the wheelchair, and all agreed he was out of order. So I took the lads to the house with me and he invited us inside. All matey, matey with him to start with. Then we bashed him up bad, and went through his pockets. Nicked some cash off him, and anything else we could find in the house. Coins, a half crown, a few shillings... and some cigarettes. The old pervert was powerless to defend himself. We never saw him outside his house again. He didn't contact the police, he couldn't. What would he have said?

We decided attacking dirty old men was easy, and I was more than happy to play my part. Already, they seemed like a magnet to me...like they were following me around. We decided to plot up in Acton Park looking for these sickos. There were often a few sat on park benches...or skulking around. Nasty fuckers, waiting for school-boys on their way home. We'd get chatting to them, and almost entice them, like a honey trap. Encourage them to take us in the bushes, and then bash them up. Give us their money, or we'd call the police.

In our gang of kids, I was definitely the leader...the boss of our little lot. I was learning all the time and becoming a force to be reckoned with. A real handful for my age.

I was always on the look out for any extra income, legal or not. I wanted to help my mum out as much as I possibly could. I blagged a job helping out most nights at the blacksmith's across the road, alongside the rail tracks. When lorries turned up with strips of metal, I'd pick up two at a time and bounce them up and down until they slotted on to the storage racks. Sometimes they'd let me drill holes in the sheet metal using a large electric machine.

*****

It was the early 1960s now. I was eleven years old, and Acton Park was base-camp for us. We kept seeing the same guy playing golf, hitting balls from one side of the park to the other. He had an Alsatian called Harry and lived in a large detached house at the other end of the park. I approached the fella one day and said we'd fetch the balls for him, if he paid us. He agreed. Anything from sixpence, a shilling, two-bob to half a crown. This fella obviously had a few quid. Then we worked out who he was. It was only fucking James Bond! Well, Sean Connery to be precise, who had just filmed *Dr No*, the first Bond film.

Connery had just bought a huge gaff, the 12-room Acacia House on Centre Avenue, which overlooked the park, and had just married pretty Australian actress Diane Cilento, so we always saw her around too.

I found some quotes online recently taken from an interview with Connery around that time...

We looked around for ages to find a house in an unfashionable part of London. You can say I'm glad to be here. In Acton nobody bothers to look over the fence to see how James Bond digs his garden.

But, of course, we were always hanging about, in and around the park. The next time the fair came to town, we watched in awe at the boxing ring as local bruisers tried their luck against old prize fighters. Five pounds if you go three rounds with one of them and a tenner if you can knock one out. We heard someone speak up. 'I'll knock him out,' and then the guy running the boxing said, 'Oh look, here's James Bond.' Connery strode forward into the ring, and promptly knocked his opponent out. Of course, it was staged, but we loved it all the same, especially as we already knew 007.

Then Connery's dog Harry gave our Alsatian bitch Girly puppies. We explained it to him, and he came to our house and gave Mum fifty quid for the inconvenience. Our dog was now a Bond girl ...haha.

But there was no room for sentiment. Being little fuckers, we decided to break into Connery's house. One day, we waited at that end of the park for him and his missus to leave. A few hours later, he appeared on the steps with the blonde and drove off in his Aston Martin. I think a DB4, the model before the DB5 he would make famous in his next Bond film, *Goldfinger*.

Three of us climbed the perimeter fence of Acacia House from inside the park and jumped into the back garden. Fortunately, Harry knew us well. I mean, we were almost related. He ran up and licked us when I'm sure he was meant to be scaring off any intruders. He wasn't going to attack us lot though, so we stroked him loads and then knew we had half a chance of breaking in. It was made all the easier because the huge windows at the back of the house had been left open. We climbed through and stood open-mouthed staring at the huge paintings on the wall, including what looked like a nude one of the wife.

We were barely 12 years old, and didn't really have a clue about the value of things, but we went in one room and saw a large cabinet containing several guns, which I later knew to be 12-bore shot guns. We might not have known the specifics of these firearms then but, of course, we sensed their importance.

We spent a few more minutes walking around the house, but took nothing. We were on the look out for any bank notes or coins laying about, but equally didn't want to fuck off Sean Connery, because he'd been good to us. He was a nice fella who took time out to talk to us.

But I did tell one older pal, Trevor, who was on his way to becoming a proper little gangster. He decided he was going to burgle the house, while Connery was away in Spain filming his latest movie, *The Hill*. Trevor took us younger lot with him, so we could take care of Harry, and show him where the guns were.

Trevor took a 'male' and a 'female' shotgun, and gave us a ten shilling note, maybe worth about £15-20 in today's money, for our troubles — a lot of money to us back then but nothing compared to what he could potentially make by selling the guns...or using them.

It came out in an article in the newspaper soon after about the burglary that the guns were from Purdey in Mayfair, who have had Royal Warrants since the 1800s, and were worth thousands of pounds in today's money. By then, Trevor had cut them down into sawn-offs.

Barely teenagers yet but already making headlines for our early blags, we quickly began to think like criminals. Mum showed me the burglary story in the Acton Gazette when it next came out. I pretended to look shocked...and anyway, I could barely read.

Sean Connery began blanking us, like he half knew we were involved in the break-in. Who else would have been able to get past Harry? He couldn't pinpoint us for sure, but he wasn't paying us for collecting golf balls anymore. We had eyes on bigger prizes anyway.

*****

We started hanging out at the Priory Youth Centre in Acton, learning how to box a bit with pads, and I got into weightlifting. I became crazy for weights from that point on. When I did go to school, now Twyford Secondary, as usual, I was always fighting.

We'd hang around Acton public swimming baths — or the fair, at those times of the year. Always scared of water, I couldn't swim, so would walk underwater in the shallow end to make it look like I could. A muscular 16-year-old bully called Brain Sigworth held me under one day, and because it took me back to my brother doing that in the bath as a toddler, I was furious. When he let me back up, I was crying in temper. He put me back down again, but I managed to wrestle free. At the side of the pool, I picked up some wooden slats swimmers stood on to dry off, and hid in a cubicle, fuming. When Sigworth walked past, I leapt out and smashed him over the head with the pieces of wood. Blood pissed from his head as he staggered and fell into the pool. The lifeguards had to fish him out and closed the pool.

The police were called to the baths, and they took me back to Mum's. The sergeant said to her, 'Your son is getting into trouble all the time. He's just attacked a much older kid. This is definitely a concern now.'

All my mates went to Twyford. One, a black kid called Leon, was getting into crime too, and also becoming a boxer like me, so we had a lot in common.

*****

My mum got a job as a dinner lady at Twyford, so always knew when I bunked off. I got suspended on a regular basis, which was fine by me, because I hated school.

The Old Bill didn't even know about my involvement in the burglary at Acacia House yet, so, although I was attracting attention personally, as a group we went under the radar for other things.

I sat down with Leon and another friend, and we plotted a robbery, aged 13. Our first one — a post office at the top of Birkbeck Road in the part of Acton close to where I'd previously lived. As Leon was good at gymnastics, we decided he would vault the counter. We ran in one afternoon, screaming and shouting, no masks and not tooled up. Nothing. Leon leapt over the cashier desks and let the rest of us through. We were opening any drawers we could see, grabbing shilling coins and five and ten pound notes. I think we came away with about £30 each. Again, a lot of money for us back then. Because I now lived in Mill Hill Road, I targeted post offices and shops in my old area, but there was only really a mile or so in between.

A few of us of got together, and said, 'Fuck this, we need money.' So we started breaking into convenience and grocery stores on a regular basis…late at night, after they'd closed. Not much security then, just locks on windows. We'd nick cigarettes and chocolates and either give them to our parents or sell them. My mum seemed quite happy to be given free fags and little bits of cash here and there. No questions asked.

We had spare money now. We bought nice clothes at Woolworths or Burtons. A pair of jeans and a shirt for five or six shillings. We were doing so well out of the robberies; we thought, wow, this is easy. No cameras, so on the face of it, not much risk.

*****

Aged 13-14, me and Leon were really into our boxing, earning a few quid holding our own at the fair when it was in town. We'd both try our luck, and were getting stronger, and lasting longer in the ring all the time. We were turning into hard kids, fighting grown men, robbing shops all the time, earning decent money. Double confident and didn't give a fuck. More boxing at the Priory too, trying to make a name for ourselves. We all wanted to be someone.

When I was 15, I decided I'd join the Norwegian Merchant Navy to try and travel and get out of Acton. I needed to apply for a passport first and that meant getting a copy of my brith certificate from Ealing Town Hall. I was shocked to read it and find out I was actually born indoors at East Churchfield Road, not at the hospital. Of course, the certificate was in my actual surname, Rowlings, and so that was the name I had on that first passport. Mum explained I was actually born at the house, minutes after she'd pushed home a pram full of coal, just over nine months pregnant.

One night at the Priory, a kid my age wanted to fight me because I'd been chatting up his girlfriend. He was smaller than me, so I thought game-on, but I didn't know he was a fucking lunatic. As I left, he smashed me round the head with a bottle. What the fuck! We started scrapping. I didn't knock him out, but I beat him up quite badly, and then he was gone.

A week or so later, I was out doing my thing...scouting robberies, etc. I walked past Woolworths and Lyons Tea House in Acton, and the kid from the Priory came from nowhere and hit me on the shoulder with a lump of lead. This time I knocked him to floor. So I now knew he couldn't fight, but he was definitely dangerous. And just like that, he jumped up and fucked off again. This happened again and again, at least four or five more times. But it was never a straight up fight. He always ambushed me, I bashed him up, and then he legged it.

One day, I was walking down by The Kings Arms in Acton and he spotted me as he drove past in a Morris Mini Minor. He turned the car round, mounted the pavement and smashed me up in the air. As usual, he left the scene quickly. Fortunately, I wasn't badly injured, just a few scratches and bruises.

The Priory kid wasn't old enough to drive, none of us were, but we were always nicking scooters and cars. My brother had a Lambretta, so I'd practise on that, and one of my older mates had a Vesper 180 SS (Supersport), which was like a jet compared to Keith's bike.

I got a slap on the wrist for pinching a scooter and then, aged 15 in the summer of 1966, I was arrested for 'taking and driving away a motor vehicle without consent'. At Acton Magistrates Court, I was fined £20 for the car theft, a tenner for having no insurance, and a fiver for driving without a licence.

I was running out of chances, but in no mood to change my ways.

In one stolen car in early 1967, we were driving away one night from a robbery on a shop, and suddenly heard bells. A big old Woolsey police car was chasing us. A few hundred yards down the road, we had to pull over. Old Bill found loads of cigarettes, alcohol and confectionaries in the boot. The three of us were nicked and banged up in the juvenile wing at Ashford Remand Centre in Kent. Incarcerated for the first time. Banned from driving too, when I wasn't legally allowed to anyway.

This was a huge shock to my system. Banged up for 22 hours a day in single cells because 16s and under couldn't be two'd up in those days. It was harsh and hard to take. My cell contained a bed with a grubby mattress and pillows all made of horse hair (so there was a shape of the kid before on the bed when I first arrived), plus a corner shelving unit, a table and chair, both with big thick legs, an aluminium piss-pot and a jug.

All the screws were huge ex-military types, and the atmosphere was as regimental as you'd expect. At the start, it was easy for kids to crack up in there. First thing in the morning, you'd have to box up your bed with the blanket, sheet and cover all squared up. Your soap dish and brush by the side of it. Never allowed to lay or sit on your bed during the day. Until such time that you heard, 'Bed!' Then you could put everything back and make up your bed again.

I tried not to get involved in fights, but had loads of scraps. Unavoidable.

At night, some of the guards would creep up on a cell, unlock it and bash up the kid inside. You could hear a fart four cells down, but you couldn't hear those screws about to come through the door.

One screw involved, Hopper, a PTI (physical training instructor) was an awful old man who made us do bunny-hops everywhere. Such a bully. One day, he came in the canteen, shouting at everyone. A few of the lads got together and smashed him to pieces with food trays, and busted his legs and knees. They nearly killed him. I thought, fucking hell, this is prison, this is heavy. You have to attack this thing head on.

*****

My case came up a long month or so later in February 1967 at Acton Magistrates Court — charged with theft, taking a motor vehicle without consent and driving with no insurance. Strangely, given my passport, all this was in the name of Raymond Hill.

Now, enough was enough. I got a 'six to 2' — i.e six months to two years. At a borstal. Fucking hell...for nicking a few sweets but, of course, my latest motoring and theft conviction was just one too many. I wasn't even driving, it was Leon, but he somehow got off with another warning.

I was sent to Portland Borstal in Dorset. One of the worst ones. Hard as nails.

I was put on a wing called Rodney House, again in a single cell. We were made to wear formal shirts, like a uniform. We had to sit at dinner with our arms crossed and were only allowed to uncross them when told to eat.

Each day consisted of a routine of 'shops' — i.e 'workshops' — where everything was colour-coded and graded, plus as much exercise as you could fit in either side. I tried to progress through the system any way I could, but it was hard.

There was a 'Daddy' on each wing, the kids who could really have a row, and were therefore in charge. Fights all the time, because everybody wanted to get known. Two kids somehow crushed up a razor blade into one boy's toothbrush, so it cut his mouth to fuck. I think being exposed to that kind of violence meant I was even more desensitised.

I stepped up and fought the Daddy on my wing...and won. So now I was the 'Daddy', who got the most tobacco, sweets and things like toiletries and soap parcels — 'donated' by other kids from supplies brought in during their family visits.

After six months, and consistently getting into trouble, and never progressing through the colour system, and so no nearer to getting released, I decided I'd try to escape, which was possible at Portland, because it was like its own island overlooking cliffs, near the water's edge. Loads tried, because it was so tough-going in there. If you got over the wall, it'd be difficult from there, though. You'd need to climb over bridges. Like most, I was caught, and the screws were like, right, this cunt can have it now. I soon realised I'd be doing at least two years, rather than six months. Nobody did six months there, no chance.

I had no visits in my whole time at Borstal. It was too far for my mum to travel, and I didn't want her to come anyway. I was allowed a double-sided one-page letter each month from her. And that letter was everything. A taste of the outside world. Confirmation that someone out there was on my side. But this privilege could be taken away at any point for bad behaviour. I didn't write back because I wasn't confident enough to put my feelings down on paper. Borstal was regimental, but hardly academic. I didn't feel like I learned much.

I was moved to Rochester Borstal, a recall centre...THE hardest one out there. The ultimate military operation. In the gym every day, all day, the screws battering you all the time. They tried to break us, but we came out so well-trained. It was the fittest any of us had ever been.

I had a gang of new friends with one common goal — to become professional armed robbers...and I hadn't ever been armed on a job yet.

I was finally released in the summer of 1969 after almost two and half years at Borstal, picked up by Leon. I was 18 and all I could think about was earning money whichever way I could, becoming a boxer...and pulling girls. The testosterone in my body at that age was crazy. I was unbelievably fit and in my mind, I was going back to robbing — one hundred per cent.

ROBBERY SQUAD

If I was determined to rob again, I also needed a bread and butter day job to fall back on. At Brentford Fruit Market, like most of my life so far, criminality was everywhere.

To start with, I had to put time in at the market, helping out in the evenings as a stand boy, until I got a regular job as a night porter on 'Northside'. The site was huge, home to more than a thousand stands, stalls and barrows. And full of 'gangsters', for want of a better word. I soon realised everyone was at it. So no chance of this job keeping me on the straight and narrow, even if I wanted it to. I'd arrive at midnight and finish at 5am, but stay on because there was money to be made.

My job at the start of my shift was to unload fruit and veg from lorries, which were meant to arrive at midnight ahead of the market opening at 4am for visiting greengrocers. I became part of a little firm of porters — skimming stuff from everywhere.

One of the managers at the market approached us.

'Anything you lot get your hands on, you sell to me, so go and make yourself busy.'

We'd break into the back of huge lorries from overseas, while their drivers slept waiting for the day porters to arrive. A lot of the night security guards were with us and onside.

The market manager took us on trips to Covent Garden and Spitalfields markets to get more stock for various traders. Always on the fiddle, keeping some back for ourselves.

We were not kids anymore, fast becoming young men, always up for any 'street-fights' held at the market. I was now boxing for London Transport in Chiswick at their big gym, trained by George Whelan.

Up to 200 greengrocers watched fights at 'Strawberry Row' on Block 6. Not for money and without a referee. All about enhancing reputations among street-fighting families. Loads of blokes who could have a row. Colin Cracknell, a great boxer and management at the market, called it on with me. One bag glove each on opposite hands. Six rounds. He smashed me to bits. I didn't mind because I wanted to learn the game, and Colin taught me how to fight. I wanted to be him. That hard.

*****

I still lived at Mum's, but also rented a room in a block of flats in Brentford and sometimes crashed at a place in Hayes too. In the summer, straight after our night shifts, we'd hang out all day at the outdoor swimming pool in Chiswick — chatting up girls until we were knackered, then sleep until our next shift at midnight. A huge bald Indian guy, all 25 stone of him, called Spike, who drove a Cadillac and reckoned he'd been a villain in a Bond film, thought he was a ladies man and would try and chat up anything in sight at the pool. He was becoming a bit of nuisance, so I told him to behave himself. He growled at me so I chinned him. He didn't move an inch and just shook his head at me, so I thought, fuck that, and kept my distance after that.

I took Leon to the market a couple of times to try and get him some work, but each time was pulled to one side. It was such a white market, so unfortunately a closed shop for my mate. A few weeks later, he was sent to Honeycomb Borstal for a robbery I wasn't involved in.

I came out of the market one day, mid-morning, and saw a Vesper SS with a key in it, so I started it up, and drove off. I headed for the Chiswick roundabout, and down to Hanger Lane and jumped on the North Circular. This thing flew. I was doing about 80 mph and suddenly realised the police were up my arse. At a set of lights, I revved up too fast, the front wheel went up. I skidded, and crashed into a fence and the bike landed on top of me. The Old Bill nicked me and I appeared at Acton Magistrates. Fined £150 and banned from driving again — even though I was already driving without a licence and had never had one.

At the market, business was good...especially our side hustles.

All we wanted was more money, so with a robbing culture and mentality always present, it just seemed natural to us to be involved at whatever level we could. We began doing really well, sometimes earning up to £200-300 a day each. Crazy cash back in the late '60s.

We were regulars at The Ivy Shop in Richmond, where we bought American brogue shoes, Doctor Marten boots, Ben Sherman shirts, nice mohair suits, trilby hats, stay-press trousers (worn with turn-ups) and Levi's jeans. All about pulling girls and being a chap.

At the market we wore long leather aprons, a scarf and a cheese cutter cap. We were big guys, we had a swagger about us, a bounce and a flash bowl from side to side.

In the evenings, we'd spend our ill-gotten gains at clubs like The Boathouse at Kew Bridge or Cheekee Pete's and The Castle, both in Richmond, where there was a Wimpy Bar nearby. We'd all end up in there after nights out for a burger meal.

One time after Cheekee Pete's with the Collins brothers and Johnny Wells, there was a group of guys standing in our way at the front of the Wimpy. I was wearing a Prince Of Wales check suit, a Ben Sherman button down shirt with a tie, and a trilby hat. Dapper. I said 'Excuse me,' to this lot and one came back with, 'Fuck me, this geezer looks like a clown.' Bobby Collins nudged his brother. 'Right, let's sort this out,' but Whacker Collins said, 'Don't worry, Ray will get this done in a few seconds.' And I did. Bam, I hit one with a right hand, then bosh, the second one with a left hook. Then, smash, I wiped out the third one with another right. A powerful combination that put them all on the floor. Of course, we had to fuck off the Wimpy, so we bowled off down the road. A few minutes later, a Ford Cortina came from nowhere and mounted the pavement. Bobby pulled me out of the way, and the car smashed into a shop front, crashing through its large windows. These idiots managed to reverse and drive off in their smashed up motor, so we jumped into Bobby's Jag and chased them down to Ham Gate, where we called it a day and headed home.

There was a knock on my bedroom window after one night out. It was Leon. Unlike me, he had managed to escape from Borstal. I let him sleep under my bed and the next morning tried to take my breakfast to my room, so I could give some to Leon, but Mum rumbled me.

'What's he doing in your fucking room?'

Because, I hadn't told my mum Leon had been put away, I said, 'Oh, his mum has chucked him out...'

'I'm sorry, Ray. Leon is trouble, he has to go.'

We were both trouble, of course. Leon was eventually caught and recalled back to Borstal.

One day I popped into see my mum while she was having her hair done in a salon in Bollo Bridge Road. A junior stylist took a shine to me so I got my mum to ask her out on my behalf. Even before our first date, the girl at Mum's hairdressers bought me a vest from Biba and a bottle of Aramis after-shave.

When Leon was finally released from Borstal, we hung out at local gyms whenever we could, always trying to bulk ourselves up.

*****

I met a stocky guy at the market called Mark and a blond fella, Gerry. Mark worked for a potato firm, lugging huge bags of spuds around all day. Colin Cracknell was fitter than him, but Mark had massive arms and could have a row.

As I approached my 20s, I started doing bits of work with Mark in and around the market. We bought a lorry and did well for ourselves as the new decade, the 1970s, began.

One night as we drove past an off licence shop in a precinct in Brentford in Mark's Zephyr Zodiac, a shopkeeper walked out into the street with what looked like two big money bags and headed for a car park at the back of the parade.

'Fucking hell, have a look,' I said.

We saw him another time after that on his own again, so me, Mark and Gerry decided to hit this late on a Saturday night, when the takings would be at their best. It would be my first armed robbery, using a bolt-action .410 shot-gun with silver cartridges, given to me by a connection at the market. No masks, and just me tooled up. We parked up and saw the guy walk to his van, as usual, but for some reason I didn't fancy it. Sometimes, it just doesn't feel right. It's in your gut, and you have to walk away.

We worked all that week, ducking and diving at the market as usual but, used to spending money now, it was becoming harder to keep up with our own lifestyles.

The next Saturday we met near the off licence shop. I'd been down there a bit earlier than Mark and Gerry, having a walk around. The boys parked up in the car park at the back of the shop, and when the shopkeeper came out, at the usual time, they left the car and stood to the side. As the guy got in his van and threw the money bags into the footwell on the passenger side, I pounced, and pulled him back. I hadn't bargained on a huge long-haired Alsatian jumping on me from inside the back of the van. Instinctively, I punched the dog in the jaw, and he let out a massive whine. I'd hit him so hard, the poor thing scampered underneath the van. I started to bash the guy up, screaming at him, 'Give me the fucking bags, give me the fucking bags.' I managed to wrestle them from him, turned round to look for the others, and they'd fucked off in the motor. Gone.

For the first few seconds I was fuming, then I realised both the bags were now mine. I started running down the road towards Acton. Within half a mile I heard, 'Beep, beep.' It was Mark.

I was like, 'Why the fuck did you drive off?', but was also delighted to see him.

Mark drove me back to my mum's, and I went inside and counted the money in my room. Two thousand pounds, in notes. A grand in each bag. As ever, a lot of money in 1970. I gave Mark £500 and kept the rest. Gerry could fuck himself. Mark ran with him, but at least he came back. He should be happy with a monkey because by the time he appeared, I could have been nicked.

In reality, those two both shit themselves because of the dog but, luckily, I wasn't scared of Alsatians.

The next day I went to The Anchor and Gerry was there, shouting his mouth off.

'You fucking cunt, you haven't give me a penny.'

'But you left the job.'

'That was all Mark.'

We were having it out in a proper villain's pub – the worst place to shout the odds about an armed robbery — especially with off-duty coppers often lurking about for bits of information.

The only way to sort this out with Gerry was to have it out in the car park. I'd heard he could fight, now it was time to find out. He was whacking me about at the back of the pub, about to give me a good hiding, so I thought, fuck this, and kicked him in the bollocks. He fell to the floor, and then I steamed in and finished him off.

The day after I took a girlfriend to the Skyline Hotel at Heathrow Airport and booked us a room for two nights. We had a great time there, sitting round the indoor pool, enjoying slap-up meals, buying clothes from the hotel boutique, getting pissed and rolling around on a bed full of bank notes just because we could.

The success of the job and the cash in my hand made me want more. I'd been watching an independent bookmaker in Hounslow for a while, and its owner depositing his cash in a night-safe at his local bank. I'd discussed it with Mark and Gerry before the off licence job but they reckoned there'd be nothing in it, so as I pretty much did the last job on my own anyway, I decided, fuck 'em, I'll take care of this one myself too. As the guy walked towards the night-safe, I came from behind and grabbed the bag, a leather pouch, and legged it home. When I got back to my mum's, I was delighted to count out three grand in cash. I hid the bags in my mum's garden later that night, with the bags from the off licence, and gave the money from this latest job to a friend to look after.

Banking was so different back then. A pal of mine came up with a blag, where he put a sticker on the night-safe, which said there was an issue, and cash should be put through the letter box. Amazingly, quite a few people did. My mate would come back in the early hours with a large piece of wood attached to the back of his car, and ram-raid the front door of the bank and help himself to the readies. Easy…but you could never get away with that now.

*****

A few days after my smash and grab, I was in bed that morning, when I heard a big bang on my mum's front door. It was her brother, Sergeant Roy Jenkins, from Brentford police station.

'Hello, Ray.'

'Alright, Roy.'

'Ray, you're nicked!'

'What!'

Privately, I was thinking…for which job? I'd done a few recently.

'Listen, Ray, we know it's you. The off licence…where's the money, Ray?'

'What money?'

'Listen, just give us the money, we'll come to some arrangement.'

Then he started putting pressure on my mum. Saying he'll nick her if she doesn't play ball. His fucking sister, really?

So I told Roy the truth. Well, for that job anyway. That I'd given the money to my mum, and it's in her room. Just a grand left in total from the off licence job. She told him where it was, and he came back in the room…and counted out £200, the wanker.

I'd told Roy where the cash was, so he wouldn't find the shot-gun, but he did anyway, under the mattress in my bedroom. So now I was fucked. Money, the gun, the shells, but they needed the money bags as proof. So I reluctantly told them where all the bags were hidden in the garden. I just didn't want to put my mum through it.

All the time Roy kept saying, 'You're nicked, Ray. Ray, you're definitely nicked.'

I was taken to Brentford police station, charged with the off licence robbery, possession of a firearm and intent to danger life, and remanded to Brixton, my first adult prison. For shouting his mouth off in the pub, Gerry was also nicked, with his bollocks so swollen they were in a truss, but released without charge. Mark didn't even get a tug.

At Brixton, I was put in a big allocation cell with about 20 others sat around a large table. I felt physically sick with a heavy migraine, and when they brought us some shitty food, I actually puked up. Then I was taken up to my wing and put in a normal cell, twos-up. Brixton was such a piss-hole, and my migraines were awful over the next couple of weeks so that fortnight is a complete blur. It's

50-odd years ago, so hard to remember, other than being visited by my barrister, who was a QC, and posh, like all of them, and head to toe in blue pin stripe.

One day, I was taken to Brentford Magistrates and given bail. Thank fuck.

To his credit, uncle Roy gave me a character witness. Gave it the old, 'I've known this boy all my life. He's made a grave error, but this is the last time he will ever stand in front of a court. He realises the seriousness of what he's done,' Blah, blah, blah. Roy was good like that, but I still hated his fucking guts.

On bail, my new girlfriend came and lived with me at my mum's, until the case came to court about six months later.

I'd lost my job at the market. Colin Cracknell came to my house and told me I'd been let go. With no official income, of course I was straight out doing more robberies. Standard. With Leon or whoever was up for it.

Ram-raiding antique shops was our new thing, based on what I'd heard about the night-safe bank job. Reversing a car close to the doorway of the premises, and wedging large pieces of wood in between the bumper of the motor and the front door. Then driving backwards through the shop front. Or we'd break into an empty flat next door to an antique shop, then use sledgehammers and industrial drills to smash through stud walls. Any alarms shouldn't go off as we hadn't come through the front door. On our first such job, the guy that gave us the bit of work was our getaway driver too. We loaded the van up with valuable vases, samurai swords and any other gold or silver bits we thought were worth a few quid...and before we could get out of the gaff, the geezer drove off into the sunset. We never saw him again. He might well have got away with hundreds of thousands of pounds of goods for all we knew.

We were doing several jobs a week. So it was a numbers game. Some you win, some you lose. Even at a young age, I felt I had to do as many jobs as possible until I got nicked. One night, we broke into the Biba boutique in Kensington High Street, through the back of the shop, and got away with loads of gear.

YOUNG OFFENDER

Three or four months later, my case for the off-licence job came up at the Old Bailey. Summer, 1970.

I arrived in plenty of time and went downstairs to surrender my bail with a court officer. He and another guy showed me to a tiny single cell, about three feet wide, and six deep. No light or door, just metal bars. Like a dingy dark dank dungeon. The original Old Bailey was built in the early 1900s, on the site of the old Newgate Prison. This was two years before a huge refurb at the site, and the cell I was put in certainly felt like it was at least 70 years old.

My barrister appeared at the bars of the cell, dressed in all his finery and, as he was let in, crouched down to step inside.

'This is not looking good for you, Mr Hill.'

And he was right, because this was as big as it had got for me so far. Uncle Roy wasn't involved anymore. The case had been handed over to the Robbery Squad. Things had escalated considerably. Guns were now involved, and I was standing trial at the fucking Bailey. I had no choice but to plead guilty.

It was all done in a day. I received three years for the robbery and only six months for possession of a firearm and danger to intent, which, even though it was consecutive, seemed light. Maybe Roy had charged me in a certain way to minimise my sentence. And I was only done for stealing £200. Roy and his boys obviously kept the rest. He may well have helped me, by helping himself, but I still thought he was a fucking shit cunt, my uncle, for arresting me in the first place.

Like so much of my time in jail, this stretch started at Wormwood Scrubs, which I quickly learned was mainly a holding prison. Most people were there for a couple of months while it was decided where they'd do most of their bird. Anyone who stays longer than that, with anything about them, usually ends up running their wing.

Still classed as a 'Young Prisoner' (or offender), I was placed on 'YP' at the end of the huge B-wing, like many at the Scrubs, one of the longest in Europe. A-wing was for remand and sentencing, D-wing was for high risk prisoners needing single cells, which were also standard for us in YP too, and there was a borstal at the other end.

Ninety per cent of the clothes I was given at reception when I arrived were too big for me. Shirts with buttons missing. All meant to undermine.

The clanging of the screws coming through the rattling gates on their way to the cells in the morning around 6am, all lively, chatty and humming and whistling songs, was the worst noise in the world. The banging of their truncheons on cell doors started an hour later. Loads of shouting. 'Check the ones, check the twos' (i.e the first floor, the second floor). Every morning. Painful.

In terms of the regime, YP seemed no different to Borstal. If you didn't have your battered bed boxed up by the time the screws unlocked you — blanket, sheet and pillow all square...soap, brush and comb on top of it — you were nicked and could lose any remission built up so far. You must stand to attention by your door, holding your piss pot and water jug, wearing a shirt buttoned up to the top, with a tie, jacket and jeans. No chance to wash yet. Prim and proper, but smelly.

I can remember being determined that first morning not to get into a fight, to try and keep out of trouble.

It was single file to the bathroom, then back to my cell to slop out again. Then down the cast iron stairs, which always shook with the weight of inmates trudging to breakfast.

The bowl, plate, knife, fork and tray given to me on day one, were mine to keep and use throughout my sentence. For breakfast, some porridge, then maybe a bit of ropey old bacon and some tired looking scrambled egg, or a crappy sausage and mushy tomatoes. Never all of it together, or as much as I really wanted. A small slice of bread with a slab of cheap butter on the side.

As I walked up the stone stairs with my tray of food to my landing that first morning, I was pushed back down by the lot up the front. As I rolled back down, my breakfast went up in the air and landed all over me. I could see a few of the lads laughing at me, so I knew

I was going to have some aggro.

I cleared up the mess and told one of the head screws, 'Guv, I've got no food.'

'Okay, well, you won't fall down the stairs again, will you, Hill? Go and bang up.'

I found out a little firm from Birmingham were responsible for my embarrassment that morning, and their top boy was 'the Daddy' of the wing. Ten lads in total, all recently given life for murder, or at least one of them was responsible, they just couldn't prove who. Either way, they really didn't give a shit at that point of their sentence.

I was back in my cell, sat at my table, hungry and fuming. When I went out to the yard for my first of two half hour daily 'exercise' sessions, I knew I was going to have a row.

I spotted one of the Brummies.

'Tell your mate, the blond guy, me and him, in the toilets, because I'm not being bullied by you lot.'

I knew I was going to get nicked, but I had to sort this out early doors.

Blondie was waiting for me in the toilet when I got there. Bam! Straight on my chin. We started scrapping. He bashed me up, but he didn't bash me up, bash me up. I was a good second best. Because he was hurt too, I felt sure he wouldn't want to fight me again.

We were both sent to the block (aka solitary confinement) and had seven days extra added onto our sentence, which was nothing really in the scheme of things, especially for him. When we got out, I went to his cell, shook his hands and said, 'Let's work together. I know I was second best, but I'm the best second best you've ever had.'

Thankfully, he agreed and, from that day, me and all the Brummies became mates.

The first job anybody had in YP was on the 'Noddy Shop', so called because you had to paint models of children's characters and toys, made in moulds, to be sent to kid's homes. Loads of big angry men painting a fucking Mickey Mouse figure. A target of 500 a week, which you could never achieve, for five shillings a week. Pretty humiliating for big lads like me, but that's what it was all about — punishment.

* * * * *

One day it was announced that 50 of us would be moved from the Scrubs to Aylesbury YP, just an hour or so drive outside of London in Buckinghamshire. Because I'd already been at a Borstal, I should have really gone into the main wing for YPs, but somehow I went to the F&G-wing, which was for first-timers (F), and lifers (G), where the Brummies, who had come too, were also allocated.

Our wing used to be a women's prison, which was usually better equipped, with more privileges. It was so clean, with an outdoor swimming pool too. I was put on the threes, which was the top floor of what was actually a huge old house in the grounds of the prison. The landings were the huge corridors on each floor of the building, each with 12 cells.

I got a job as a cleaner, but because this prison was spotless I had to make sure the toilets, the taps on the sinks, the copper pipes and any areas with glass were all scrubbed and polished by hand to the highest standard. Then pull and push ten foot long buffers backwards and forwards to get the floors gleaming. I liked the physicality of the job. It kept me busy and fit, and, if I was lucky, I'd maybe get seven shillings a week.

Every morning as a YP at Aylesbury, we had PT (Physical Training) in the outside yard. Our chief instructor, Dyer, was also the head PTI of the whole prison service in England, and nutty as a fruitcake. Everything we did was outside, particularly when it was fucking freezing, and including football with one team each week in 'skins'. When we'd finished a match, Dyer would blow his whistle and scream, 'Right, swimming.' Even when the pool was iced over. 'Take your shorts off, and jump in.' It was better to walk than swim, otherwise the ice could cut you to pieces. Thankfully, the showers were always nice and hot.

If it was raining really hard, we'd be taken to the main wing to play murder ball: two teams of ten, wrestling a huge medicine ball from each other. It got a bit lively sometimes, but it was a legitimate aggression release I loved.

After PT it was into our 'uniforms' to start working before lunch around midday. Then bang up at 2pm or work in the afternoon if your job needed you to. Dinner would be around 4.30pm, then association — gym, snooker, television…or a fight in the toilet. For me, it mainly meant going to the gym, which was in a separate hall in between F & G-wing.

In our cells each night, we were allowed to listen to an hour of *BBC Radio 1* on a small transistor, the size of a bar of soap, bought with privileges. Normal batteries would only last about 20 minutes, so we were allowed to buy a larger PP9 battery, which we attached to the radio with an elastic band, and that lasted much longer. You could try and work your way up to a larger Hacker or Robinson radio, but you'd have to be lucky and completely stay out of trouble, to have enough privileges to afford one of those.

Any wages or 'spends' you had could be used at 'Canteen', on things like soap, toothpaste, tobacco or confectionary.

On a Sunday, our cells were inspected by prison chiefs. One white glove, looking for dust. It felt like some of the top brass took it in turns to perv over us fit and strong young lads.

Like Borstal, I didn't really want my mum visiting me at YP, but she did a few times. It was my old mum, wasn't it? I didn't want her to see me banged up like that, nor my girlfriend.

The visiting room was primitive to say the least. The seat was a plank nailed to a wooden base and I had to talk through a wire mesh divider to the visitor on the other side, sat on a bench.

At Borstal, it was one letter for one letter, but I could send and receive two each month now. For visiting orders, one VO and one PVO (Privilege Visiting Order), which could only be used midweek, and could be taken away for bad behaviour. As usual, any privilege could be removed. Like you'd take something away from a naughty kid.

The Brummies tipped me off that a guy on my wing, Pardo, who made teas for the screws, was a serious sex offender, or 'a nonce', as they called him. The oldest YP was 21, but Pardo was bald and probably in his late 30s. Something was going on. In the end, the Brummies got to him, and they nearly killed him. Stabbed him up with all sorts of things. They were all transferred out of Aylesbury with immediate effect. I never saw them again, nor Pardo.

I was later told the term N.O.N.C.E stands for 'not on normal courtyard exercise' and back in the day was written on the slate on the wall outside the cells of sex offenders to indicate they were to be exercised away from the general prison population. Given my circumstances, I didn't fancy the chances of any nonces I came across inside.

*****

Fed up with my cleaning job, I managed to get transferred to the laundry. A short 16-year-old kid in there, Andrew, was part of a father and son burglar team both doing life for murder. Barely 5ft, Andrew's dad lifted him through small open windows of properties so he could clamber through and open the front door. One time, Andrew hit an old lady coming down the stairs with a metal bar, and it killed her. Borderline schizophrenic, I don't think he should have been with us at YP. When working on the big washing machines, we used huge safety pins to bunch up smaller items, like socks and even knickers from the girls' Borstal, which we got very excited about. Andrew used the pins to stab people he didn't like, or he'd actually push someone into a washing machine and switch it on. They'd scream and shout as they span round and be in a right state when he finally drained the water and let them out.

Andrew got too many privileges for my liking, and got away with loads. I reckon he was letting the old screw who ran the laundry give it to him. I soon realised there was loads of that going on.

Me and Andrew had a nice little sideline. Charging lags to starch the collars on their shirts, iron their clothes, and even get their standard issue blue and white shirts adjusted to have smaller collars. So they looked better on a visit, especially if they wanted to impress their missus. Keep her on side.

From the laundry window, I noticed a huge screw talking to a YP called Sid Lane, who had massive, powerful legs. My mate told me Lane was Olympic level and the screw, Smith, managed the power-lifting team.

Smith fixed it for me to try out for the team and when he realised how strong I was, I was straight in.

A Welsh guy, Malcolm Peace, who was amazing at squats and a great fighter, who could really march forward, was an impressive powerlifter. He would have smashed up Lenny McLean and Roy Shaw. I was useless at squats, but a very good dead lifter and solid on the bench. Smith and the guys loved me, and it felt amazing to be part of the team. That year we won the Inter-Prison Southern Area championships, beating a team from Parkhurst with an Olympic lifter. All done under supervision with adjudicators in our own prisons.

I was now bench-pressing about 400 pounds, squatting 420 and deadlifting 800. Starting to get massive. Powerful, but not yet 21 years old. Importantly, as part of the powerlifting team, I was now allowed in the gym every night from 6pm - 7.30pm, before supper and bang up.

About a year into my sentence, I got a job in the metal shop dismantling huge copper cables, working with a prisoner called Steve, who drove the forklift. Every couple of weeks, a lorry would come to the prison and we'd load it up.

In Aylesbury, there were no high fences, just a wall about ten foot high. Steve was doing life for killing someone on the door of a club in Manchester, but he always argued he'd acted in self-defence and was fitted up.

One day Steve said, 'I've got to get out of here. I've done four years, I can't take it anymore.'

So we hatched a plan. We put some bins at the entrance where the weekly lorry was due to come in, so it couldn't quite pull in fully. Usually the screws could see the wall, but this time they couldn't. Steve loaded up the lorry with metal from the forklift truck. Then the rest of us started causing murders in the metal shop, banging things, creating a commotion. The screws came rushing in just as Steve, out of sight, drove the forklift truck up against the wall, raised the forks, climbed out of the cabin, on to forks, and jumped over the wall.

Steve was on the run for 20-odd years. He was eventually nicked for something else serious, got another life sentence, and had to finish off his original one too.

*****

At one powerlifting session, we were told we were going to the main room for a game of murder ball. Screws Dyer and Johnson, who played rugby for Leeds, and Rodwell, another gym instructor, were all referees. A big guy steamed into me when I had the ball, and punched me on the chin. I thought, you dirty cunt. It wiped me out, and I saw stars. After, in the showers, I stabbed him in the back with a pencil and cracked him on the chin too. He stayed down, job done. Back at the wing, nothing was said. Six weeks later, I'd forgotten all about it. That morning we were told we had to use the canteen in the main wing. As I walked in, the geezer jumped me and bit through my left ear, leaving it half hanging off. That's why to this day, each ear is a different shape and I have big scar down the back of my head. I grabbed his bollocks and squeezed them so tight he screamed again like a baby. The screws ran in and found him on the floor unconscious and my face pissing with blood. I was taken to the hospital at HM Grendon, just outside Aylesbury on the Oxfordshire border, which was also a nut house, worse than Broadmoor at the time. The medical guy stitching my ear back up was bonkers too, and specialised in removing prisoner's tattoos, with a blade. He said he was going to use a local anesthetic, but didn't. The pain was nothing I'd ever experienced before. I undid the stitching soon after, and my ear popped back out again.

I was told to get on with it, and was taken back to YP at Aylesbury. My hospital visit seemed to defuse any punishment I might face, but from that point on, I was fighting all the time. Something took hold of me. I was always down the block, a particularly secure unit at this nick, where they had kept the Great Train Robbers. Like any adult prison, you could still get visits when you were on the block. They're meant to take them off you but if you had one booked, it usually went ahead, because the screws couldn't be bothered with the aggro.

The two screws on this block were really horrible. Bissington, 6ft 9ins, huge 14/15 size feet and Stone, with a big bushy moustache. Both as regimental as they get. First thing in the morning, no boxing up required. Just put your mattress and bed frame outside your cell. Just you and your table and chair left inside. Then they brought in brass bins. I'd always noticed them around the prison, and wondered why they were so gleaming. Now I knew. That was our job for the day. Spit and polish with an emery cloth. Hours of cleaning and polishing those bins in our cells. Your bed not allowed back in until 8pm. Day in, day out.

Old fashioned names like Gladys or Doris were carved into the brickwork lining the small segregated exercise yard attached to the block. There were marble tiles in the grass, also with names on. We were told women waiting to be hanged in the 1930s and '40s stayed there previously and were also buried in the grounds.

With one of my good friends on his toes and enjoying some kind of freedom, it was only another couple of months before I was made up to full adult prison, or starred up...when a star is put on your blue jacket.

And then I was moved back to the Scrubs, with another former YP, a Scottish guy, and we were put twos-up together on C-wing. I got a job in the stores, and, as usual, spent as much time in the gym as possible.

Five or six months later, in the autumn of 1972, my time on this stretch had come to an end. I'd done two and a bit years out of three for the robbery and four months out of six for the firearm possession. I was 22, and had spent most of my young adult life banged up.

Aside from my involvement in the powerlifting team, it felt like I had worked all day and slept all night. It didn't feel like there had been any time to talk about my mistakes constructively or any ambitions I might have. Most conversations with other lags were about crime and especially robberies. Always trying to climb the ranks or making myself someone in there. Bashing people up, or trying not to get bashed up too. Making sure everybody knew who I was, so I was feared when I walked the wing.

The only time I thought about going straight was during a visit, when Mum might say, 'C'mon Ray, this is not for you...'

Colin Cracknell also visited me, which was big of him. It was great to sit down and catch up, and hear about the comings and goings at the market.

Now it was time to get back out there and test myself. No more small-time robberies. I wanted large jobs, to become a career criminal and work with the big boys.

Between 1968 and 1972, the annual rate for bank robberies in the London area rose from 12 to 65...one every five days. So it seems my release was perfect timing.

SWEET FREEDOM

As I walked along my mum's road in a short-sleeved T-shirt, tasting freedom and the Spring fresh air, a dog ran up to me excitedly. A new decade and maybe a new dawn for me. I was 22 years old. Fit, muscular and powerful.

Mum was delighted to see me. With Bob still by her side, I was welcomed with a new baby brother, Bobby. I could only hope he would have a much better start to life than I'd had.

I wanted to try get a job back involved at Brentford market so I got in touch with Mark, who was still active. We sorted out a truck in his name and began using it to deliver potatoes.

I'd been soaking up information from other criminals the whole time I was locked up. Now I had to do what I needed to do. Earn money, try and get ahead and do things better this time. I felt strong enough, I felt invincible.

My cousin Terry Nelhams/Adam Faith was now the star of hit TV series *Budgie*, playing an ex-convict just released in the world, trying to make a living any way he could. I was surprised Terry didn't visit me in prison for some research, but perhaps that wasn't the done thing for a celebrity like him, and maybe I wasn't the best person to ask about finding your way again in life.

Each week, in the opening credits of the show, *Budgie* dropped a suitcase full of cash and was shown trying to grab bank notes as they blew in the wind. A feeling I would become to know all too well.

Obviously, I was delighted for Terry, but didn't have any time to be starstruck. Other than crime, my main focus was boxing. Two worlds that literally went hand in hand.

My time was split between my mum's place and my hairdresser girlfriend, with whom I had quickly rekindled our on-off romance. I started to train at the gym at The Noble Art pub in Haverstock Hill in Hampstead, a few miles away in north west London. I was lucky enough to spar there with Joe Bugner, who had just enjoyed a 15 round points decision against Henry Cooper. Mohammed Ali had famously trained at Noble Art in 1966 before his fight with Brian London, and Joe Frazier would also use it for training a year or so later when he fought Bugner, before Bugner fought Ali himself.

It was amazing to feel the energy of these heavyweight legends. I held my own with Bugner and also Billy Aird, the British, European and Commonwealth champion.

Leon was about to turn pro at The Wellington in Highgate, and would have a dozen fights, trained there by George Francis, and under the management of Micky Duff and promoter Jarvis Astaire. Leon took me down to The Wellington, and I caught the eye of the guys.

George was a real character, and someone I could relate to. A bareknuckle street fighter in the slums of Camden in the 1940s, he had juggled his own boxing career working as a porter in Covent Garden Market, and had also spent time in the Scrubs.

A few weeks later, George, Duff and Astaire turned up at my mum's house, wanting me to turn professional, which was a lot to take in. The guys would go on to work with 16 world champions, including Frank Bruno, John Conteh, Joe Calzaghe, Barry McGuigan, Lloyd Honeyghan, Charlie Magri and Alan Minter.

Duff told me, 'We've seen how hard you work in the gym, how hard you can bang, and we think you can do opponents a lot of damage.'

Like an idiot, I said I needed to think about it, and also check with my trainer George Whelan, who I felt loyal to. In reality, I was probably more interested in chasing girls than boxing. I did apply for a professional licence through the British Boxing Board of Control but was refused because, unlike Leon, I'd done time at an adult prison, not just Borstal. I was told to keep my head down and to apply again in the future.

Staying out of trouble would be difficult. While I was inside, Leon had been hanging around Ladbroke Grove, breaking into places around that area. He now specialised in 'loiding' locks. The name comes from 'celluloid', i.e plastic. You cut a long rectangular shape of plastic from a washing liquid bottle, and then use the curvature and flexibility of the plastic to slip the lock. This tool could even do Banham locks, if they were off.

But it took over Leon's life, and it fucked up my boxing, really. We were meant to be training at the gym every day, but more and more Leon would say, 'Let's go and earn some money today instead.' I was mainly on look-out, then Leon would break in and we'd hide any jewellery or cash in our boxing gloves around our necks.

*****

I wasn't a big drinker, but hanging out in pubs was essential for getting bits of work, settling scores and, of course, meeting girls. But the sort of characters those pubs attracted meant trouble was never far away.

The Anchor in Acton was a proper gangster's boozer, where scrap dealer and demolition guy, Dennis Haley — another local 'businessman' I worked for and with — was a regular. Dennis had a big yard and metal merchants in Ashburton Grove in Holloway, which is now the site of the Arsenal's Emirates Stadium. He had 40 members of staff, and at one time was also partners in the Anchor with landlord, Charlie Harris.

Dennis could have a row, but could help calm things down too. A guy known for sorting stuff out. His son, Terry, was 15 years old at the time and would sit in the car park in his dad's Jenson, a beautiful dark blue brand new L-plate, which cost five grand back then, when you could buy a house for that much too. A really exclusive motor. Terry and his mates were getting into bodybuilding, so they looked up to me because of my size.

Dennis gave me bits of demolition work on various jobs. One at Heathrow Airport, dismantling old Vickers Vanguard planes for BEA and another taking down a factory in Park Royal. Dennis reckoned I was more effective than his Cat bulldozer, because with a sledge-hammer I could knock the top of walls over, and then push the middle brickwork through with my hands. Dennis was a big character who, at a time when pubs still shut in the afternoon, would take half of the Anchor back home with him in between.

Poor old Terry's mum, June, would have to feed them all while Dennis snuck off for a nap, before the pub reopened again.

Dennis had the top of his ear sliced with a broken light ale bottle, trying to stop a violent fight between his mate Snowy and another dangerous local, One Eyed Neville. Snowy needed 300 stitches after being hit by everything on the bar — glasses, ashtrays, soda syphons...the lot.

Another time my nemesis from The Priory shot up The Anchor after his brother was arrested following a brutal fight in the pub. Maybe someone from The Anchor was suspected of grassing. My arch-enemy clearly wasn't the full ticket, but I already knew that. A few years later, he was being chased by Old Bill after a robbery, and jumped from the passenger seat to the back of the motor, shot out the back window, and then started shooting at the police. He got a long old stretch for that.

*****

A pal of mine from The Anchor, Danny, worked for a guy called Bob Coleman, who provided staging for events through his company, Octopus Productions. Me and Danny became great mates, but I never 'worked' with him. He had been away for a stint in Borstal when he was younger but unlike me, he was now on the straight and narrow.

Danny got me some work, knocking down walls and digging out the gardens of houses Bob was chopping into flats, all over London. For a few weeks at least, it felt like I was going straight. Danny and Bob were great influences on me.

Danny and I started to go to The Cromwellian casino, bar and nightclub in Cromwell Road, South Kensington, which had three floors, and had been a popular celebrity hang out since the late '60s. The likes of Elton John, Jimi Hendrix, Eric Clapton and Stevie Wonder had all performed exclusive gigs there. Compared to our working class base in Acton, we loved the glamour of a night out in the Knightsbridge area. On our fourth or fifth visit, we spotted John Bindon on the dance floor.

Bindon was from Fulham and, a bit like me, had been in and out of Borstal as a kid. The usual car thefts...and also for living off a prostitute's immoral earnings. In his late teens, Bindon had a spell in Maidstone prison and earned the nickname Biffo, because of his links to violence and love of scrapping. Since I'd been away at YP, Bindon had become a well-known face through his various acting roles, usually playing violent criminals or hard-nosed coppers. He was spotted in a pub by director Ken Loach and cast in his film *Poor Cow* without any acting experience. He was a natural — literally playing himself. While I was away, Bindon had played a violent villain alongside Mick Jagger in the film *Performance* and starred as a London gang boss in the movie *Get Carter*. He'd also been in the TV series *Z-Cars*.

Bindon was famously very well-endowed. Around 13/14 inches long, all told. His party pieces including hiding his prick in a buffet tray at a function and then offering a guest a sandwich, or hanging five half-pint glasses on it.

It was said Bindon earned £20k a year in the late '60s/early '70s from acting, and another ten grand from a protection racket — intimidating pub landlords in and around the Kings Road area.

With his surprise acting career well underway, Bindon was cock-sure, literally, and oozed confidence at The Cromwellian, with dolly birds swooning all around him.

And Bindon was used to female attention. A couple of years earlier, he had famously infiltrated royal circles via a girlfriend, the actress and socialite, Vicky Hodge. Princess Margaret also fell for Bindon's roguish charm, and he reportedly visited her two times at her holiday home on the Caribbean island of Mystique. While the princess always denied an affair with Bindon, there is that famous photo of them on a beach, with Bindon wearing an 'Enjoy Cocaine' T-shirt. The relationship allegedly continued back in London, where it has since been claimed that the firm behind the famous Baker Street robbery of 1971, on the vaults of a branch of Lloyds Bank, had intel that compromising photos of Bindon and Margaret were in a security box down there. The 2008 film, *The Bank Job* — starring Jason Statham — is based on the raid and the supposed incriminating pictures taken in Mustique. Stranger things have happened, so who knows.

As me and Danny moved onto the dance floor at The Cromwellian, late 1972, Bindon's group shimmied and shuffled nearer. With a huge sexual appetite, a raging temper and, like me, predisposed to criminality, Bindon was a ferocious character.

When he bumped into us, the inner thug quickly came out and Bindon had a go at Danny. I stepped in and calmed it all down, but I could tell Bindon was put out. I decided it was best we leave as I thought he could erupt at any point. We were still only kids, really, but fresh from my daily powerlifting sessions in prison, I was 19 stone and very strong. Bindon was seven years older, 6ft 2in and probably 17 stone. A good looking guy in great shape. When we got outside into the street, Bindon appeared in the corner of my eye and started shouting the odds. I turned towards him and he landed a perfect punch square on my chin, which floored me. I got straight back up, but out of respect, and because we were out of our manor, I stepped back. My instinct was to go back in, but for once I left it alone. Our cue to stay away from The Cromwellian for a while.

But it didn't seem like I could stay out of trouble for long. The next night me and Danny popped into Deli's — a late night Chinese restaurant in Acton we'd hang out at after The Anchor. At one end were a dozen rugby players from Wasps. Big lumps. Really loud. Dancing around. Deli asked Danny to have a word, so he shouted at them to keep it down. Well, they took offence to this, and a few came over. Danny got up, and squared up to two of them, and wallop, one of them smacked him. He punched one back, so now I was involved. Ping, ping, bop, I knocked a few down, but they're like Weebles, they kept bouncing back up again. Which rugby players are used to doing, of course. We were trying to get out of the restaurant, and they kept dragging us back in, and bashing us up some more. Deli called the police, and although Old Bill were not my favourite people, they were good for us that night, and broke things up. A lot of rugby players are police themselves, so it could have gone either way, but it was defused and everyone was told to go home.

Another night out nearer to home also ended up outside in the street. Me and Danny had been to the Carlton Club in Harrow a few times. It was owned by local face Mickey Green and pals of his like Bryan

Turner, Bertie Smalls, Bobby King and Jimmy Wilkinson were in there most nights. Together, in our world, they were known to be successful bank robbers. I'd bowled into the club that night all lairy, like you are when your young and big, and said hello to Mickey Green, who knew my face by now, but I upset Turner when I knocked into him accidentally on the way through to the toilets. He gave me some verbal and told me to fuck off. Because all that lot were older than me, in their 30s and 40s, and much more established, I bit my tongue. It was a good job I knew Jimmy Wilkinson from the fruit market and his family greengrocers in Hanwell, because he tried to calm things down by introducing me to a few of those boys, but they were all drinking pretty hard and I could tell it was going to kick off. After a while, I decided we should leave so I waited outside while Danny got the motor. But Bertie Smalls and Bobby King followed me out. I looked over at them and Bertie was already walking towards me. Bang, he threw a punch, straight on my chin and it put me on the floor. A right fucking liberty. It was a hard punch but not hard enough to knock me out. I got up and Danny tried to pull me back but I thought, no, I'm active and I can have a row. I'm not leaving this one. Let's go...

And I thought I bashed Smalls up. I was smashed to pieces and had to get off the floor again, but I thought I won the fight. I was still a boy really, but I had to fight like these tough men. Turner, King and Jimmy Wilkinson broke it up. I was sure Bertie Smalls wouldn't want to fight me again.

A few weeks later, I was casing the Unigate Dairies depot opposite Ealing Common with a pal and I spotted Jimmy Wilkinson sat in a Jag parked up on the roadside. For a few weeks, we'd been trying to work out when the weekly cash takings were collected by a security van. I walked over and Jimmy wound his window down so I explained why we were there. 'We are too...best you fuck off.' So I did. Frustrating, but I was beginning to understand that sometimes it comes with the territory.

* * * * *

Mark and I sat down one day to try and work out how we could find out more about bank processes. And specifically how we could gain official access to the rear of banks. One idea, with the help of our truck, was to get involved in maintenance at such banks or something related. Amazingly, Mark secured a refuse contract with a group of banks, collecting rubbish and hopefully useful paperwork too.

One of the main cash management companies at the time was Security Express. Their guards would throw big bags of cash from their vans through the front or back doors of the banks, and in fact the front doors most of the time, because of the lack of access to the rear of most of those properties. It seems crazy looking back now.

We were doing a collection at one bank in Notting Hill shortly after a Security Express visit and a bank worker walked us past big bags of cash just left on the floor before being processed. I said to Mark, 'Is this is a fucking joke? There's definitely a bit of work here.'

One that got away was a job in Hillingdon. We were in position waiting for a Security Express van to arrive. I was outside a church across the road, and Mark was on the other side of the street by the entrance to the bank. As soon as the first cash bag was thrown across the road to the security guy at the door of the bank, Mark would pounce and hold his gun to the guard. I was holding too, and now with the other guard aware that his colleague was in trouble, and now staring at my thing, I'd grab the rest of the bags from the van. I might only have time to take two or three bags before an alarm is activated in the bank or via the van, but it could still be a very nice amount, because there could be up to £100k there in total.

The SE van pulled up and the guards were about to start throwing the cash bags when suddenly a load of Old Bill walked out of the church, uniformed up. How was our luck? It was only a fucking police wedding. A couple of officers were getting married with dozens of colleagues as guests, dressed in full regalia. Good job they were, because if they were plain clothed, we'd have still done the job. Either way, they're the sort of witnesses you really don't need. They would feel compelled to get involved. Instead, I had to give the signal quickly, so I touched the top of my head repeatedly, which means, 'On top, on top'.

These kind of setbacks came with the territory. It was very much a numbers game. There were loads of jobs I had to give up on. One reason might be if kids and women suddenly appeared on the scene...or I just wasn't feeling it.

Our main thing then was following security vans or cash management vehicles and spending time working out their movements. Jobs on the spur of the moment aren't always the best ones. It's all about the planning — Borstal did that for me. We'd try to grab a bag of wage packets that had already been made up in cash by banks, often with wage slips in them too. We'd open them up and be like, 'Fuck me, look how much this poor cunt is being taxed,' or, 'Oh look, this bloke got a bonus. Nice one.'

All the time, we were considering how we could go back to the bank where we had the refuse contract...once we'd fully worked out their systems and processes.

*****

Bob Coleman offered me some work doing staging in, of all places, Finland, for a big political event, with a dozen other guys but not Danny. Travelling to Helsinki was the first time I'd left the country, been on a plane or used my passport under the name Hill, but I can't remember where we flew from. Helsinki was fucking freezing, but had loads of jewellery stores, so not the best place for someone like me. It was like a mini Hatton Garden with about 30 prime shops, all with no alarms. I did think about coming back on my own, but, unlike London, they had armed police as standard. We still managed to pinch quite a lot of stuff out of our hotel — ornaments, vases, and even kettles from the rooms. Also designer watches from display units, dotted about the place. I was a thief, so it was in me. I couldn't help myself.

One day, Leon introduced me to a guy called Chilton who came from a large Jamaican family in Grove. His mum was a real matriarch. The smell of jerk chicken and yams in her house near Portobello Road was amazing.

I sensed that Chilton and Leon had never really hit it off, mainly, I think, because Chilton knew Leon could bash him up. I took a fancy to Chilton's pretty sister, and also to Leon's sister-in-law, who was beautiful too. Hanging around with these girls and their female siblings, made me realise that I had a thing for black girls... but then I liked all kinds of women. Maybe being locked up for so much of my young life already meant I was permanently on heat.

I started doing a bit of work with Chilton — armed robberies to earn money for our families. Some of Chilton's pals used some of the cash to set up an illegal drinking club in the area.

'Raymond, you want a job?'

'Yeah, yeah, doing what?'

'Running the club with Chilton.'

So I went down there and I thought, this is going to be easy. The place was packed. Full of the local Caribbean crowd. Reggae music blaring out, a pool table, everyone smoking weed downstairs. Nice and chilled. Me and Chilton did the door together. I was always the only white person there.

Then it started getting tougher. Heavy guys coming in and out who wouldn't be searched.

One night one of the family elders said to me, 'Be careful tonight. So and so is coming down.'

Now, I knew all about this fella. He was one of the main men in Grove at that time. A serious, serious guy. Sure enough, he appeared with about eight or nine others. I said, 'You can come in guys, just behave yourselves,' but they didn't give a fuck, kissing their teeth, and walked straight downstairs. The boss gestured for me and Chilton to go down too.

To this day, I'm still in shock at what happened next. I can still picture it clear as day.

The group that had just arrived were clearly looking for someone in particular, and they quickly found him. The poor fella was surrounded and then lifted onto the pool table and laid on his back. With the guy physically shaking, everybody else stopped what they were doing, and watched as the main man pulled a machete from inside his coat. He held the large knife above his head and then, quickly, with one lethal action, plunged the blade into the neck of his victim, pretty much clean chopping this guy's head off. And when I say 'off'...the machete had sliced through his jugular vein. It was only the skin at the back of his neck that stopped the head from becoming completely detached. Blood was spurting everywhere. The man let out a huge scream, and then the scream kept going. That was the worst thing: the scream lasted a lot longer than it should have.

Me and Chilton's arseholes went. We ran up those stairs for our young lives. I could have a row and I was dangerous, but I didn't fancy taking on this lot, who were now chasing us, probably because we were witnesses and were worried we might grass. We were running so fast it felt like ten paces at a time...all the way down Harrow Road towards Harlesden. Fortunately, they gave up seconds after, obviously needing to get out of the area as quickly as possible too. God knows what they would have done to us.

We carried on running though...down Scrubs Lane, where Car Giant is now, past the *BBC*, into Shepherd's Bush, up Uxbridge Road and into East Acton, where we laid low at a pal's place.

We were told the police had arrived and we were needed there for questioning, so Chilton drove us back down. Let's just say there wasn't a lot we could or were prepared to tell the police, who had taped off the venue.

Not surprisingly, that was the end of the club. I was told it was shut, and didn't ask any questions. Standard.

Me and Chilton carried on doing armed robberies. We'd done about four or five by now. Mostly taking bags of cash or cashboxes from post offices or shops. During that time in the early '70s, it was quite straightforward.

Me aged 9 with my tortoise, Grandpa.

(Above) Sean Connery, the then James Bond, practising his golf swing at Acton Park, a familiar sight to us kids.

(Top right) The house at East Churchfield Road, opposite the park, where I was born and grew up.

(Right) In recent times outside the impressive Acacia House, Connery's home in the 1960s, overlooking the other side of Acton Park, and where our little gang were uninvited guests.

(Above) The kind of Post Office counters we jumped over and robbed as kids in the 1960s.

(Right) Ashford Remand Centre in Kent, where I was sent after one such crime.

(Right/below) The kind of exercise and hard labour each day at the borstal I was sent to after.

(Top) Brentford Fruit Market, 1960s (Below left) Terry Nelhams/Adam Faith and mum, Nell.

(Below right) Outside our old family house in Mill Hill Road, Acton in 2024.

(Bottom) An Adam Faith record sleeve and the plaque marking where Terry was born in Acton.

(Top) The Wimpy Bar in Richmond, with The Castle venue in the background.

(Above right) The Ivy Shop in Richmond, early 1970s.

(Above left) The site today on Cromwell Road of the infamous Cromwellian bar and discotheque.

(Right) The dance floor at The Cromwellian in full swing in the late 1960s.

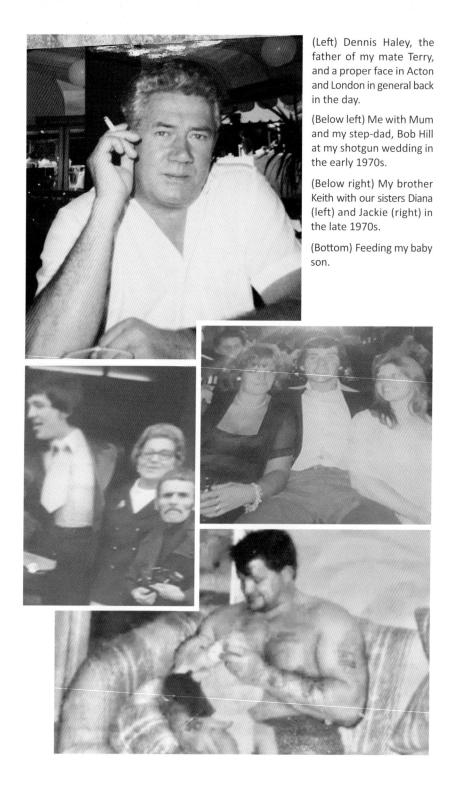

(Left) Dennis Haley, the father of my mate Terry, and a proper face in Acton and London in general back in the day.

(Below left) Me with Mum and my step-dad, Bob Hill at my shotgun wedding in the early 1970s.

(Below right) My brother Keith with our sisters Diana (left) and Jackie (right) in the late 1970s.

(Bottom) Feeding my baby son.

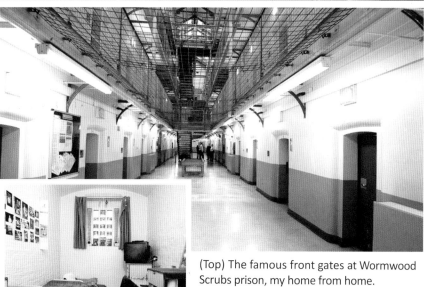

(Top) The famous front gates at Wormwood Scrubs prison, my home from home.

(Above) One of the wings at the Scrubs.

(Left) A typical Scrubs single cell in the 2000s.

(Top) This is actually an image of one of the cells that Nelson Mandela was locked up in, but when looking for an example of a typical segregation (or 'block') cell, this is about as close as I could find to some of the block cells I was put in on a regular basis.

(Above) The waxwork reconstruction at the Chamber Of Horrors exhibit at Madum Tussauds in London of Graham Young in prison. (Right) Graham Young's sinister 'mug shot'.

INSURANCE JOB

Mark had an insurance guy who tipped him off about properties with specific high value items on their policies. He told us about a jeweller from 'the Garden', who had a load of gold bars and expensive watches in a safe at his house in Bridstow Place, just off Westbourne Grove, a few miles down the road from Acton.

In the spring of 1973, we decided to hit this property and pull the safe out. Ambitious, but doable.

Tucked Away in leafy Notting Hill, Bridstow Place is a narrow mews-like street of detached and terrace two-floored cottages, with gardens that back on to larger town houses on Chepstow Road.

We parked up in the truck at the start of Bridstow around lunchtime on a fresh sunny day. The plan was to first suss out the area and lay of the land. Who was in and who wasn't. I walked up a small flight of stairs to a flat and knocked on the door. A young fella with glasses appeared and I asked him if he had heard of a Dr Logan or if he knew of a Dr Logan living on the street, which was a blag, of course. He shook his head, and shut his door so I went back to the lorry.

Our main aim was to find someone who had loose lips and might tell us if there was anyone home at our target house, which was a bit further down the road. We'd been assured that there wasn't, but we still needed to be careful. We would rather it be a burglary than an aggravated burglary. If there was someone in the house, and it went tits up, we could be looking at 15 years. For just a burglary, then it would all depend if they found anything on us.

We moved the lorry and parked outside the jeweller's house. I left my thing behind the passenger seat, and walked through the gates at the front of the property, while Mark kept watch. I knocked on the door. No reply. I could see through the glass some lovely antique furniture inside. I wasn't surprised there were two Banham locks on the front of door, one at the top and one at the bottom, with a Chubb lock in the middle. It looked like we had come to the right place. With a small crowbar, I tried to gem open the door. I went for the hinges side because sometimes there are bolt locks on the inside too.

Suddenly, I heard, 'On top, on top,' so I slid the crowbar into a huge plant pot, and walked back towards Mark, who I watched being bashed up and thrown into the back of a police van. I shouldn't have been too surprised, but I stood there open-mouthed as Mark out-muscled the officers and suddenly jumped out of the police van, and legged it down Bridstow Place, in the direction our truck was facing.

There was no point me doing anything but try to run the other way and escape through the back of the property. I saw a ten foot wall in front of me and managed to jump up and scramble over it. Then, rather than run through the back gate of this garden and into the street where I expected the police to be, I did a sharp left alongside a garage and was faced with another similar-sized wall to climb over. I looked back and could see Old Bill appearing over the first wall so I panicked, and turned around and approached the copper. 'What's up mate?' He grabbed me by the neck of my top and, as I tried to pull away, smacked me on the chin. What? I had to give him one back. Bop. He went down and was crying like a child. Maybe because I was a fighter, all I wanted to do was bash him up. I didn't know what was happening on the other side of the wall, but I knew there were more police coming. There always is.

I was on top of this copper, giving it to him. How dare he hit me? I bashed him up so bad, I split the roof of his mouth from top to bottom.

Now I had to get out of there. Through sheer adrenalin, I found the strength to jump over that back wall of the property and landed on Chepstow Road. I ran towards Talbot Road, and then down to Portobello, and across to Ladbroke Grove Station. I took the tube to Hammersmith and then the 226 bus, and got off not far from Mill Hill Road

As I walked towards my mum's house, it seemed quiet down there. Unaware there was a police cordon at the end of the road... especially for me.

As I walked up the garden path of my mum's house, I heard cars screeching. More Old Bill arriving...and the proper lot. The armed boys. I thought I saw my step-dad, Bob, in his usual blue security guard shirt, through the glass in the front door, but it was police actually inside the house already. As I turned my key, I was grabbed from behind. My mum was standing in the hallway, helpless, as I was smothered by officers, both from inside and outside the house.

I wriggled free and immediately stripped naked, as Old Bill stared at me mouths wide open. I was stood in the hallway of my mum's house, with no clothes on, saying to her, 'Look at me, mate. There's not a mark on me.' Because I knew the plan would be to bash the fuck out of me, as soon the police possibly could...for what I did to their pal.

I was thrown in a motor, one of half a dozen cars which flew down to Paddington police station. I was put in the cells in the basement there, normally reserved for terrorists or other serious offenders. Five Old Bill walked in with truncheons. My jeans were removed and my handcuffs taken off. I decided to fight fire with fire, so I tipped over a table, snapped off a leg and said, 'C'mon, you cunts?'

The station sergeant calmly said, 'Guys, leave him alone, he's only been here a couple of minutes. He's going to Harrow police station soon.'

I really thought they would have done me there and then, but another couple of cars took me to Harrow, all gunned up again. As I was chucked in a stinky old cell there, a copper poked his head in and said, 'You're in fucking trouble, mate. You've nearly killed a police officer.'

'Not me, mate — don't know what you're talking about, mate.'

At this point I still wasn't sure they had anything on me.

But this copper kept baiting me, popping his head in and out. After a while, I said to him, 'If you think I did it, come in here and tell me to my face. C'mon, you've got keys. Open up and shut the door behind you...and let's have it out.'

In the early hours, the cell door did open, and an Inspector Treen walked in, his badge tucked into the pocket of his shirt.

Treen was right up in my face and I said 'Fuck off, your breath stinks.'

He was trying to provoke me and wanted me to kick off. So I grabbed him and threw him up against the wall. I wanted to whack him, but if I had, that would have taken it to another level.

Old Bill separated us.

Treen walked out calmly.

Then I heard someone call out, 'Ray?' from down the corridor.

It sounded like Mark. I didn't even know whether he'd been nicked yet.

'Who's that?'

'It's Mark...'

'Hello, mate. What you doing here?'

'You're a cunt, Ray. You've nearly killed a police officer.'

'What you talking about, Mark? Wasn't me, mate...'

'Ray, you've got to get me off this. It wasn't me. What did you hit him with a paving slab for?'

'Paving slab? What do you fucking mean, mate?'

Mark shouting the odds was the last thing I needed. I could tell they'd got to him. They must have. I reckon officers were in the cell with him.

Minutes later, a furious Inspector Treen was back in my cell with a cardboard box, with cling-film over it, which he held out in front of me. Inside, was my thing...the sawn-off.

'I don't know anything about this, governor. I don't know what's going on.'

'Well, put it this way,' said Treen. 'We're going to charge you with attempted murder, with threats to endanger life, and carrying this weapon.'

I hadn't made a statement yet, but I was clearly fucked. As I suspected, Mark already had. I knew if they were talking about the paving slab, even though I didn't use it, that they must have something to link it to me. The Old Bill was smashed to pieces. The only thing in my favour, was that they didn't find the gun on me, but it was on my side of the truck.

They took me and Mark to a special court at The Royal Courts Of Justice on The Strand, which houses the High Court and the Court Of Appeals, with no brief. Detectives were in and out of my cell there, trying to fuck with my head.

At this point I was deemed 'Poss A', which stands for possibly Category A, a new level for me. So I was put in the book for the first time too, which was usually a small red booklet which logs everything you do and everywhere you are in the run up to a conviction. Mark would have been Cat-B, because his offences were lesser. We were then taken to the Bailey in a police escort in separate cars to get a date. I pleaded 'not guilty', and then we were shipped off on remand to Brixton.

Mark wasn't on my wing, but a couple of days later I heard he got bail. He'd grassed on me, hadn't he? It was obvious. He had a wife and two kids, so I can understand to a certain extent, but he went too far.

When my 'depositions', or 'deps', arrived at my cell, as usual, with my dyslexia, it took me ages to go through it. Normally, half a day to understand one fucking paragraph.

Eventually, I was able to piece everything together. That Mark ran towards Paddington train station, jumped down on to the tracks, fucked his ankle and the police finally caught him. After being told the Old Bill I attacked was going to die and we'd both be done for murder, it appeared he told them everything and, I should imagine, some options of where I'd be. He would have been worried that if he didn't give a name, he could be done for the lot. And that's a lot of bird for killing Old Bill.

It also turned out that the guy who opened the door to me in Bridstow Place was studying for the bar and was suspicious so he called the police. Just our luck.

I was on remand in Brixton for another eight weeks, a hard few months in Cat-A and another summer inside with some tough and notorious characters. Including my 'mates' from the Carlton Club — Brian Turner, Bertie Smalls, Jimmy Wilkinson and Mickey Green, plus Sam McCarthy and Frankie Fellows, so most of the 'Wembley Mob'. So-called because of their involvement in the £140k robbery of Barclays Bank in Wembley the summer before, in 1972. They had eventually been arrested for that job and many others because Bertie Smalls had 'super-grassed' on more than 30 bank robbers and associates to get a deal for himself. In total, he had confessed to being on 15 jobs, and gave details of seven others. I knew he was a wrong-un.

Bertie recognised me and kept his distance to start with. Even though it was only a few months since our fight, I think he could see I'd really developed physically, even in that short space of time, and that I would really hurt him now. He did shake my hand eventually, but he wasn't there very long. He kept getting taken out loads and when he came back said he'd been with his solicitor, but he must have been with the police doing his deal. He did do a lot of damage, grassing everyone up like that. Awful. There's an excellent book on the whole story called *Cops And Robbers: An Investigation Into Armed Bank Robbery by* John Ball, Lewis Chester and Roy Perotti, which was first published in 1976. It's a great read.

The rest of the Wembley Mob were okay with me. I got on really well with Sam McCarthy, who was a British Featherweight boxing champion boxer in the 1950s. He used to sit on my shoulders while I did press-ups.

On remand, especially in a Cat-A where it's stricter, when everyone's looking at a long bit of bird, there's often a tight bond between us all, because nobody wants any trouble before their case comes up. The Cat-A screws are usually more experienced and older and know how to handle serious criminals. Because they didn't want any aggro with the Wembley Mob, they turned a blind eye to visitors bringing in alcohol and meals like pie and mash.

When that lot went to trial, Turner got 21 years, Green 18 and Wilkinson 16, although Jimmy's conviction was quashed on appeal. Smalls probably got a new identity. What an arsehole. His evidence had secured sentences totalling 308 years for more than robberies worth almost one million pounds, a helluva lot cash back in those days.

*****

All the time the critical condition of the copper hung over me. Updates from solicitors convinced me I was looking at a long stretch.

A couple of months later, my girlfriend's granddad somehow managed to stand bail for me at the Strand, paying several hundred pounds to get me out. I couldn't believe it when I was told I could go. I was so grateful to see my other half's face.

The old boy also suggested we get married as it would look

good in court if I was in a solid relationship. Looking back, it was a silly idea because those old judges are not stupid. But we tied the knot at Acton Registry Office at what was a low-key event, with just a few close family members present.

*****

I remained active with small little unarmed jobs, usually jumping counters at bookmakers. Six or so months later, early 1974, my case came up.

My first day at the Bailey, another one, and I was slated to be in front of a judge called Mervyn Griffith-Jones, who at the time was the Common Serjeant of the Bailey, the second most senior permanent judge of the Central Criminal Court after the Recorder of London.

And these judges were well known in criminal circles — celebrities almost, and as famous as some of the A-list criminals they put down. During my time in prison, I heard old lags talk about the pros and cons of various judges in the run up to each other's cases. Nobody wanted Melford Stevenson — he'd made an example of The Krays just a couple of years earlier.

Since my last visit to the Bailey, a huge refurbishment had taken place. As usual, I'd headed to the basement of the original court building to surrender my bail, but was told to report to the South Block extension. At least the cells weren't like something out of the last century anymore.

My barrister came to introduce himself.

'You're in quite a bit of trouble, Mr Hill,' he said, looking over his glasses at me.

No shit, Sherlock...

'Let me tell you, Mr Hill,' continued my barrister, an accomplished QC. 'Judge Griffith-Jones and I and a lot of other QCs were out at a function last night. We all drank too much, so we're a little bit worse for wear. Mr Griffith-Jones is a very good friend of mine. With that in mind, we could certainly look at doing a deal with him.'

'Really?'

After the morning session, my QC came into my cell looking all flustered.

'They're all knackered and want to call it a day.'

'No deal, I'm staying not guilty.'

Very early on in the proceedings, photos were produced of the police officer, with big black eyes, his nose smashed all over his face and what looked like scaffolding holding his head together.

Even I was shocked, and I'd seen a lot in my relatively short life by that point, but I still said, 'No way, no deal, I'll take my chances.'

Well...

The police officer I'd bashed up appeared at court on the second day. I wasn't expecting that. He could barely talk, and mumbled that he hadn't been able to eat properly since. As he shook his head disapprovingly at me, the jury gasped while they looked at more damning photos of his injuries.

The final nail in the coffin for me was that cunt, Mark, the grass. They read out his statement and it had me banged to rights. The prosecution said, 'A gun was found on your side of the vehicle. Mark says it was yours and that you were there. The officer's blood type was found on your jeans so that also suggests you were there. I put it to you...that you were there.'

What could I say?

'Mr Hill, you hit a police officer with a paving slab, didn't you?'

'No, I didn't'

Then they brought out a corner paving slab and a smaller piece of concrete paving, each in separate plastic bags. The court was told the small piece had blood on it.

This was a decade before DNA was used to prosecute in a UK court case. My barrister, defending me, said the blood had dripped on to the concrete from the officer's nose or from a cut on his head, after I'd punched him.

The prosecution found it difficult to argue against that, but Griffith-Jones had other ideas in his summing up. I thought he was meant to be impartial, but he asked the clerk to bring him the items, which he held in his hands, as he said, 'Members of the jury, the prosecution may have failed to confirm how the blood came to be on the smaller piece of concrete, but I am of the opinion that it was originally attached to the paving slab and came off on impact.'

Then I remember the old wanker picked up the photos of the

police officer and, addressing the jury, said something like, 'You've seen the photos of the police officer. You've actually seen him in person in this court. It is for you to decide whether it is conceivable that he would have sustained his facial injuries only by a fist and punches?'

But, fuck me, I really had only punched him. If I had actually used any paving, like they suggested, that Old Bill would have been dead, for real. There would have been open wounds, not just cuts here and there.

The prosecution painted such a bad picture, I began to think I should have gone for a deal.

The next day, judgement day, literally, and not surprisingly I was found guilty.

My barrister said to me, 'This case is on its fifth day now. You didn't want to discuss an offer. This afternoon, you will go in front of the judge for him to pass his sentence. Good luck.'

Griffith-Jones asked Mark to stand up. He was given three years, and taken away.

I was sentenced to seven years, courtesy of the 'old boys club'. Attempted robbery, possession of a firearm, and grievous bodily harm — better known, of course, as GBH.

And don't forget, I still wrongly thought I was sexually abused as a kid by a copper, so there was no love lost between me and the police. It all felt so fucked up. Even if they had caught me on that street, outside a property, with a gun in the motor, I'd be looking at three years. But because Old Bill was involved, I had been given a lot more. Seven years was my biggest yet, and my first straight in as an adult prisoner. With three or four months on remand already done, I was looking at least another four years, if I was lucky. I had to look on the bright side. If that gun had gone off in front of a police officer in a uniform, I could have got life.

*****

So I was back at the Scrubs, and on that first morning, when the gates were rattling and the screws were singing, I had a familiar sinking feeling. Here we go again.

I was put on A-wing, threes-up with two decent fellas. I was given the top bunk because they had obviously already taken the bottom one and the single bed. Nobody really wants the top bunk, because when people are farting and shitting below you, the smell rises.

There were no toilets in the cells in those days. One aluminium pot, a bowl and a jug. I learned very quickly that if I wanted to do No 2s, and I just had to go, to rip up single sheets from a newspaper, put them on the bed and shit on that. Fold everything up, make a parcel, maybe also using a ripped bit of the end of your bedsheet and then throw it out of the window. Hence the phrase 'shit parcel'. There could be dozens of shit parcels on the ground below, which some poor lag had to pick up. You'd look out in the morning and see hundreds of cockroaches scuttling in and around the parcels.

On my first full day I was given my EDR (Earliest Day of Release) and my LDR (Latest Day Of Release). A screw who I knew from my YP asked how I was.

'Not too bad, mate. I just got to get through this bit of bird.'

'Are you still the same?'

'As what?'

'A right little fucker?'

So I knew he wanted me to do something for him.

A few days later, the same screw started explaining about a couple of fellas, one doing 12 years and the other 14, for sexually abusing a young girl in a graveyard. He reckoned they left this girl paralysed. 'Like a cabbage,' he said. The family was known to a couple of the screws, and they needed these sickos sorted out.

'Ray, you'll be well looked after with tobacco and food.'

Exactly the two things that were king in prison in those days before drugs were commonplace.

'Right, Ray, 'the threes', where one of the nonces is, will be unlocked first. Then we'll let you out of your cell on 'the ones', and you can go and find him in the toilets. All the other screws will know what's going on...and won't interfere.'

So that night, I knew in a matter of hours in the morning I'd be called to action, but I kept that quiet for now. I was playing cards with the guys in the cell and unbeknown to me, one of them, who was a joker, drew a heart on the back of my shirt in red biro. For a laugh.

As planned, first thing in the morning, our cell was the only one unlocked on our landing and, before disappearing, I told the other two I was going to sort out a bit of business and they'd be looked after, so they were sweet.

In the toilet on the threes, I filled up a bowl with piping hot water. The first water out of those taps in the morning was so white hot you could make a cup of tea out of it. When the nonce came through. Bosh. In his face. He screamed liked nothing I'd ever experienced before. Everyone could hear it. Anyone still locked up was banging on their cell doors. The whole wing knew something was going down.

I grabbed his head and smashed it on the urinal. I had to be careful I didn't kill him, because I didn't know my own strength. Then, because of what he did, and with my own abuse flooding back in my mind, I pulled down his trousers and stamped on his bollocks. I wanted to damage this guy down there, as much as possible.

By now, about 15 guys were watching. As arranged, the screws turned a blind eye and I legged it back to my cell, where I was banged up again.

A few hours later, I was taken to one side by the screw and given some supplies. The fella was taken to Hammersmith Hospital on Ducane Road, next door to the Scrubs. Job done.

'Now, Ray, the other fella, he's on the 'twos' and they're exercising with the 'ones' today, so we need him done too.'

I decided to wait to see if this guy used one of the two toilets on the exercise yard, and he did. I watched him walk into one of the cubicles. The doors were split and not lockable, so I barged my way in, armed with a scrubbing brush with a pointed end. The peado was mid-poo, so I got shit all over my trousers as I grabbed him. The same as his mate, I punched and stamped on his balls... repeatedly. I didn't want either of them to be able to do again what they'd done to that poor girl.

I had to be careful because I'd quickly worked out some of the screws on the exercise yard were actually not in on this. Fortunately, I was able to get out of the toilet, back into the yard, and to my cell, to clean myself up without any problems. I had a good wash and put on a clean pair of jeans.

Later that afternoon, as I came down for my dinner, the governor, the deputy governor and some other screws were waiting for me. They asked me to turn around, and pointed to the red heart on the back of my shirt, which I didn't know anything about, and which the second nonce had identified me by.

I was banged to rights. Kicking and screaming, feffing and blinding, now banged up on the block.

Loss of any privileges...again...not that I was likely to get a visit any day soon from anybody other than my mum. My darling new wife certainly didn't want to know and hadn't shown her face yet.

Shortly after, the door to my cell opened up and the governor came in. I went into auto-pilot and recited my prisoner number, which I knew off by heart by now. '131549, Hill. Yes, sir.'

As I waited to hear my fate, what began to come out of the governor's mouth was surprising.

'Do you accept, Hill, that you verbally assaulted one of my officers at the bottom of the stairs?'

So the charge was only for what I said when I was ambushed by the screws, not for anything else. Result.

'I can't accept threats to kill one of my officers. So, Hill, you'll be down on the block for ten days, and then you'll be shipped off to another prison.'

Fucking hell. Amazing. That's only what everybody wants at the Scrubs anyway...to be moved on.

Back in my usual cell on the block, I decided it was time to get really fit. Press-ups and sit-ups constantly. One of the screws had competed in Mr Universe so showed me how to do press-ups properly, all kinds of different ones. Another screw would always give me a decent plate of food. Like macaroni cheese and ham. Cups of coffee and cans of Coca Cola. Lovely. It was like they were trying really hard to look after me, which is unheard of on a main wing, let alone on the block. I was then given quarters of tobacco, good portions wrapped in clingfilm. It seemed like they were making it easier for the move to my next nick.

*****

The block had its own exercise cages, connected to the main yard. A bigger one that four people could use and two smaller single person cages. One day, me and a guy, who looked like a member of the Hitler Youth, were in each of the small cages. He asked me through the metal fencing if I had any tobacco. I didn't know who the fuck he was, but he was exercising on his own, so I knew he was heavy.

I said, 'Yeah, I've got a quarter here…'

'Great, I'll make it up to you…'

The next day, I was out exercising and the shout came out, 'Hilly…IN…'

Back in my cell, the screws brought me my tea tray…and I had two buns rather the usual one.

'The guy in the yard you've been talking to, Hill…he's given you his bun.'

'Okay, sweet.'

'Hill, let me tell you something. The guy who has given you this bun is Graham Young, who has killed people by poisoning them. He could make poison out of the weeds in that yard.'

Then another screw stormed into my cell, waving some tobacco at me.

'You gave this to Graham Young, Hill, are you fucking crazy?'

I didn't know who the geezer was. Nobody told me. Both buns were taken away, thank God.

I later found out Young was born and bred in Neasden in north west London, not far from me. At the age of 14, he had become one of Broadmoor's youngest ever inmates when he poisoned his father, sister and a classmate. All survived because Young hadn't perfected his potions yet. While at Broadmoor, there were a number of suspicious cyanide poisonings, leading to the death of an inmate, but staff could never prove it was Young. In 1971, he was released after nine years, deemed 'no longer obsessed with poisons, violence of mischief.'

Well, they got that badly wrong…

A few years later, Young was convicted of killing at least three people with thallium, including his step-mother, claiming, 'I suppose I had ceased to see them as a people. They were simply guinea pigs.' He was convicted on two counts of murder and two counts of attempted murder and sentenced to life imprisonment. Like many of us, Young began his latest bit of bird at the Scrubs before being allocated, and that's when we met. Young died in his cell at Parkhurst prison in 1990 in his 40s. They reckon he either poisoned himself or was murdered by prisoners or prison staff who didn't feel safe around him.

That night in my cell on the block, all I could hear was 'click, click, click.' I was told the next day that it was notorious child killer Ian Brady, writing his memoir in the cell above me, using a typewriter generously given him by the prison. I was fuming. A guy who killed all those kiddies, and hadn't even told the families where the bodies were, was allowed a typewriter to write a book? Outrageous.

When I was next let out for exercise, I ran up the stairs to try and find Brady. There were three screws outside his cell. I could see him in there and I wanted to kill the cunt, but alarms started to go off and screws appeared from everywhere and marched me back down to my cell. I really really wanted to smash up Brady, but the screws told me I was getting shipped out soon, and urged me to hold it down. It was so difficult because all the time I channelled what happened to me in the past — what my uncle and those people at the children's home put me through. How close had I come to being snuffed out like those poor young girls and boys abused and murdered by Brady and Myra Hindley? Maybe some of the kids at the home weren't returned to their families?

I later discovered that around the same time, Brady had somehow befriended Graham Young in the Scrubs through a shared fascination of Nazi Germany. Brady even devoted a whole chapter to Young in his finished published book, *The Gates Of Janus - Serial Killing and its Analysis*. He talks about 'a stay in London' — which is a unique way of describing a spell at the Scrubs — when he 'had the opportunity to interview some prominent English serial killers'. Brady describes with fondness his time spent chatting with Graham Young. Fucking sickos, the pair of them. Apparently, Young was delighted when a waxwork of him was added to the Madame Tussaud's Chamber Of Horrors.

Retired prison officer John G Sutton talks about an encounter with Graham Young at the Scrubs in 1975 on his interesting *YouTube* channel *Tales From The Jails*.

SHIPPED OFF

After four or five days on the block, I was on a ferry to Albany prison on the Isle of Wight, which I didn't know enough about, although I had heard it was next door to Parkhurst prison and part of the overall HMP Isle of Wight set-up. Being sent straight from solitary confinement at the Scrubs to a fresh new nick could only be a blessing.

Not before the nightmare trip on the ferry over to Cowes, though. Cuffed up in a cubicle in a Black Mariah police van in the hull of the boat for the whole journey, I couldn't see where we were going, and heard every wave crashing in — the loudest, most disconcerting noise I've ever heard, especially with my fear of water. If that boat had gone down, us cons would have been helpless.

Finally on dry land after that horrific hour-long crossing, it was just a short drive to our new home.

At reception I heard, 'Hello mate, how it's going?' It was Tommy, a larger than life well-renowned armed robber from Bermondsey. I'd dated his sister.

It was nice to hear a familiar voice and see a friendly face. Tommy really sorted me out with some nice clothes, not the usual stuff you get given, which never fits.

I was put on A-wing and could immediately tell Albany was a clean and modern prison. Lovely single cells with electric doors... click...operated by screws in an office. During the day we could come and go with our own keys, then...click...the screws were in control again by the evening. We all used wooden wedges with metal tips made in the workshop, or nails, under our doors, as our own little security feature, so that once the doors were unlocked another inmate, or screw, couldn't steam in unannounced.

I made friends with a camp guy called Terry, who gave me some tobacco I could use to trade for some bits and pieces. I soon found out that C-wing at Albany was known as 'Marriage Quarters' because so many guys there hooked up together.

As usual, I asked the fitness manager if I could join the gym, and he told me to be there at 6pm the next evening. I was delighted to bump into Sam McCarthy, who was a gym orderly. It was great having him there. That first night, I clocked some huge guys playing basketball, including a 6ft plus black fella called Tank. A lovely, lovely guy. I went on the weights stage and impressed them with my powerlifting, having not lost any of my strength since my stint as a YP.

At the gym in the evenings chatting to the other guys, it didn't feel like being in prison. Not everybody could be arsed to use the gym. I'd say a total of 50 guys out of the 600-odd prisoners on the five or six wings at Albany actually bothered to work out, so it felt quite exclusive to be there. Because Albany was so laid back, there were other regular activities like being allowed to cook on your wing, in an area with two or three stoves, which made the gym less appealing.

For something extra to cook up, some guys on the threes would catch seagulls with their bare hands through their cell windows, which were casement in style, but obviously only opened so much. They'd attach pieces of bread to some cotton via a little hook and throw them out to the gulls hovering outside, some of them big old albatrosses you get down on the coast on the Isle Of Wight. Once the gull had bitten and the hook was embedded in its beak, they'd drag the poor fucker through the gap in the window, and garrot it. Snap. I witnessed it a few times, an unbelievable spectacle. They'd boil the seagulls first, and then roast them for dinner later that night. Pigeons too, which were much easier to catch.

As usual, I was deadlifting around 700-800 pounds...bosh bosh, five or six reps at a time. The others were lifting a lot more, but they noticed me. As I banged out more and more weight, now two 100 kilo plates on each side, so 880 pounds, I got bigger and bigger.

I asked three huge black guys in the corner with strong Jamaican accents if I could train with them. 'Okay man, sure,' said a guy called Tom, with a huge scar down the side of his face, and an inch across. He was only 5ft 8in tall but it felt like he was that wide too.

Over the next few weeks other inmates started to tell me that

Tom was actually called David Lashley, and was dubbed the Beast Of Shepherd's Bush when he was jailed for 12 years for a series of rapes, robberies and assaults on various women. Tom strongly protested his innocence. We were mates by now, so I believed him.

Tom was later released in 1976 but banged up again 12 months later for another 18 years for the rape and attempted murder of another poor female victim. Upon his next release in 1989, Lashley was re-arrested at the prison gates and finally jailed for life, due to admissions about a murder he'd made to a fellow inmate. I found out later that the scar on Lashley's face was caused when two inmates attacked him with the jagged top of a pineapple tin hidden in a bar of soap. They must have known all about him. When I found out stuff like that after striking up a friendship with someone, it was tough to take.

*****

Being so close to Acton, my wife had visited me a couple of times at the Scrubs, but the Isle Of Wight was much more of a mission, and she hadn't come yet. The set-up in the visiting rooms at adult prisons were a step-up from the plank and wire mess during my YP, though. Now, I could sit across a table from my visitor, but still no kissing or touching allowed.

It was at Albany that I first heard about 'vicar visits', which could be requested every now and then if you were able to claim you were having marital issues, and needed the prison vicar to mediate in a special room to the side of the main visiting area. In my case, I was actually expecting 'the wife' to leave me at any point, so my claims of so-called domestic problems weren't far from the truth. The key to a vicar visit was how relaxed they were compared to a regular visit. No divider and much less supervision. Once inside a vicar visit, the aim was to have such a heated discussion with your other half that the vicar offers to give you ten minutes on your own to try and work things out. And a charitable vicar is much easier to manipulate than a hard-nosed screw.

When I heard my wife was making the trip over by ferry, this was my chance. Sat around a normal table with her and the vicar, the plan worked perfectly, and he left the room. There was just about enough time for a kiss and a cuddle and possibly a quick handjob, which of course would last only a matter of seconds. My wife was not best pleased, but we had managed to compose ourselves by the time the vicar reappeared.

My wife wrote to me soon after and said that I had degraded her in that room. But I was desperate...and, anyway, I thought everybody knew what went on during a vicar visit and how to play the game. If someone was pulled aside for one, while we waited to go into the regular visiting room, a big cheer would go up. 'Go on my son...get in there, my son. Nudge, nudge, wink wink...'

My wife told me she would not be visiting me again. I had begun to find visits bittersweet anyway. Often, they took days, if not weeks, to get over. It almost felt better not to have them.

*****

Then one day, I was told to get my stuff together. I was being moved to C-wing. Marriage Quarters. I quickly made friends with Peter Kelly, another accomplished armed robber, doing a 14 stretch. A massive guy and very dangerous, we later became friends on the outside.

Peter hated the screws with a vengeance. In Wandsworth, he threw his shit at them each morning. Literally. Everybody else would throw theirs out of the window, but Peter would shit in the pisspot, save it, and when the screws unlocked in the morning, he'd chuck it at them. After a few days of this, the screws had enough, dragged him down to the block and smashed him to pieces. When they opened his cell the next morning...wallop...he threw his shit at the block screws too. Peter didn't give a fuck, he did the same thing five days running on the block.

One day, the No 1 Chief (the boss of the screws) came to his cell and said, 'I want no more shit or piss thrown at my guys. I know the governor is the most important person here, but I run this prison. The next important person is the doctor, who I know very well. If necessary, he can come to your cell tonight and certify you dead.'

Peter told me it sent a chill down his spine, because he knew the No 1 Chief meant it. Then he was sent to Albany, also a result for him, albeit his sentence was extended considerably because of his dirty protests.

One night on C-wing, I heard the worst screams imaginable, echoing around the prison, sounding like they were coming from the threes or the fours. I could also smell smoke.

Someone was about to be moved to a lower category prison and was distraught at leaving his boyfriend on the wing. So he set fire to his mattress, which in those days didn't come with a fire protector, so his cell had gone up in flames. Screws rushed to the landing, but the electrics on the cell door were burned, so an officer had to bring a manual key from the gate lodge, about a quarter of a mile away. When they eventually got in, the prisoner was himself alight. He was virtually dead already, but the adrenalin allowed him to stagger out of the cell, leaving footprints of sticky black patches of skin from his bare feet on the floor, as he collapsed and died in front of the screws.

*****

At Albany, I came across more and more faces and names I'd heard of. People I wanted to get to know, because they could help me, or maybe we'd work together one day. That's one thing you can try and do in prison...spend the time trying to build a trust with someone, that can be used on the outside.

There were already some big firms at Albany, like the Barry brothers — Anthony, who I knew as Parkie, and Johnny. They owned The Regency nightclub and restaurant in Stoke Newington during the 1960s and paid protection money to close associates the Kray twins, who were infamous regulars along with (allegedly) Princess Margaret and Lord Boothby. Parkie Barry was acquitted at the Krays trial in 1969 of the murder of Jack 'The Hat' McVitie (which the twins were famously both sent down for) because he was 'forced to help the Krays by fear'. When I first saw the Barrys at Albany, I thought they were the Krays. As tiny as Ronnie and Reggie, they looked identical and were dangerous cunts too.

I first met Pat Adams when he arrived at Albany, wearing a

massive gold cross around his neck. A lot of people were saying Pat's name. His family was just starting to make it, so a lot of guys at Albany wrapped themselves around him because they knew the Adams were on their way up.

Pat settled in quickly and wasn't a bully. He knocked on my door one day and asked me to come and have a chat in his cell, and from that point on we got on really well and became pals. We started training together, doing weights in the gym, and Pat got really fit. It was clear Pat had some very good people around him and got everything he wanted inside. He'd do his own thing, and then pop up at the canteen and empty it.

The Barrys were the first firm I knew to bring drugs into a prison. Cigars full of acid tabs, usually stuck up someone's arse. For the next few weeks, everybody was out of their nut — apart from me, because I wasn't into drugs then.

By now, Albany being a cushy prison, we were allowed record players, made by PYE or Phillips, in our cells. An electrical engineer con would sell their services with the help of someone from the paint shop, and chase the wall — maybe cover it with a page 3 girl during the process — and hardwire from the record player, up the wall to the light fitting. Then someone else would re-plaster it. A team effort. Job done. We were able to buy certain records, or get them brought in at visits. The most popular albums were Pink Floyd, Led Zeppelin and the reggae artist, John Holt…everyone had that one.

One guy who had taken some acid, came to me the next morning and said he was in my cell with me the night before, and told me exactly what records I was listening to and the book I was reading. He said it was an astral projection. I didn't have a clue what he was on about.

I went into another pal's cell and he said, 'Can you see him?'
'Who?'
'The little green man in the corner…'
'What?'
'The leprechaun. The Irish fella in green? Can't you see him, Ray?'
'Oh, yeah, the guy in the green hat. Yes, I can see him now, mate.'
I had to play along, because this guy was fucked, and I was trying

to help him get through it. He denied all knowledge of it the next day.

A few days after the cell fire, John Barry heard a trans guy called Jackie screaming. It sounded like another protest. We ran to her cell and looked through the window in the door and saw blood everywhere. We tried to get in but Jackie had about 20-odd wedges under her door. Most of the screws were upstairs repairing all the damage to the last cell. When a couple of them appeared trying to smash the door in, we argued that might make it worse. Eventually, with the help of a metal acrow prop, used to support a floor or wall, we were able to isolate the door, and open it. Inside the cell, Jackie was on the floor, blood pouring from an arm she'd been slashing with a tool she'd made herself. Another protest at soon being separated from her lover.

A few months later, me and John Barry were told that the Home Office would be taking time off our sentence for helping to save Jackie's life. We both sat outside the governor's office, excited about what reduction we might get. Johnny went in first and after a few minutes, I heard him shouting, 'Fuck off, you wankers,' and then he stormed out.

Seven days...seven poxy days off our sentences. Johnny told them to keep it. I said, 'If he don't want his, I'll have both lots.' Haha. But it was a pisstake. You could get seven days added on for not having a shave, or growing a moustache without asking permission. What a joke! We hadn't helped Jackie to get any time off anyway.

*****

The summer of 1976 was the second hottest on record in the UK, so prison was not the best place to be. London had an amazing 16 consecutive days over 30 degrees. When it reached those sorts of temperatures, we weren't allowed on the exercise yard because the tarmac was just too hot. So, instead, we were allowed to sit on the grass next to it. That's where I met Jimmy Reid, another trans guy who had been allowed to grow his hair and had been prescribed Estrogen tablets to try and grow a little pair of titties, which were now trying to pop out of the boob tube Jimmy had fashioned from her standard issue T-shirt.

A lot of heterosexual guys in prison are turned by the gay or trans guys. Maybe it's something to do, and because after all that time away, they become attracted to these fellas running around looking like women and doing things to them that women would. Everyone has needs, so these things happen. We all do our prison sentences the best we can. It's not for me to say what is right or wrong. I reckon on C-wing, out of 100 prisoners, at least half had been turned. And some you could have never imagine would.

I could become pals with a geezer and wouldn't know they'd been turned the other way, until someone told me. By then, you're mates and you think, well, he's alright, and he's not trying it on with me.

Some of the gay lot might be cooking a nice meal and you think, hold up, I can be part of that, and you can't be if you've already distanced yourself. Prison is all about food…and survival. Before drugs were widespread, prison was run by food.

So me and Jimmy Reid became mates and spent a lot of time chatting on the grass that summer.

*****

A big Irish fella wanted to get back to a prison in Ireland, to be closer to his family. He was huge, 6ft 6ins tall, handsome, God-like. He decided one hot sunny day to climb up on the roof to make his own personal protest, and five or six guys followed him up there, including my pal Johnny Pattern. Like I said, probably just for something to do. Everybody else was immediately banged up.

The 'protestors', who had scaled drainpipes, based themselves on the gym roof because it was flat, and they slept there on that first night. For whatever reason, the screws weren't in a hurry to get them down. The guys lowered down pieces of rope made from bedsheets past the windows of different cells, so lags could send up flasks of tea or sandwiches or whatever food they could attach.

I now had a job in the kitchen, in the bakery, so any old bits that would get thrown out at the end of the day were sent up to the boys too — sausages, bits of bacon and buns.

A warning went out that anybody caught sending stuff up to the roof would get nicked, but we argued they needed water. It was boiling hot, they could die up there. I can't even imagine what they doing for the toilet, despite being used to having limited facilities.

They were on that roof for at least a week. It was a crazy time at the prison. Most jobs were put on hold while the protest continued, but thankfully in the kitchen, we had to keep going, so that meant we could keep feeding the guys. Them being on the gym roof also meant no gym for anybody, which was very frustrating, but we had to try and support the protestors and what they were trying to achieve.

The gym was connected to a walkway which splintered off to the various wings, which the boys moved around on. If the screws came up on ladders on top of the walkways, the protestors would run to the gym roof, in the middle.

Under instruction from the home office, the prison put up scaffolding and barbed wire to stop the boys jumping from the gym roof to the roofs of the wings, where they would be able to access the food and water we were sending up more easily.

A police helicopter began to circle above, and I was told another chopper appeared with reporters in it. There was also a cartoon in one of the tabloid papers, picturing a prisoner with a gorilla's head, grabbing a helicopter out of the sky, like he was King Kong.

Even in those record temperatures, there was little compassion for the protestors. Four of the boys came down first after about five to six days, leaving the big Irish fella and Johnny Pattern up there for another 48 hours. Pattern was the last man down. The sun had burned his liver and kidneys, and he was taken to the hospital at Parkhurst and put in a cage next to Charles Bronson, where he later stabbed and killed a guy because of an argument during a game of cards.

I don't know what happened to our Irish friend. He definitely wouldn't have got his wish to go back home. He was doing life anyway, so his chances of parole at some point would have been a lot less after that little episode.

*****

One night, I was in my cell with a pal, Togi Ludlow, and a couple of other guys, drinking some hooch. There was a knock on the door, and Jimmy Reid came in. She explained that her 'friend' George Cockle wanted a gang-bang with her and another prisoner. Jimmy was in bits, because she wasn't up for that.

She explained, 'I don't want anyone else involved. I'm in love with George, but he says if I don't go along with it, he's going to hurt me.'

By now, I considered myself the governor of our wing so I reassured Jimmy, 'You tell George, that if he hurts you, I'll hurt him more.'

Now, George Cockle was known as 'Catapult Charlie' because he and his wife robbed jewellers by firing a catapult at their shop windows, so he was a tricky customer. The next day, I was in the kitchen, and the alarm bells went off. I had nicked some steak the night before so I thought they might be after me. Suddenly the gates opened up and a load of screws came running through with Jimmy Reid, her hair all over the gaff, blood all over her boobs. Five minutes later, they brought George out on a stretcher, a sheet over him. He'd been stabbed 16 times with a quarter inch chisel. While Jimmy had been working on a lathe in the wood mill, George came from behind and gave her loads of aggro about the gang-bang. Jimmy let him have it, his male strength taking over her female sensibilities.

George was taken to Parkhurst and died at the hospital there. Jimmy Reid was taken to Winchester Prison, because she was going to be tried at Winchester Crown Court. Both aged in their 20s, it had been a brutal end to their relationship.

Because Jimmy had come to me the night before the incident fearing for her life, I decided to put myself forward as a witness. I couldn't bring George Cockle back, but maybe I could help Jimmy get the best sentence possible.

I was actually moved to Winchester myself for the week of the trial, which I wasn't too happy about because it was a piss-hole compared to Albany, and it also meant another miserable trip back and forth on the ferry. I was twos-up there also, and banged up a lot more, but it was what it was. I wanted to try and help Jimmy.

I was taken to court most days and quickly believed that both the judge and prosecution were the other way, I could just tell. Jimmy might have a half a chance here.

When it was my time to give evidence, it was nice to be in the dock as a witness for once — without my neck on the line. I told the court Jimmy had come to me the night before, worried about what George might do if she didn't agree to the gang-bang…and that I believed she had acted in self-defence the next day.

When it came back as guilty I thought, fuck, Jimmy could get life here, but the judge did ultimately find kindly in Jimmy's favour.

'Taking into account diminished responsibility, I am sentencing you to two years.'

Probably because it was a woman, as such, attacking a man, after refusing his sexual advances. A crime of passion…

At the time, I thought, that's something a judge will never say to me — 'Diminished responsibility', the actual definition of which is…

An unbalanced mental state that is considered to make a person less answerable for a crime and to be grounds for a reduced charge, but that does not classify them as insane.

It could be argued that I've had 'an unbalanced mental state' ever since the abuse I suffered as a child. Whether that makes me 'less answerable' for any of my convictions is, of course, debatable, because it always comes back to the argument that the vast majority of people who are sexually abused as children probably don't go on to lead a life of crime.

I later found that Jimmy was actually inside for chopping a security guard's hand off…to get a money bag. The two years she had just received was nothing on her original sentence, because she'd only serve an extra two-thirds of that — around 15 months.

*****

Back at Albany, everything was sweet. I was working in the kitchen and, as far as prison goes, I was enjoying my time behind bars again.

At the end of one breakfast sitting, I'd been serving up eggs, bacon, sausages, tomatoes, beans and fried slices. Tank, the basketball player, came in. I actually had quite a bit left that day, so I loaded up his plate, with a couple of extra eggs for good measure. Then I put a plate with about six or seven eggs on the side for me and one of the other kitchen staff, and left it there while I sorted out some other stuff. I turned back round and Tank had nicked the extra plate of eggs.

'Hold up, what you doing? Put that back.'

It was the only time Tank had used Jamaican patois aggressively in my direction.

'Bloodclaat...bumboclaat...fuck off...'

'Mate, put the fucking eggs back...'

Tank kissed his teeth and walked off.

I put my tray of food down by the office door, caught up with Tank and said, 'In the toilet...'

I couldn't let him have that over me, so I had to fight him now. Two screws had worked out what was going on, but they're weren't bothered. They were going to let us have it out.

Inside the toilet, this fight became more of a wrestle, so I had to start boxing Tank. I began punching him all over the place. He then ducked at a big right hand I threw, and my hand crashed into an aluminium post and I was worried I'd broken my knuckle. The screws eventually pulled us apart, took us both back to our cells, and there were no repercussions that day.

The next morning, as usual, the cell door went 'click'. A few minutes later, my door came open a little bit, but only so far, because of the wedges I had got in place and also a nail in a hole in the floor. It was Tank, pushing the door so hard that the nail bent over and the wedges went everywhere. He was in the cell so quickly, and tried to stab me in the head with a plastic knife he'd made, as I laid in my bed, half-awake. He legged it back to his cell and I ran after him, but he'd wedged himself in so well I couldn't force my way in. But now I knew for sure. If I didn't do him, he would do me...all because of some eggs. But that's prison — all about food... that and surprise knife attacks. In the winter, we'd be issued with overcoats, especially for people who worked outside in the gardens. We'd put books or a couple of towels down the back of our trousers, which couldn't be seen under our coats, to protect us from plunge attacks.

My latest job was in the laundry. The main task each day was to get together all the inmates' clothes that needed washing. As I walked down a flight of stairs, Tank appeared out of nowhere and shoved me, sending me tumbling down six or seven steps to the bottom. As I lay on the landing, with two of the other basketball lads as his back up, Tank stabbed me three times in my stomach with a modelling knife he'd managed to blag from somewhere. Fortunately, no screws witnessed the attack and I managed to scramble to my feet and run back to my cell, where I ripped a bedsheet and wrapped it around my wounds.

It was really on now. I had to retaliate.

I knew Tank was on 'the works', aka maintenance, and that he finished late. I decided to wait for him in the television room, where there was a broom handle with a piece of wood on the end, used to wedge open the door. As Tank walked past...bosh...I pounced and smashed him round the head two or three times with the broom handle, splitting his head open badly. Tank was out sparko, so I ran back to my cell. This was survival. If I was going to get a big bit of bird for this, then it was going to be for killing him or maiming him for life.

Tank was taken to the hospital across the way at Parkhurst, and I was banged up, like everybody else. Click, click, click.

Quietness for a moment.

Then one more click, and I knew the screws were coming for me.

I pulled back a little bit in my cell, in readiness, and as my door finally opened, a big fat nasty block screw walked in, an ex-rugby player, and hit me square on the chin, just to be a bully. Fair enough, he was entitled to come and pick on me for what I'd done, but not punch me square in the face, just like that. I stepped back to the wall, and then moved forward and punched him in his solar plexus area, so in the middle of his stomach, just above his belly button. I hit him so hard, it burst his spleen. He was in bits.

As the other screws pulled their colleague out of my cell, I knew I was really in shit street now. I knew they were going to come back in with something. It's part of the system.

Minutes later. Click. My door opened again, and two or three screws came at me and shot me in the arm with a tranquilliser gun. I hit the floor. I wasn't unconscious, but I was paralysed. I couldn't even blink. As they started bashing me up, I was powerless. Those screws were out of order. That tranquilliser shot should have been administered by a medic, but they didn't give a fuck about the rules at that point. They had one of their men down. Next an actual doctor came in, put a shot in my neck commonly known as 'a liquid kosh' and knocked me out fully. Now I was really fucked.

It was my turn to be taken to the hospital at Parkhurst. I woke up in a straight-jacket, lying on the floor, with water being chucked over me. It felt like a scene from a mafia movie.

Suddenly, I was dragged along a tiled floor, with no socks or shoes on, into another room. I was stood up against a wall, and the AG (Assistant Governor) came in and said, 'This is an offence which could easily be dealt with by the police because you have seriously injured a prison officer. But we're not going to involve the police. We will deal with this internally.'

Which basically meant they were going to do what the fuck they liked to me.

The AG continued, 'We're going to put you on an indefinite order, which means we can send you to every block in the fucking country…if we want to. For 28 days at a time.'

First up the block at Parkhurst, where I was pretty much tortured for the next few weeks — constantly dragged in and out of different rooms so I was always disorientated. I began to not care where I was or what was happening to me. It was the same shit every day.

I know I was back at Winchester Prison at one point because I had to endure that horrific ferry crossing again, even worse in my battered state. As I was dragged to the block there backwards by my feet, so my head banged on every step, I noticed riot mattresses and truncheons on the wall, which they regularly used to bash me up with during sudden ambushes in my cell.

Breakfast, tea and dinner were all the same. One plate of horrible slop, which smelt disgusting, and a 'pudding' in a bowl, which was basically the same slop. Plus a cup of water with a sedative in it that knocked me out within minutes.

I wasn't allowed a piss-pot so I had to wee on the floor. The screws came in and bashed me up constantly, so I regularly rolled around in my own piss as the punches and kicks came flying in. All I could think was, when will this ever end? More prisons, more blocks, more beatings. If I got taken to a new prison and another block there, I'd be bashed up all the way in the van. The worst block by far was Dartmoor.

Thankfully my mum kept on at the prison service, and always tracked me down eventually. That probably kept me alive, because since I'd been at Albany, I'd written to her and called her whenever I could. If that ever dried up, she knew something was up and that she needed to keep the pressure on. She even got our local MP involved.

I ended up on one block, God knows where, but the screws were a bit more civil and gave me some decent food, which I desperately needed. It felt like I had lost half my body weight. Maybe I just wasn't a threat by that point.

Then they told me I was on the move again.

STARTING BLOCK

I woke up in a bed in the corner of a cell on the block at Chelmsford Prison — a Cat-B. There was a chair and a cupboard. Wow, this didn't even feel like a solitary confinement unit. Maybe I could look forward to some regular jail time again. Some decent bird. But I was properly fucked. So bruised...black and blue. So undernourished, I'd lost loads of weight. I didn't realise how skinny I looked, because I'd had no mirrors to look in. I was told I weighed nine stone.

And old PO called Jack Sad appeared in my cell and said, 'Son, it's over.'

I burst into tears, because up until that point I hadn't allowed myself to cry. All through that horrifying period, I daren't give those screws the satisfaction of seeing me blub. It would have shown weakness.

The prison doctor came in and said I was lucky to be alive. I was 26 years old.

I really believe the only reason I hadn't been killed was because of my mum. If she hadn't been looking for me, it would have been very easy for me to be lost in the system. Especially back then.

I haven't a clue what happened to Tank. Dead, alive or still inside. Who knows?

After ten days, I was taken up to C-wing, and I quickly realised that Chelmsford was the best prison I'd come across yet. Single cells again. Do what you want, go where you want. And I thought Albany was good?

Thankfully, Togi Ludlow, my mate from Acton, had also been transferred from Albany to Chelmsford, so I had a pal there already, which always helped. He brought me some decent food, which helped to start build me up.

I was given a job in the kitchen, starting on washing up and cutting potatoes, working my way up to a really good role as a baker. So as much bread and cake as I could eat, making loaves and desserts every day. Just what a scrawny former bodybuilder needed.

My huge muscles had just about disappeared under saggy skin all over my body. I couldn't even lift a hundred pounds. But a combination of working out again and eating small balls of yeast every day to thin my blood out helped me pile on weight...and muscle.

I joined the Chelmsford powerlifting team and trained with them every day. I became so big again that the Senior Officer in the kitchen, Mr Mitchell, gave me the nickname 'Honey Monster'...after the character in the popular breakfast cereal TV advert, Sugar Puffs. Mitchell even collected coupons from the cereal packets we had in the kitchen and sent off for a Honey Monster doll, which he proudly put on display.

*****

Chelmsford prison itself was a mad old nick and held just 300 prisoners at the time. Shortly after I arrived, they opened a brand new church there.

It was meant to be a prison chapel, but it was the size of a normal church, and they employed a nutty vicar to run it, who had to deal with some big characters banged up then. Mad Frankie Fraser, Ronnie Bender, who helped dispose of Jack The Hat McVitie's body for the Krays — as well as the Dixons, the Tibbs and Lou Swallow, to name but a few. The screws let Bender and those kind of boys have what they wanted. Scotch, cigars, cigarettes, whatever.

With everyone undone all day, Chelmsford had a real feel-good factor to it. Lots of music and laughter. Alan Dixon was renowned for staying up all night singing Frank Sinatra hits like *My Way*. A few of the other boys played the guitar and the mouthorgan, while Lou Swallow played the same prank every Sunday morning. He'd appear in the kitchen, grab a couple of hard-boiled eggs and put them between his bum cheeks, before making chicken noises as he danced half-naked around the place, before eventually 'laying' the eggs.

I was always up to some sort of mischief, and I loved trying to wind up Frankie Fraser, who was just two cells down from me.

I pinched two sheep's eyes from the kitchen and planned to put them on his pillow before he got up, which was tricky because Frankie was always up early cleaning his cell. That's how a lot of people do their bird…by hours. Clean for an hour or exercise for an hour. Whatever. Just to make the time seem quicker. The idea behind the prank is that when the victim wakes up, they're so dozy they think the sheep's eyes are theirs. It's meant to be a real mindfuck. One morning, I snuck in his cell early enough. Frankie screamed the place down when he woke to those eyes next to him. It was bitter-sweet because while Frankie couldn't fight, he was a dangerous little fucker, so I'd have to watch my back. I just seemed to get off on the thrill of a joke like that, and the potential repercussions that may come my way. I think I just liked the drama of it all.

Tony Lawrence became my best mate at Chelmsford. Tony was a key player in the Richardsons' protection rackets and known as The Brown Bear, because he'd turn up at a boozer wearing a big fur coat, with a pump action shot gun and shoot it up, until landlords paid up. Only one visit required.

Frankie Fraser somehow ran with both The Richardsons and The Krays. He could be a bit of a turncoat, but Tony was exclusive with The Richardsons and was very dangerous. He told me Johnny Bindon was petrified of him, and I could see why.

Tony, who owned scrapyards, famously had a big battle with a firm from Fulham. He was shot first with a .303 rifle, which has such big bullets they can easily go through and out the other side. Tony fell down a flight of stairs and was then shot three or four times in the head with a .22, a small calibre gun with bullets that are so small they can ping around your body and bounce off your bones. But Tony survived. At Chelmsford, he still had some of those bullets in his head.

Tony and Frankie Fraser were always at loggerheads, so Tony asked me to watch the door if he was having a shower. He was worried that Fraser might try and stab him, and he didn't want any trouble so close to his release in a few months. And Frankie did come to the showers a few times, trying his luck. He was a persistent little fucker, but he was also only about ten or eleven stone and I was building my size back up again, so there was no way he could get past me.

When Tony left, as a thank you for looking out for him, he gave me a weight he'd made in the workhouse out of metal cogs, which had a wooden handle. I kept it in my cell and trained anytime and anywhere I could with that weight. In the toilets, tucked away on a landing...wherever. Doing bicep curls and tricep extensions.

I also played for the Chelmsford prison rugby team as prop or second row. I had most of my top teeth knocked out across two or three games, and had to be given a plate of a few false crowns by the prison's visiting dentist to tie me over until I got released and could get them fixed properly. We played the second and third teams from London Irish, London Welsh, Wasps, Harlequins, Saracens, and beat them all. We played the police, the army, all of the services, and won, but lost to the barristers and solicitors team. The police had some hard bastards playing for them. I bashed up a few, but I was surprised how hard some of the police were. Every time in the scrum, as a prop...whoop...I'd clock one, when nobody could see.

*****

Shortly after the huge prison chapel opened, the vicar booked a group of ballerinas to perform there. Was he serious? Loads of fit athletic young ladies in their early 20s in tutus? You can imagine. Every inmate wanked themselves silly that night.

A few weeks later, we were told we would be attending a concert at the gym. After the ballet turnout, what the hell did this crazy vicar have for us next? Well, he certainly had something different up his sleeve. Only the fucking Sex Pistols. Sid Vicious, Johnny Rotten...that little mob. Back then, we didn't have a clue who they were, just that a new punk band was coming to perform at the prison. At the time, and even now, it just seemed such a stupid idea on so many levels. Johnny Cash had made prison gigs a thing in the 1960s, so I guess the Pistols were trying to do their own take on it. We all went to the show, of course we did, just for something to do, but what a racket!

I remember a bloke with a big mouth, I think it was Sid Vicious, saying stuff on the mic like, 'How do you wankers allow these fucking screws to bang you up?' I mean, c'mon mate, didn't he realise just how many dangerous nutcases and lunatics he was performing to?

At times, some of the guys stood up and I thought it was going to kick off. How it didn't, I'm not sure. At the end of the performance, the screws came running on stage and escorted the Pistols to a safe area of the prison, where they got to meet a few well chosen lags, some of the gym and visiting orderlies, I think. The rest of us were taken back to our wings. The music had been so awful, it was one of those rare nights when everybody was happy to get back to their cells.

Johnny Rotten, aka John Lydon, talks about the event in his autobiography *Anger is an Energy: My Life Uncensored* and has some sympathetic words for us cons...

How odd that Chelmsford prison invited the Sex Pistols to play there — to killers and psychos. I loved it. These were real people contaminated by a shitstem not of their own making and caught up in the problems there accordingly. It's very easy to become a criminal without understanding the guidelines. I see everybody in jail as a victim one way or another. Talking to them after, there was no kind of control, we weren't separated from them. They meant no harm to us, and quite a few of the fellas were expecting me to become a fellow prisoner. 'You're on the road to ruin, you are!' I've since proved differently, but they understand society and how society can turn against you.

The sleeve notes on the band's LP, *Live At Chelmsford Prison*, released years later, says, 'Their opening number was 'Anarchy'... at the end of the number there was a barrage of catcalls, boos and screaming.' I'm told the sound engineer over-egged that, and also dubbed in police sirens, shouting and breaking glass to the final recording of the performance, but there was certainly a lot of barracking and tension anyway.

At Christmas, the vicar threw a party for deprived local kids, and a few of us were asked to attend and give them presents. Togi Ludlow tucked me up in the toilets an hour or so before. There were about eight of them smoking some opium black, a combination of marijuana, opium, and methamphetamine, through a copper pipe. I told them I didn't touch drugs, but they said it was Christmas, so to make the vicar's festive tea party seem a bit more interesting, I took a couple of puffs. I floated the whole way to the chapel. Fucked. I didn't have a clue where I was. I told the vicar I wasn't feeling well and was taken back to my cell. I played the Pink Floyd album *The Dark Side of the Moon* on my record player all night and stayed in bed 'sick' for the next 24 hours.

*****

One day, Mr Mitchell gave me a little nod, that I was wanted down the wing by the No 1 Chief...so I went to see him.

'Ray, there's a guy coming in called Wilkinson, and we want you to look after him...'

I thought it might be Jimmy Wilkinson, from the Wembley Mob, but it was a George Wilkinson.

Now, what they didn't tell me, and what I should have suspected, was that George was a few years short of a full jail sentence. The lift didn't go all the way to the top. A big muscular guy, like me, with a bold flash of red hair, he had been in and out of juvenile institutions and prison most of his life. Uncontrollable during a lot of his time inside, it seemed that George had been heavily medicated by screws in the various prisons he'd been held at.

I was allowed to take a cup of tea down to his cell on the ground floor, and he was often kicking off. I'd regularly find him with a chair, table or cupboard above his head. Threatening to smash someone up. Always with the various pills he'd been prescribed for his injuries all over the floor.

There's a chapter about George in the book, *Frightened For My Life: An Account of Deaths in British Prisons* by Geoff Coggan and Martin Walker, which also references my friendship with him. Here are some excerpts from it...

George was hard and given to bouts of drinking and patholog-ical violence. At the peak of his fitness, he was six foot one inches tall, weighed some seventeen stone and boasted a sixty two inch chest and twenty one inch biceps.

A body covered in tattoos, scratched and badly executed in wavy blue-black lines, the cartography of self-contempt. An eye above each nipple; a crude linear nose at the base of his sternum; a set of almost unrecognisable lips around his navel; colourless flags of Britain; 'Janet' on both arms; a stone cross 'In Memory of Bill'.

The incident which must have inevitably followed Wilkinson through the prison system, was him taking a prison officer hostage at Parkhurst. There is something in the collective consciousness (of prison officers) which demands that they seek retribution in the long term from individuals who have attacked one of their number.

Of course, I was only just recovering from the retribution disgruntled screws tortured me with after my own prison office 'incident' at Albany.

George had taken a female welfare officer hostage and demanded a helicopter take him to Newcastle so he could see his old mum, who was now too frail to visit him. The authorities were having none of it, but George had a makeshift knife to the poor woman's throat so the screws did 'a deal'. If George agreed to swap her with a male officer, then they'd arrange the chopper for him. Naively, George agreed and during the handover, was recaptured. I'm told the screws nearly killed him.

Now he was at Chelmsford Prison, I was surprised they'd asked me to look after him. It was fine with me, because it seemed an easy way of earning some 'good behaviour' towards my parole.

I tried to take George to the gym, but he was weak as fuck and couldn't lift anything. He loved the TV room, but that was problematic too. He never agreed with what the others were watching. Evening association became a pressure three hours in the day...6pm - 9pm. All the crew would be in there. Fraser, Bender, the Tibbs and the Dixons. Because they'd clubbed together to pay for a decent television, the boys wouldn't let George change channel one night, so he grabbed the TV off the wall, and smashed it on the floor. It might take ages to get a new TV so this lot wanted to kill George, and were all very capable. In reality, the screws were so cool at Chelmsford, they had a joint whip-round with senior inmates to pay for a new telly themselves because it kept those boys quiet and made the screws jobs and lives easier.

In *Frightened For My Life: An account of deaths in British Prison*s, it explains...

From the beginning of his imprisonment, Wilkinson was given drugs in an attempt to calm down his violent outbursts. During his remand period in Durham he had been given Largactol —100mg, four times daily. This was the beginning of his medical treatment, which was to continue until the end of his life, in ten different prisons.

Wilkinson's four week-stay (at Chelmsford) was brought to a sudden end when, while having association, he smashed the colour TV set. The officer, who dealt with the incident, explained in his report:

'By the time I arrived on the wing, Prisoner 131549 Hill had managed to get Wilkinson away from the TV area and was talking to him in his cell, and said, 'He's all right now,' whereupon Wilkinson was returned to his own cell.'

On January 3rd, Wilkinson was transferred to Pentonville, it seems, because of threats made by other prisoners.

George got put on the block for that little episode. I was told they often put him in a straitjacket but he was able to rip them off his body. I tried to calm George down and I could tell he was scared. He was slurring his words and said, 'Ray, Ray, Ray. Please don't let them take me away.'

I went to see the No 1 Chief to ask him how long George would be on the block, and he said, 'Ray, he's going tonight. He's being shipped out. He can't stay here, he's too much aggro. We haven't got the facilities to keep him.'

George wound up in 'The Ville', and I was told he eventually died in there because he was so drugged up.

*****

With George gone, not having to look out for him any more left me with a lot more time on my hands. When I couldn't be at the gym, I trained with Tony Lawrence's homemade weight whenever I found a discreet place. A guy called Dennis, a heavy cunt from Bermondsey who was with the Tibbs and that lot, dug me out all the time.

'All that muscle and that stupid weight won't help you. Ray…'

He'd thump his chest and say, 'It's all in here. Heart. That's what matters.'

This Dennis guy was alright sometimes, but at other times he really fucking annoyed me. And with me, it would only take that one spark. That moment came as I worked out in the toilet. Dennis was in my face going on about 'heart' again and I thought, I can't take any more of this cunt. I hit him on the chin so hard he flew back through the closed main toilet door, crashing through the frosted glass and landed in a heap on the landing floor of the wing.

As I came out of the toilet, fuming, Dennis jumped over the railings on to the cage netting to grab an old metal tray that been collecting dust for a year or so. He leapt back over, swung the tray at me, missed and I knocked three or four of his teeth out with one punch. I went back in the toilet and carried on training, but shortly after the screws banged us back up in our cells.

The next morning, Dennis' mouth was all over the place. The governor at Chelmsford, a good bloke, had us in the office and said, 'Right, you two, shake hands.'

Always trying to avoid anyone going on the block, that guv. So we shook hands, but I knew it wasn't really over. It rarely is.

Dennis was in with Frankie Fraser, the Tibbs and all that lot. They all gambled fortunes in the card school at Chelmsford with Mickey Green who, following our last few dealings, looked out for me. They'd also bet with watches and rings brought in by visitors in the card games, usually held in Ronnie Bender's cell, which was eight down from mine.

When he got out, Mickey became one of the UK's biggest drug dealers, overseeing a huge international operation, and was said to be worth £75m at one point. He evaded the authorities for more 20 years and was eventually arrested by the FBI in Beverley Hills. Renowned for his tan and love of the Costa Del Sol, Mickey was said to be an inspiration for the lead character in the film *Sexy Beast*, played by Ray Winstone.

*****

During my time in prison so far, my mum was the only family member who came to visit me on a regular basis, but I didn't feel let down. I'd been away before, I was a big boy now. Keith visited me once during my YP, but I think that was it. Thankfully, Acton wasn't a million miles away from Chelmsford, and now I was settled there and able to keep in touch with Mum regularly, for once, she was able to come and visit me on a consistent basis.

My sister Jackie and her friend began bringing my mum, and Jackie came in a few times and introduced me to her mate, and then the friend would come and see me on her own every week.

Traditionally, my family have all been straight-goers. School teachers, security guards, engineers, cooks. My brother Keith and I became very close in later life, but I didn't see him much in between prison terms. Because he was a bully to me as a kid, I think when I became older and bigger he shit himself a bit, because I had become a very violent man. If he'd have got nicked for anything, I'd have visited him. Made sure he had money, but I had none of that support. I just had to take it on the chin, and do my time.

Chelmsford was the only prison in the country that allowed visitors to bring in meals for prisoners, which could be eaten at the table as you sat and chatted to them. A roast dinner. Ham, egg and chips...whatever. We were even allowed one alcoholic drink with that meal. Crazy. The governor was quite regimental, but he ran the nick in such a way that it almost ran itself. It had the potential to blow up any minute, but nobody wanted that, because we had such a cushy time in there. Frankie Fraser's mum was lovely. She brought him up a whole chicken with boiled potatoes on a plate each time.

*****

One night in March, 1978, I was in the gym and the lights went out. I could smell smoke.

'Right, everybody back to the wing. There's a fire in the prison. Wait for further instructions there.'

Back on our wing, the screws told us to go back the other way, and we were led towards a visiting room away from the nick.

Just at that very point, that fucking nutcase Dennis decided, because there was chaos, and he believed there was a good chance it would go unnoticed, to whack me on the side of the head with a dumbbell weight-lifting bar.

Fucking cheek. I hit him on the chin and he went down. I couldn't bash him up, bash him up, because there wasn't time. It was bonkers. As we were scrapping in the corridor, other panicking inmates rushed past us.

I just about made it to the visiting room in one piece, and that was it. We didn't go back to the wing, to the cells or back to Chelmsford Prison again. Everybody was shipped out in Back Mariahs that night. To the Scrubs, Wandsworth or 'The Ville'. It was awful. I lost all my letters, photographs and any keepsakes I'd managed to collect.

It was a huge shock for all of us. Thankfully, nobody was seriously injured or died in the fire. But to a man, we were gutted about leaving Chelmsford and without any warning too.

The 1979 TV film of *BBC* hit comedy *Porridge* was filmed almost entirely on location at Chelmsford a few months later while the prison was still being refurbished after the fire.

In my van, as we left, there were some proper faces, including Terry Millman, one of the guys who attempted the ambitious heist at the Millennium Dome, and who famously bought a speedboat for the job in the name of Mr T Diamond.

By now I was too big to sit in one of the five cubicles either side of the van with bench seats in them, so they had to handcuff me to an officer on a chair in the middle. Another arduous journey, every bump in the road felt and, like any time a prisoner is suddenly moved, such a weird experience to be looking out at the road after all that time…and only because you're about to be banged up somewhere new again. We were all on large-ish sentences, so we knew whatever nick we were taken to, it would first be a holding prison.

Suddenly, we pulled up at Wandsworth.

A cry of, 'Fucking hell,' went up because we all knew Wanno was a piss-hole.

I was the first one off the bus, and as I clambered out, trod on the foot of Mr Dixey, the No 1 Chief.

'I'll be having a word with you later, prisoner Hill.'

Not the best start.

There were a couple of boys some of us knew in reception, trying their best to sort us out decent clothes, but we were allowed to wear civvy jeans at Chelmsford, so with all the will in the world, with the bits we were given, we felt like we were going backwards. I was massive again now — 21 stone, with a 24-inch neck and 22 inch biceps. The screws were fascinated by the size of me, but I could tell they were also a little apprehensive. The buttons around the neck and wrists on the only shirt that fit me wouldn't do up. One screw lost his temper and said, 'Get a needle and cotton tomorrow and move the buttons,' but the collar was about 18 inches at most so that wouldn't work anyway. The only shirts that were any good were loose around my waist, which was still only about 36 inches, but everywhere else I looked like The Incredible Hulk, about to burst out everywhere.

About a hundred of us came from Chelmsford to Wandsworth and we weren't happy at all. We'd been used to decent curtains, lights and bedspreads and the record players we'd first had at Albany. Coming from single cells, they daren't put us threes up, so most of us were twos up in three man cells. The look on my new cell-mate's face when I walked in and towered over him was a picture.

Loads of the Chelmsford lot went mad that night, ripping their cells to pieces. Wandsworth couldn't really handle veteran cons who knew the regime. They really don't like to put guys who have done a lot of bird in other prisons suddenly, especially a holding prison like the Wandsworth or Scrubs. We're just too set in our ways.

Wandsworth was an old fashioned prison, with a cast iron central hub where the screws stood, which had to be polished every day, without fail. No con was allowed to walk across the 'centre' without permission, or they'd get bashed up. The only two that ever dared were Roy Shaw and Frankie Fraser, who had come with me from Chelmsford.

Frankie was taken to see the governor at Wanno, known as 'the Beast', and denied his offence.

'Listen, if one of my officers said he saw you driving down the landing on a motorbike, I would believe him and want to know where you got the fucking petrol from.'

Frankie called him 'Beast by name, beast by nature,' to his face, and walked out of the office.

Frankie told me at a club in Paddington called Angelo's in the '80s that a few years later he arranged for the Beast's dog to be killed and hung from a tree near the prison.

BREAKING BAD

On this latest stretch, I'd now been away for just over four years.

One screw at Wanno was obsessed with the size of me. I bowled out of my cell wearing a just a vest, because my shirts were too uncomfortable, and he rushed me back in and said, 'How the fuck did you get that big — roids?'

So I explained to him about the yeast I'd taken, working in the bakery in Chelmsford. That it thinned out the blood and got it pumping quicker around the body, and about drinking cabbage or carrot water. Like a posh smoothy you'd have for a detox these days.

A couple of days later, the screws informed me that the No 1 Chief, Dixey, whose foot I'd trod on, wanted to see me. I was found an extra large T-shirt to wear for the meeting.

In his office, Dixey cut to the chase.

'I know your brother, Keith.'

'Really?'

'Yes, my son, John, is an electrical engineer, who works in the prison, and he knows your brother Keith, so you can't be here.'

There was no arguing with him. He'd made his mind up.

So I was sent to Lewes Prison, another Cat-B, near Brighton in East Sussex, which as soon as I got there seemed a nice little gaff. Single cells, good screws and the cons were okay too — a lot of respected boys in there who'd done a lot of time.

On top of my recent experience at Chelmsford, I now realised that there wasn't always the need to prove myself on arrival at a new place. Sometimes it just clicks like that, especially in a smaller prison. It was calm, for a while at least. I had a few punch-ups, standard, but no need to become the Daddy in there, which was a result because, as I kept telling myself, I didn't have long left now. Of course, it could kick off at any point at any time, because like on the outside, in prison there's a lot of dangerous people who can't necessarily fight but they can cause lots of problems. Sometimes it's the quiet ones that cause the most harm. They're the ones who'll throw a jug of boiling hot water with sugar in it. A face-changing, life-changing assault. Or from nowhere, stab you in the back with a makeshift knife. But on arrival, Lewes was sweet and I got a nice job in the kitchen.

After three or four months, I fancied a change and managed to blag a job at the gym, which was a first for me. It meant cleaning the office, and the gym floor and its apparatus, which was mainly wooden. Then setting up work-out circuits for gym users, mainly YPs — younger inmates who had been told to exercise or who had specific injuries, which various bits of gym work could help. The standard of the gym was quite good. No machines yet, but lots of free weights and a punch bag in a loft-type store room, where we'd put all the equipment back in at the end of the day. Keeping everything nice and tidy. Prisoners were encouraged to come and take their aggression out on the punchbag, which was one way of looking at it. For some, getting fitter and stronger was counter-productive, though, because it meant they had more strength to unleash on the rest of us, and when they got out.

*****

I got friendly with a guy using the gym called Fred, who was doing a 16 for armed robbery. A big lump too, we'd chat for hours, and back in our cells also. Fred kept saying because there were no alarms that it was easy to escape from Lewes. We didn't even discuss a lack of cameras because we didn't know a world, inside or out, with cameras.

From playing rugby on the nearby sports pitch, we were both already well aware that one side of the gym roof ran alongside fencing and a parameter wall that separated us from freedom. Fred had a plan and said that everything we needed to escape was in the store room at the gym — long wooden benches and rope. If we could smash through the plaster roof of the store room, we'd be on the main roof and yards from the fence and then the wall.

The more Fred talked about this elaborate plot, the more I got into the idea. Fred had about four or five years left so he had loads of incentive. I had a year or so to go, but the temptation was still strong. Everybody inside loves of idea of escaping, however long they've got left.

I was really fucked off at the time because my wife was always writing letters, talking about divorcing me, and telling me what a cunt I was. In my darkest hours, it felt like I had nothing to lose. Our plan needed to be discussed over and over again, but of course we only knew so much, in terms of what we'd be escaping from and to... so we had to assume loads. Not the best preparations.

One night, we were as ready as we'd ever be. During recreation around 7pm, me and Fred walked onto a small wing, which came out of our main one. It led to the kitchens and the gym, which a few nights a week was already shut around this time. Fred had worked out the entrance to this wing was never manned by screws, and that there was something wrong with the locks at the bottom of the double doors leading to the gym. It meant we were able to push the bottom of the doors, reach a hand in and slip the lock. Then we could push the doors just about open enough for us to squeeze through and shut them again, still locked together halfway up.

Once we were through, with the doors locked behind us, it was just ten yards to the entrance to the gym, which we barged through. This time we didn't give a fuck what state we left the doors in. Now it was all about being quick and efficient.

Inside the gym, we headed across the floor towards the staircase leading to the store room loft area. We stacked one of the wooden gym benches, around ten feet long, on top of another. Then we both got on top, and used another bench each to smash through the plaster board ceiling below the flat roof. When the hole was big enough, Fred climbed through and up on to the flat roof, where he'd be able to monitor the pair of screws and their dogs, who patrolled in between the fence and the parameter wall. Fortunately, in the distance, he could see that they'd only recently passed through and that, luckily and somehow, him crashing through the false roof hadn't disturbed them.

I passed two more gym benches through the hole in the ceiling and joined Fred on the roof. Now we had a few minutes, who knows, five or six maybe, to execute our plan, which at best, was based on pure guess work. The edge of the building was about ten feet away from the fence, which had standard prison circular barbed razor wire on the top. Then there was about another ten feet to the wall. We had estimated the gym benches were at least about ten feet long. But that's all we had... 'about'.

As we stood on the edge of the roof, our aim was to lower one bench on top of the fence, but it just wasn't long enough, probably by about six inches, so it wouldn't take hold. I suggested sliding down a bench in between the building and the fence so, with the help of the other bench, we could try and climb up to the fence. Fred threw the extra bench down and slid down himself. Even if we could make it over the fence and then the wall, on the other side of that were 'ankle breakers', i.e broken slabs of concrete, which were brutal to land on. We'd hoped to use the benches to counteract that, when actually the benches had been little help at all, apart from bashing up the ceiling in the gym. We'd done all this double fast, with no time to think. It was like a bad task on *The Krypton Factor*.

We quickly realised our plan was fucked. The fence was higher than the building and the wall was higher than the fence. We also knew the screws and dogs would be back round again any moment. There was only one option left. To try and break back into the prison. For fuck's sake...

At least the benches helped us scramble back up the wall and on to the flat roof. Fuck knows how we did it, but we managed to lower ourselves back through the hole in the roof, smash through the gym doors once more and unlock the double doors back onto the wing. But what would greet us on the other side? The screws may have been shouting our names out for some reason, or had realised we'd disappeared, which would mean a full scale inquiry was underway.

But nothing.

As usual, no screws on that little wing, which was empty. We'd managed to get back in, thank fuck. It was an achievement in itself, but not the one we were looking for.

We tried to compose ourselves as we walked calmly back into the recreation area and towards our cells. The relief at not getting caught was huge, but, of course, mixed with the disappointment of not getting away...and then lots of, what the actual fuck were we thinking?

We needed to get back to our cells, so we could have a cup of tea and sit chatting like we would normally...and then wait for it all to kick off. Of course, there was a huge mess in the gym, a hole in the ceiling of the store room and one bench left in between the building and the fence.

The next morning, there was an announcement that the gym was closed. Everybody on our wing was banged up for the rest of the day, because there had been an attempt to escape. The three of us working in the gym were called separately to the PO's office on our wing. I was asked what I was up to that night. I just kept it straight. In my cell, usual stuff.

But the other two gym workers were lifers and just didn't have as much recreation as me, so I must be the prime suspect. However, with no cameras and no reports of me being missing at any point, there was just no proof.

*****

The day after, I was told to go back to the PO's office, where I was served divorce papers, which I refused to sign. My missus had obviously decided she wasn't going to wait for me, and who can blame her? It was fine. It happens.

It was a kick in the teeth, though, because I knew this wouldn't help any parole hearings in the future because she hadn't visited me or written for months.

The screws, who already suspected I was involved in the attempted escape, really wound me up. Saying my wife was fucking every Tom, Dick and Harry, that sort of stuff. So I lost it, and I really gave it to them, not physically, but verbally. I think I shit a few of them up. It just touched a nerve, because me being fucked off about my wife was the reason I wanted to escape in the first place.

For the usual 'threats to kill' when having a ding-dong with screws, I was sent down on the block...and the next morning I was suddenly shipped out to Blundeston Prison in Suffolk, a Cat-C. I later heard Fred was sent somewhere else too. They knew we were behind the attempted escape, but were unable to prove it. They just wanted shot of us.

I was put on a coach with five or six prison officers for the three hour drive, and handcuffed to one screw. But this greedy bunch decided to stop off at a greasy spoon on the way, when they definitely should have been driving straight to Blundeston. The screw I was cuffed to wasn't missing out on the caff, so I was left with another screw who, pissed off at not joining his pals for a Full English, decided to hold the handcuff instead of locking me up to him.

Once the others were sat inside tucking into their breakfasts, I punched the screw next to me in the mouth, which knocked him out sparko. I ran to the front of the coach, but I couldn't manage to disable the locked doors. The screw at the back came round and radioed to the boys in the caff, who rushed out, opened the coach up and overpowered me with their truncheons. At that point, I probably could have got away if I'd really tried, but I thought, fuck it. Just not worth it.

Everything calmed down, so the journey continued. When we reached Blundeston, the screws couldn't admit what happened, because they'd have had to come clean about stopping off for breakfast. Result. No extra time added, nor put on the block. Thank God.

*****

Blundeston was punishment enough, though. An absolute shit-hole, and full of nonces. I caused so much trouble in there, I was shipped out within a couple of weeks, and sent back to the Scrubs and D-wing. Home again.

I was given a nice job on the works as a bricklayer with a Welsh screw called Taffy Breeze. As usual, trouble followed me around...or rather, the various bits of trouble I'd got myself into inside over the years, followed me around.

During my YP in Aylesbury I'd got into an argument with a kid over something stupid, and knocked his front teeth out in the showers. This time at the Scrubs, his brother was a lifer on D-wing, and had already done eight years. My parole wasn't far away so I had to keep my distance, and try and keep out of trouble so close to my possible release.

One day, watching a film in the gym, the brother tried to stab me with something he'd made. When I got back to the wing, I went to his cell and bashed him up. Thankfully, he left me alone and the screws turned a blind eye too.

Out of the blue, Taffy said I was wanted in the kitchen, which we were renovating at the time. The No 1 Chief in the kitchen, Reeves, whose brother was the same rank in the kitchen at Wandsworth, pointed to a homemade weights bar I'd used for training and had built out of empty fruit boxes full of concrete, hidden under a table.

'There's only one person, Hilly, who is strong enough to pick that up. How do you plead, Hilly?'

'Okay, fuck it, guilty.'

I'd only made the weight because I wasn't getting in the gym enough.

Reeves said, 'Okay, thank you. Now, because I know you're coming up for your parole, I'm not going to nick you, but you are off the works now, because if you can make that weight, then you can make something to help you get you over a fence.'

I was gutted, because losing my job on the works meant I had to move wings from D to C, but at least it got me away from any bother on D-wing, and potentially a load more bird for all the trouble I might be drawn into.

Two days later I was taken to the office and told I was getting parole, and leaving very, very soon. It really hit me — the sheer euphoria. I was supposed to do four years six months, two thirds of seven years, and did just over five years, with a few bits added on.

The screws said, 'We know the clothes you came in aren't going to fit you, let alone any you've been given here, so a few days before your release, we've arranged for you to be taken to High &

Mighty in Edgware Road to buy some new gear.'

That was a lovely touch. I'd heard of the shop, it was somewhere a lot of bodybuilders had started to go. So I was taken out, un-cuffed because I only had days left. Another amazing feeling, driving into the West End in a black cab with a couple of screws, also in civvies, which was nice. I loved being in High & Mighty. They sorted me out a nice jacket, a shirt and a pair of jeans. New shoes. One whole outfit. I looked good and I could taste freedom. However, I was shitting it also, because, even though I only had days left, I still couldn't trust myself not to suddenly run out of the shop, and leg it down the road. I felt more comfortable in prison than in that store. It's a funny old feeling. Most people wouldn't understand, because they've never been in that situation, but presented with the opportunity, my natural instinct, still, was to escape.

Thankfully, I got back in the car, but I thought, fuck, I've got to go back inside for another couple of days. It was made worse because Edgware Road, Paddington, Ladbroke Grove, Shepherd's Bush — the places I drove back through to get to The Scrubs — was my manor. When I got back to my cell, those few days felt like months. When you're doing bird on a long sentence, you don't think about getting out, you just get on with it. When you've only got a couple of days left, you feel every minute, every second. That's why people on a shorter sentence can sometimes feel worse than if they'd got a bigger one.

FIGHT CLUB

When I left the Scrubs in the spring of 1979, they gave me the princely sum of £14.06…after five years of my life locked up. As I stood outside the prison on Ducane Road on a nice sunny day, about to get the No 7, a mile and a half home, I thought, fuck the bus, and walked instead.

As I went across the A40 and into Acton, it felt like I could walk a million miles. That's how you feel, when you finally get out.

I was big and strong and on top of the world. As I strolled past people on the street, they looked at me like a normal regular person. It was a great feeling.

The last contact with my soon-to-be ex-wife had been the divorce papers. You get to hear things in prison and I knew she was with a new fella. He got my missus pregnant while I was away — like I said, it happens — and by the time I was released, she was mother to a beautiful little girl.

A few months before, I was unloading bricks from a truck just inside the prison entrance at the Scrubs…topless. I saw a mate's bird coming out of a visit so I shouted 'hello' to her. Apparently, she told my ex I was huge, tanned-up and had a six pack.

Halfway home to my mum's at Mill Hill Road, I decided to pop to Perryn Road to see my ex's grandparents.

'Oh…hello…Ray.'

Poor old grandma and grandpa's faces were priceless. I could see a million things going through their minds. The baby? Does he know?

They sat me down, bless them, and nervously explained the situation. I was like, 'Right, okay…'

There was no way I was going to kick off there and then. I always got on well with the grandparents, who were good as gold. The old boy stood me bail last time, of course. But they were very set in their ways. I was always made a bacon and beetroot sandwich, popular in their traveller world, and cups of tea that were so fucking milky, they were almost white. In heavily stained tea cups. No point asking for a glass of water — you'd be given it in another grubby cup.

'So, I want to see your granddaughter…'

'Well, you've got to be careful, Ray. She's got a baby now, and she's seeing the dad.'

The thing was…I already knew this guy was active. Like I said, you hear things in prison, people tell you stuff.

When I got back to my mum's, she was waiting at the gate. My Alsatian Girlie hadn't seen me for five years. She was like a whippet running down the road. Whining, like you've never heard. So pleased to see me, so loyal.

I went upstairs to my old bedroom, had a little wash and came down in a vest. Mum couldn't believe my physique. 'Oh my God, Ray,' as she touched my muscles to see if they were real.

Later that afternoon, I went to the hairdressers, but my ex was nowhere to be seen. I could tell everyone at the shop was on edge when I walked in, and stopped what they were doing — frozen to the spot.

Okay, so I'll try and find her new bloke instead. I was pals with his brothers before I went away, so he really shouldn't have gone there. He should have known it would catch up with him at some point. They say all's fair in love and war, and it can work both ways…

A lot of guys who go away have girlfriends on the side. They might have got a little flat for that bird, and spent a lot of time there, pretending they were out doing bits of 'work'. Then they get nicked and find out they've been grassed up by the missus, because she'd already found out about the bit on the side and the other gaff. Now they're in prison, doing ten years, after spending twenty, thirty grand on the love-nest. The new girl fucks off, then the missus comes to visit them in prison, sees them at their worst, and fucks off too. I've seen it happen loads.

I've seen some big gangsters completely fold up inside. If you've got a good sort, everyone on the outside knows you're stuck in there, so other guys make their move. These women have got used to a certain lifestyle, and there's always someone willing to step into your shoes, because they think your release date is years away.

But it creeps up...

A little bit of digging around and, whad'ya know, the new boyfriend had just been nicked for something, and was on remand to appear at Acton Magistrates Court. His hearing was the next day. I didn't know which way it was going to go, but I thought, if this cunt gets released, I need to be there when it happens. I wasn't on license, no probation officer to report to, so, if I was able to, I'd break his fucking neck.

I arrived at the court, and I could see the panic set in among his family as I took a seat in the public gallery. The boyfriend's face was a picture when he was brought in and turned round and clocked me. He called his solicitor over, and then Old Bill came in the court room, glaring at me. An officer came over and said, 'Excuse me, sir, do you mind leaving the court?'

'So why's that? I'm in the public gallery, I'm not causing any problems.'

But I had to leave. I was later told the defendant changed his plea. He ended up with a nine-stretch, I believe.

*****

A week after my release, my sister Jackie was married. I was pleasantly surprised to be invited. Before I'd gone away the last time, I was worried she would get with some of the criminals I hung around with, or someone like myself, who would take liberties. She was my younger sister, so I kept her close to me at all times, but that only exposed her to the wrong sort of people, and some of them were pals of mine. Now she was a marrying a straight-goer... so at least that.

I nearly didn't go to the wedding, because by now those sort of events and the people there weren't my cup of tea. I worried I would find the normal conversation awkward. But I did go, and it was nice to catch up with the family again, even if we really didn't have anything in common.

However, seeing Aunty Gladys and Uncle Don again was very unsettling. I still didn't really know by then that the abuse in the attic happened in their house, and I still believed my Uncle Roy's brother-in-law, a copper, was responsible. At the wedding, Gladys and Don were over-friendly, particularly towards someone who had been in and out of prison ever since. Instinctively, I felt something wasn't right. I've also only found out in recent years that Don was a security guard at the Bank of England, in charge of the gold bullion — a fact that was kept away from me for very obvious reasons.

*****

I finally tracked down my ex to a property in Gunnersbury Park.

'Now he's gone down, let's make a go of it,' I suggested.

Because of my imminent release, and thinking she had a bit more time, the missus had already moved out of our area to Lewisham, because she was worried about me coming out. She reluctantly agreed to me moving south of the river too, which was not her original plan, but anyway...

Moving from west London to south-east London wasn't an easy thing to take on, certainly with form like mine, but because nobody really knew who I was, or my past, and I had a bit about me, it was actually a blessing in disguise. I had got the girl and almost a fresh new identity too. Well for a while, anyway. With that clean slate, I got straight at it from the off...doing a couple of armed robberies on my own shortly after I arrived in south London. Nothing major, but enough money to get the flat together. I really think my ex would have been happy if I was caught and put back in prison, as long as she could keep the proceeds.

But I was out...and making up for lost time in many ways. I told my ex I would support her and her daughter and a few months later she was pregnant with our own child.

Predictably, I also started seeing my sister's friend, who had visited me so much in Chelmsford, and who lived back in west London in Greenford. I got a job working on the door at Crispin's

Wine Bar in Ealing, just around the corner from her, and I'd pop round and see her before my shift.

Despite my work and fling back in west London, I quickly settled into life in south London and started to make the most of my new freedom from a fitness point of view, building further on my gym work in prison. Every morning, I filled an old rucksack full of large stones and ran up to Black Heath and back, or to Hilly Fields, near where we lived on Brookbank Road in Lewisham. I started to get really fit and ripped as fuck, going down from 21 to 18 stone. I was hearing more and more about unlicensed fights and wondered if I could get involved.

I'd pop into a local pub called The Swan, ran by a couple of gay guys, both also called Ray, to get a feel of what was happening locally, and who was up to what. I didn't really drink alcohol still, because I didn't want people taking liberties if I was drunk. On my first visit, I could tell there were some serious guys sat around.

I got talking to one geezer, who commented on my size, and introduced himself as Eddie Richardson, and then his older brother, Charlie. Nice, I'd come to the right place. 'The Richardson Gang', also known as 'The Torture Gang', were known to be brutal, far more so than the Krays, and ran south London (and beyond) in the '60s.

I explained to Eddie and Charlie I'd been inside with Frankie Fraser and Tony Lawrence and told them a bit about myself. Out of respect, because I'd just come out of prison, the guys — Dave and Johnny Holde, Terry Combes and Terry Sharpe were there too — had a whip-round and, between them, gave me about two hundred quid, which was so good of them.

Eddie said we should keep talking about boxing. I got back to the house and gave most of the money to the missus...as you do.

I started training at the Thomas a' Beckett pub in Old Kent Road, where Henry Cooper had been based. Other famous visitors included Joe Frazier, Mohammed Ali and Darth Vader actor and bodybuilder Dave Prouse. It was Beryl Cameron-Gibbons' pub, the UK's first female boxing promoter. On the bag there one afternoon, I got chatting to Jimmy Tippett, who was training some younger guys to street-fight. I told him I used to spar with Bugner at The Nobel Arts and Jimmy said he'd get me some fights.

I won my first two unlicensed bouts at Harvey's Social Club in Woolwich, wearing eight ounce gloves, boxing boots and shorts, and for the first time bare-chested. Normal boxing until something happened. There was a referee who could disqualify you after two warnings, but by then you could have done someone a lot of damage. With an elbow, you could smash someone's face to pieces, and because it was unlicensed, nobody followed what rules there were.

Rules or no rules, it was at the Beckett where I really learned to punch properly.

ACTING THE PART

The likes of Jimmy Tippett, Eddie Richardson, Terry Coombs, the Holde brothers, Gypsy Tom, and going back to Johnny Bindon, were all proper old school gangsters who were advised to apply for equity acting cards, so they could basically play themselves in TV dramas and films.

At one of my unlicensed fights in the south-east London area, Jimmy Tippett introduced me to Brian Cox, a young actor who had taken a big interest in the unlicensed fighting scene.

I couldn't imagine what a successful stage, TV and film career Brian would go on to have, most recently starring in the huge TV drama *Succession*. In his autobiography, he talks about moving around London in the early 1980s. He directed a play in Richmond and performed at The National Theatre, and even took a job at health club Holmes Place in between acting jobs. I was beginning to meet interesting people, like Brian, from all walks of life.

Jimmy naturally introduced me to some proper faces. Next up the Haward brothers — Harry and Billy, except I already knew Billy because we'd been in Chelmsford together. Harry was renowned for starring in *Harry's Out*, a *Thames Television* documentary which filmed his release from 'The Ville' in 1971, and his bid to go straight.

Harry had been in and out of prison in the 1960s, most notably for stealing a lorry load of cigarettes worth £90k. Billy served time for affray and being in possession of a loaded firearm during the infamous Mr Smith's nightclub shooting in Catford in 1966, which left the Krays' associate Dickie Hart dead. Frankie Fraser was one of those charged with the murder of Hart. Although acquitted, he did receive five years for affray.

Then the 'Torture Trial', as it became known, a follow-on from the Mr Smith case, saw Eddie Richardson sentenced to a total of 15 years...so when I met Eddie he hadn't been out long himself.

Harry Haward was already away when the Richardsons visited Billy at Mr Smith's. Jimmy Tippett was present, though — a doorman that night, who took Billy's gun off him.

Of the Mr Smith's shooting, which left six or seven others with gunshot woulds, Billy, who was also badly injured, explains in the *Harry's Home* documentary...

I was in a position where I couldn't do much else than what I did. I could have gone to the police, I suppose, but that's not me kettle of fish, so I did the only thing that I thought I could do...at the time...and had a row.

There's also a lovely interview in *Harry's Home* with a Detective Superintendent John Cummings, who explained...

He's a very likeable rogue and chap, Harry. He was an active criminal, but he never squealed or grumbled when he was caught. He took his punishment, no complaints. A good example of an old-type villain, and a wonderful personality. He is a violent and strong man. Other criminals fear him, but I don't think he would extend that violence to law-abiding citizens.

Meanwhile, a pub regular points out in the doc...

Thieving is forced upon people by circumstances, and the environment they live in. If you're brought up in an area around here (Lewisham), you're very very lucky to find someone who don't thieve.

A car dealer backs that up...

You cannot keep out of the way of villains, because Lewisham is a villainy area. Harry's the greatest hearted man, to his friends, but if you cross him, well, he's not worth knowing.

While Harry, always the campaigner, delivers typical words of wisdom, when he reasons...

They keep talking about going to the moon, but we've still got piss-pots in our cells. They aught to put some toilets in prisons.

Fast forward ten years or so and Harry was still going straight…well just about. He had taken on the Harp & Erin pub in Deptford. I was told recently that one of Harry's secrets of being a straight-goer was the 'cell', like a proper prison one, he installed in the basement of his pub. If Harry ever thought about doing a piece of work, he would go and sit in that cell and think long and hard about the job and its potential implications. He was challenging his own thoughts, many years before myself, or anyone else, was eventually taught that in prison.

*****

In the summer of 1979, Jimmy Tippett arranged a fight for me at The Mayfair in Tottenham, an old cinema, against an experienced pro called Brian Hall.

Brian Cox had become a big fan of mine, and was very fond of my sister, Diana. Brian gave me the nickname 'Basher' or 'Bash' for short. He also suggested *Cool For Cats* by Squeeze, a big pop tune that year, as my ring record, which I quickly adopted. Some of the lyrics were fitting, to say the least.

In and out of Wandsworth with the numbers on their names
It's funny how their missus always looks the bleeding same
Credit: Chris Difford and Glenn Tilbrook

I smashed Brian Hall all round the gaff, and I thought I'd won, but it was given as a draw. There's an old video on *YouTube* called *Box On* which features me at the start of that fight.

As I got out of the ring, a guy all dressed in black was standing in front of me.

'Who the fuck are you?'

'I'm Lenny McLean, I'm The Governor.'

'Not of me, mate.'

Lenny, a year or two older than me, came straight to the point.

'You wanna fight?'

'You'll have to see my manager, Jimmy.'

Lenny was with Frankie Warren, who was his second cousin, and just starting out as a promoter. He was tied in with local publican, Vic Andretti, who had a pub called The Spread Eagle in Shoreditch with a boxing gym upstairs where I had sparred before. He also put on boxing bouts at The Ring pub in Southwark, which was a tribute to The Ring boxing arena, the first indoor boxing ring for the working classes, which was built opposite the site of The Ring pub in the late 1700s.

A former British champion at welterweight, Andretti had an impressive record of 41 wins from 49 licensed fights, and went on to train Nigel Benn.

Jimmy and Frank arranged for me to spar three or four rounds with Lenny upstairs at The Ring, the frist of several sessions. Lenny might have had seven or eight unlicensed fights by now, while I'd had three.

Lenny was loud, always screaming and growling, but it was like neither of us wanted to go full at it. The so-called 'Governor' knocked me around a bit, and after three or four sessions, I started to hold my own and began knocking Lenny around a bit too. When I boxed him he was 16/17 stone, roughly the same weight as me. He later blew up to 22, 23 stone on the roids. We didn't form any kind of relationship. Lenny was just too aggressive, a big powerful man, who could be an intimidating bully. I didn't try to talk to him, I didn't want to.

In 2017, I was interviewed for the book *The Guv'nor Revealed: The Untold Story Of Lenny McLean* by Lee Wortley and Anthony Thomas, and explained...

We had words quite a few times, and we sparred together many times. We trained at a pub called The Ring, which had a boxing gym upstairs. Lenny and I wanted to get it on, but we always held back when we sparred because it could have ended in a war. I always thought I was the better boxer, but Lenny could sell the tickets — he was good at that, he could fill the place.

Next Jimmy fixed a sparring session with a guy called Lloyd Waltham at the Thomas a' Beckett. He hit me hard on the chin and knocked me down. I bounced back up and later drove to Lewisham, but when I got there, I was so concussed I thought I was in Acton.

The other draw I had on my record, was against Kevin Paddock, a very talented fighter, who I later watched beat Lenny.

I continued training down the Beckett and then they said, 'Basher, we've got someone else for you to spar with?' They pointed at a stocky guy in the corner. It was Roy 'Pretty Boy' Shaw. He'd been in prison and was known to be a right nasty bastard, so I respected him. Roy was renowned for ripping cell doors off their hinges. He'd put a book in between the door and door frame, and smash them off with his hands. My party piece was snapping handles off a cell door, for a wind-up, so someone couldn't get out. Depending on what time of night it was, the poor fucker could be stuck in that cell until the morning. Sometimes to people I knew and liked for a giggle, and other times as bullying tactics.

When I got in the ring to spar with Roy it was the same as with Lenny. He bashed me around a bit to start with, and then I bashed him around a bit back. Roy was a great puncher and I went on to spar with him loads at the Beckett.

I wasn't as interested in fighting Roy as I was Lenny, because Roy wasn't giving it the big'un. Lenny was always shouting the odds, that he would beat me, so taking him on appealed more.

There were about 20-25 decent unlicensed fighters and ex-pros from the south-east London area alone, where I was based, who Lenny and Roy didn't fight, but yet they become the legends of that scene.

Cliff Field was widely thought to be THE man, much more so in our circles than Lenny or Roy. Cliff fought Lenny a couple of times and bashed him up badly, chucking him out of the ring one time and, so I heard, almost bankrupted Lenny the next time, because he'd put his own money up for the fight.

I really wanted Lenny. We were meant to fight twice, but he didn't show up to either. The first time was a Warren Sports Promotion on Monday September 10th, 1979 at The Rainbow Theatre in Finsbury Park. It featured Cliff Field against Tshaka at the top of the bill, fighting for a 'Heavyweight Championship Of Great Britain', and supposedly licensed by *The National Boxing Council*, which had actually been set up by Frank Warren in opposition to respected regulator, the *British Boxing Board Of Control (BBBofC)*. Me and Lenny were next on the card for a heavyweight clash of 10 x 3 minute rounds, him billed as Lennie 'Boy' McLean from Hoxton, continuing his fight back to the top', and me, 'Ray Hill from Lea', with two KOs to my credit in two fights, which I can only think referred to Lee High Street in Lewisham, and had been spelt badly. My local pub at the time, The Red Lion, had sponsored me by paying for my gown, shorts and boots. All a waste, because Lenny no-showed.

The other time I was supposed to fight Lenny was on an Eddie Richardson show at Harvey's Social Club in Woolwich, but again it didn't happen. It might not have been Lenny's fault on either occasion. Maybe Frank or Vic Andretti were worried I'd iron him out?

I was now getting around £300-£400 a fight — big money in those days. Lenny would get at least a grand, and Roy was around that level too, being managed by Joey Pyle. At this point, Frank Warren and Joey really started pushing their star men.

There were reports in the October of 1979 that pro boxer Paul Sykes, a notorious ex-con, who spent 21 years out of 26 in prison in the UK in the '70s, '80s and '90s, was considering taking up a lucrative offer to join Frank's *National Boxing Council*.

Earlier that year, Sykes, after another stint away, was devastated at losing a British and Commonwealth title shot against champion John L Gardner, and felt the pro boxing scene was against him.

His manager Tommy Miller was quoted as saying Sykes had received 'a ridiculous offer' and explained that sums of £3,000 or so were being offered for 'washed up' fighters to box street-fighters who were otherwise ignored by the boxing establishment.

Personally, I loved the adulation and attention I was getting as a prize fighter…and enjoyed taking the cash back to my girlfriend and telling her all about it. It beat putting guns in people's mouths. And licensed by the *BBBofC* or not, it was much more legit than anything I'd been up to in recent years.

At another unlicensed show at Harvey's Social Club, I was asked to be the compere in the ring, which I was quite happy to do and very confident about. Lenny McLean was meant to fight Harry Starbuck, but Lenny was another no-show again. They asked Harry to fight a huge 6ft plus guy, with massive arms, but he didn't fancy it. Terry

Combes got hold of me and asked if I'd fight this geezer instead and I said, 'I haven't come down to fight tonight, I'm the compere.' And then Eddie Richardson got involved and I couldn't say no. I threw my first punch, then fell into the guy and bit his ear lobe straight off. Claret everywhere. The geezer leapt out of the ring as my corner guys leapt in, all saying, because Lenny hadn't fought again, that I was now 'The Governor'.

Maybe I should have starred *Lock Stock and Two Smoking Barrels* instead of Lenny? A lot of people have said I should have had a part in that film.

Meanwhile, my own 'stock' was rising. Jimmy Tippett would take me to pubs and clubs, where I'd prop up the bar with just a tonic water while he chatted to the bouncers, trying to fix fights. If Jimmy pointed a guy out to me, I'd gesture, 'Yeah, okay.'

I'd bash these guys all over the ring, mainly in bouts at Harvey's or The Cat Whiskers in Streatham, usually lasting two rounds at the max. These doormen got a couple of hundred quid for their troubles, and they might have to work six or seven nights on the door to earn that much usually, so everybody was happy.

Except my ex, who was really my ex this time. She'd had enough of me again, and moved back west to Northolt to get settled there before giving birth. I'd still been seeing my sister's friend, but Jackie told me her mate was also pregnant, and it could be mine, so I needed to calm that down.

*****

In November 1979, John Bindon stood trial for the murder of south London gangster Johnny Darke of the Wild Bunch Gang, who was stabbed multiple times at The Ranleigh Yacht Club underneath the arches at Putney railway bridge one Monday afternoon.

Bindon was arrested and charged, believed to be the 'hitman' behind the killing. It had been an eventful end to the '70s for Johnny. In 1977, he was sacked as security for Led Zeppelin after fights with crew members and journalists.

I'm told Bindon had been having a party that night in Putney with a sample of cocaine he was shopping around for a heavy firm, who weren't best pleased, so was tooled up and then got into a nasty fight with Darke and his lot.

Vicky Hodge talks about blood pouring from Bindon's chest and neck. Apparently, somehow through IRA contacts, he was able to escape to Ireland by telling airport officials he'd been in a really bad accident in a rugby match.

Pleading self defence, Bindon was eventually acquitted of all charges after celebrity actor pals like Bob Hoskins were character witnesses at the Old Bailey.

*****

I got another door job at The Venue in Victoria, Richard Branson's club, which had only just opened. It had a nightclub feel to it, but audience members sat at tables and could wine and dine while watching some amazing live acts of the time, sometimes two performances a night.

I was now earning around a grand a week. Amazing money in the late '70s/early '80s. I didn't need to do armed robberies anymore, but I still kept my hand in, mainly bits and pieces on my own.

I loved unlicensed fighting and wanted to be the bollocks at it. One of my losses, November 29th, 1979, was to a guy called Dave Strong. I had become over-confident and I'd also started taking black bombers — speed in a capsule, or wrapped in a Rizla paper — at The Venue. I was on a comedown when I fought Dave Strong, and he smashed me all over the place.

One night me and the head doormen Frank were backstage at The Venue, and Motown legend Marvin Gaye appeared in the VIP area, with three bodyguards, who were asking if anyone had any coke Marvin could buy. Frank had a nice little sideline going by this point, pushing some lovely Peruvian flake, which came in quarter ounces wrapped in rice paper. I'd started having the odd line here and there, courtesy of Frank. It was so nice, it wasn't difficult to get a taste for this stuff.

Marvin bought three grams, but within an hour was back, wanting the same again.

'Nah, nah…no more, mate. I got some regulars coming down tonight I need to look after,' said Frank.

Marvin wasn't happy. One of his lumps squared up to Frank, giving it all that, so I punched him on the chin. I could half hit by now, but this guy didn't go over straight away, it was like slow motion. I'd never seen anything like that before. He stood there for a second, and then slowly collapsed into a heap on the floor, with his head between his knees.

I looked up and one of Marvin's other boys pulled out a thing. My arsehole dropped. Everybody's did. I couldn't tell if the gun was loaded or not, you just never know. Fortunately, Marvin persuaded the guy to put it away. He didn't need the aggro, not on all that gear. So the piece was back in this idiot's jacket, but I now I wanted to punch this one's lights out too. Frank calmed it down, and sold Marvin another three grams. When they all left, we were like, thank fuck for that.

Bad Manners were at The Venue for two shows, and the first night about four hundred skinheads turned up. Part of the act was larger-than-life frontman Buster Bloodvessell getting smashed over the head with a fake bolster-wood chair. As door staff, we should have been told about the stunt. When an outraged skinhead rushed the stage, Frank knocked him out and all hell broke loose. A load of skins jumped up and it all kicked off. When we were clearing the place up after closing, we found loads of cut-off broom stick handles with knitting needles stuck in them, so the skinheads had obviously come prepared to cause trouble. Thankfully, they didn't use them on anybody.

Another time, the country singer Joe Ely somehow managed to get up on the roof of The Venue with a couple of his roadies, who were chucking cans of beers at cars driving past on Victoria Street. Me and a couple of the door lads climbed the caged metal staircase that wrapped around the building and used dustbin lids as shields as the crazy roadies hurled cans at us too. We found out later that Joe wrote a record about that night at The Venue.

It was all par for the course. A lot of crazy things happened at The Venue, with some of the best up-and-coming British bands performing like Cabaret Voltaire, Depeche Mode, Level 42 and The Smiths, plus American stars like Hall & Oates, Ramones, Herbie Hancock and Chuck Berry.

As usual, I had a nice little sideline on the go. When I was on the front door collecting tickets, I'd resell them to touts or punters.

Freddie Mercury came one night and I didn't have a fucking clue who he was, because I'd been away so much. He was quite taken by me and started asking me loads of questions.

'Have you got any tattoos?'

'Yeah, I've gotta a few,'

'Please show me, I'd love to kiss them'

I pointed to my crutch area and said, 'I've got one down there,' and Freddie said, 'Oh really,' and roared with laughter.

He was a lovely, guy, Freddie, and he flirted with me all night. Good fun.

When Hot Gossip, the dancers, appeared, I was out the front that night, so I missed all their costume changes backstage. Gutted.

Tina Turner was lovely. I think she performed on the same night as James Brown. Fred was selling packets to Brown all night too... proper on the gear, like Marvin Gaye

*****

During my time at The Venue, my ex gave birth to our son at London Bridge Hospital. At best we were on-off, but mostly off. I was present at the birth...but only just. I was asked to leave the hospital just before, because I kicked off and accused a doctor of perving over my ex-wife too much, when she was laying there with her legs open. As I stood outside the hospital, ranting and raving, it hit me that I wasn't the full ticket. I was only just allowed back in to see the baby. It was a magical feeling to see that little boy come into the world, but, of course, I'd done my best to try and spoil it.

I was confused. I wanted to make a go of it with my ex-wife, because I just thought we had so much unfinished business, and such a deep connection, but when I came out, like any guy in his late 20s, who'd been away so much, I wanted to get amongst it.

Shortly after, my mum told me that my sister's friend had given birth to my second son. I hadn't seen his mum for several months now, so, as I hadn't been invited to come and see the baby or be part of its life, I decided to keep my distance.

*****

I moved back in with my mum, and decided to approach Bob Coleman, to ask if he was interested in doing a joint unlicensed boxing promotion in the Acton area. He agreed and came up with the name Hillman Promotions, which I thought was great.

Bob offered me one his properties, a large house in Ealing, so I could try and make a go of it with my ex-wife and our son, so we moved in for a couple of months. It was so generous of him.

I also talked to Bob about opening our own gym, opposite Ealing Broadway Police Station, in an old carpet warehouse, Bufflao's, which was closing down. I wanted to keep the same name as I thought it was perfect, and Bob was up for it too. I thought setting up a business like that around my love of bodybuilding and powerlifting could be my chance of finally going straight, a few years before fitness member-based gyms really started to blow up in the UK.

We decided to concentrate on the boxing promotions first, with our first event at Acton Town Hall at the end of October, 1980 and the second just before Christmas. I fought on both cards, the second against Colin Cracknell. I went to see him to fix up the fight and was delighted when he agreed. I gave him a load of tickets and between us we sold the event out. A lot of the locals were excited to see me and Colin fight. They knew it would be a good punch-up.

Colin had a quick start in the first round and, to be fair, he bashed me to bits and busted my nose. I now knew this old-timer could still fight. In the second round, I upped the stakes, throwing him in the corner and nutting him on the top of the head, bashing up my own face further in the process. For the third round, Colin said, 'I'm not getting back in that ring with you, Ray.'

I persuaded him to continue, nut as soon he was back in the ring, I kicked him in the face, and it ended up a right old tear-up.

I'd always wanted to beat the governor of the fruit market, one of my fighting mentors, and I did. I don't think Colin was best pleased with my tactics, but, for me, that's what prize-fighting is all about. Trying to win at any cost.

I was pleased to win both bouts on those promotions, but I just had to on my own turf. Leon also fought and won both times.

For the second show, we even made it into the local newspaper on a double page spread— written by a young Charlie Sale, who went on to become a celebrated Fleet Street sports columnist.

Here's an extract...

It was a mixed bag of bouts for the prize fight fans, and it looks as if prize fight boxing is here to stay in West London.

The promoter, Acton boxer Ray Hill, wanted to turn professional as a heavyweight. He worked with top coach George Francis in the same Highgate gym as former world champion John Conteh.

But Hill, 29, had his boxing licence application turned down by the British Board Of Boxing Control. He said it was because of his criminal record. He spent five years in prison.

Instead, Hill turned to prize-fighting and became well known in the boxing game and as a co-promoter, which helped attract the fighters for the two Acton shows.

Hill, who is in the car business and works part-time as a bouncer at Crispin's Wine Bar in Ealing, sees prize fighting as a chance to channel his aggressive energy into the ring rather than elsewhere.

He said: 'There's a lot of money to be had from prize fighting if you're prepared to take on the best. In Scotland there's a 10 stone 7lbs boxer who's ready to put up £10,000 to take on anybody in a winner take all fight.'

Hill says there's now a big demand for the sport in West London.

'A lot of boxers on our shows are local lads, so it gives the audience a lot of community involvement, cheering on their own favourite. Everybody likes to see the bully from their club meet his match in the ring.

'In the licensed fights, a lot of the boxers are from abroad and mean little or nothing to the punters. Prize fighting is full of disillusioned for-

mer professionals who got fed up with the recognised version of boxing.'

Hill defends criticism about the age of some of the prize fighters.

He said: 'We wouldn't let them box if they weren't up to it, and the ones on our bill are in very good condition for their age.

'We're hoping the two West London shows are the start of the something big in the area. We're looking to stage fights at other venues. The Old Brentford Market would be an ideal site.

'Prize fighting is a very entertaining form of boxing. We keep mainly to the rules but they're amended slightly to allow for more entertainment for the fans.'

In reality, the success and momentum of the boxing shows was just too slow for me. Life on the outside was so fast-paced. Then our third promotion was cancelled because of police objections. I'd split up with my ex-wife again and I was a man in a hurry, so I decided to go back to Lewisham...and that could only really mean one thing.

ENFORCE FIELD

Me and Jimmy Tippett got very close, hanging around Hayes in Bromley, where he came from, and decided to do some work together. Jimmy was a great enforcer, the best, and I learned so much from him. He got Cliff Field into enforcing too.

Jimmy had various ways of torturing people, cutting the tops off fingers with secateurs his speciality. Good clean cuts. Before they knew it, the victim could be a couple of fingers down. Jimmy was very good with a hammer too. I picked things up as we went along. We did a lot of work for Eddie Richardson and all that mob, and loads of debt collecting for Harry Haward, including at card schools, where large amounts of cash changed hands. When two brothers got lairy with us on a staircase, Jimmy took one out and I threw the other over the bannisters.

We had some run-ins with posh self-made Brighton-based property tycoon Nicholas van Hoogstraten, who became Britain's youngest millionaire in 1967 at 22, and who did time in the '70s, after a business associate was assaulted. By the time we came across him, it was estimated he owned more than 2,000 properties, mainly in the Notting Hill area. Jimmy had words with van Hoogstraten but it's hard for the likes of us to row with people that powerful.

*****

Jimmy also introduced me to a colourful character called One Eyed Johnny, who lived on a huge plot of land on the borders of Kent — multi multi'd up from caravan and mobile home parks.

I started working for Johnny as an enforcer – he needed a lump who could collect money from travellers, as well as bringing stolen goods back to their rightful homes for a finder's fee. Not easy work, but well paid, so right up my street.

One day, a traveller said to me, 'You're Ray Hill, aren't you?
'Yes, I am.'

'We got someone who will fight you.'

'I'm not here to fight, I'm here for the jetskis.'

When I returned to John with the goods, I told him they wanted me to fight this guy, and he said, 'Be careful, Ray, these boys can scrap, you know...they're not idiots, that's what they do.'

I went down there with a few pals. This guy was stood there, wearing a trilby hat, looking like an extra from *Lock Stock...*, and he said in a thick Irish accent, 'So, you want a fight, then?'

'Let's do it...'

I could see punch bags, medicine balls and weights by the side of the fella's caravan.

Then he said, 'You took them fucking jetskis?'

'Yes.'

'I nicked them fucking jetskis, and I want them back. I'll fucking fight you for them.'

'Nah, nah, I'm not fighting for the jetskis. They're not yours...'

'Okay, put some fucking money on the table.'

So I went back to John and he said he'd put up a grand for me. He said he knew the fella and that he could fight. I argued that he was only about 13 stone, so I could take him.

John, Jimmy Tippett and a few others came to support me on a big bit of grass on the traveller site, with loads of their lot watching. I was wearing jeans and a T-shirt, hands bandaged up.

Well, let me just say, this geezer absolutely smashed me to pieces...bashed me up properly. I haven't lost many fights, but this guy...well, I'm convinced it was because there was no ring. He was quicker and more agile, and able to dance around...bosh, bosh, bosh...then run back out again. He didn't put me on the floor, but he did bash me about. I gave up in about the ninth round, because my nose, lip and cheeks were split. My elbows were smashed up to bits too. Just to rub salt in my wounds, he came over and said, 'See you... you're a fucking wanker.'

John just laughed and said, 'I did warn you.'

* * * * *

On a bit of enforcement work, I was sat with a pal in his car outside someone's house on a west London housing estate, with a baseball bat tucked away with me in the passenger seat. We saw the suspect enter his property and my mate got out and knocked on the door. The guy didn't open up or come out, but he did call the police, who appeared 15 minutes later and started questioning us. They found the bat and that was that. It was all over for me. If it had been in the boot of the car, I would have had half a chance. Arguing that I was off to play baseball wasn't going to cut it.

I was arrested and they came up with a charge, which sounded strange to me. Something like, 'Causing GBH to a person unknown, with a person unknown.' It's such a long time ago, I can't remember if I did chase the guy with the baseball bat or not. It's possible.

From Acton police station I was taken to Brixton. My lucrative boxing career was on hold again and, in fact, I wouldn't fight again. My last official unofficial fight, the one against Colin Cracknell on one of my own shows.

I wound up in a cell with the most untidy fella I'd ever met inside. He rarely washed so he was grubby. The cell was like a fucking pigsty, clothes everywhere and never scrubbed down either, yet he never got bollocked for it. This guy smoked weed all the time too, so much so, I started smoking cigarettes. All we did, the pair of us, was puff all day and chat. But I loved this guy, an absolutely lovely man. A proper diamond geezer and complete one-off, certainly when it comes to jail. His name was Howard Marks, and he'd been charged with importing puff on an industrial scale — 15 tonnes of it!

Me and Howard — better known now as *Mr Nice*, the name of his best selling autobiography and film in later years — sounded each other out, and then he told me loads of bonkers stuff, including hiding tonnes of Thai hash in someone's loft and his crazy travels around the world.

Howard's story was fascinating, and he seemed to have some serious clout in prison — relationships with the screws I had never seen before. They even let him out to get married.

There were deliveries to our cell all day, every day, and Howard generously shared everything. In return I emptied the pisspot each morning. Tins of fruit and corned beef. Bottles of mineral water.

Handmade sandwiches brought in by the screws, made that morning by their wives, and lots of chocolate. Howard loved his chocolate. Probably through years of having the munchies, smoking all that weed. And boy did Howard love his weed. I was sure the screws were bringing that in for him too, because he always had so much of the stuff, and happily shared it with other lags. Howard rolled huge joints, which I daren't take a puff of. I'd get nicely stoned breathing it in just talking to him. When he had legal meetings with his solicitors, I don't now how he coped, but fair play to him, he did. Probably just used to it.

Howard explained in *Mr Nice...*

The prison authorities had no objection to me getting married and even went so far as to let me out, escorted by two prison guards, to a Welsh Congregational in South London to perform the deed. After the wedding, I begged the two guards to allow me to attend the reception. They would be very welcome guests and I promised not to escape. In a chauffeur-driven Cadillac, Judy, a guard, and I were driven to the Basil Hotel. Champagne and congratulations flowed. Judy and I were allowed to spend some time alone in a hotel bedroom. The guards and I got drunk.

I got on with most of the guards at Brixton. There were lots of perks. I was allowed out of my cell for most of the day. The screws brought me little presents of harmless contraband. Danish blue cheese and dirty magazines. It was easy to smuggle in dope with the food. I still had quite a lot of cash that the authorities hadn't confiscated.

* * * * *

One afternoon, three or four weeks after arriving at Brixton, I was collected from the cell I shared with Howard and taken to Streatham police station. I was told I was under arrest, suspected of shooting at a police officer, with intent to danger life, something I simply wasn't involved in.

Put in a cell with five other guys, we got chatting for a few hours and all discussed our cases. One guy was pulled out of the cell, but we didn't know why.

I was told I was going to be put on an identity parade, but was arguing that I needed a brief first. They got me a duty solicitor, and he rejected their idea of the victim coming to the holding cell and picking one of us out. He insisted that we do a proper ID parade another time, at a different prison, maybe Wandsworth, where there might be similar looking people.

I was handcuffed to a prison officer and walked to a police car in the car park. As I sat in the car with my solicitor, about to be driven to Wandsworth prison for a few nights, a top Old Bill came up to the car and shouted through the window, 'Mr Hill, we have reason to believe you were involved in an attempted shooting of one of our police officers.' Standing a little way away, now in a uniform, was the guy who got pulled out of the cell. I shouted out, 'Fucking hell, it's you,' as the car pulled away.

I was in Wandsworth for a couple of days in a normal cell, then I was sent back to Brixton and put twos-up with Keith Barry, one of the Barry brothers, on a different wing to Howard Marks. Despite, all his perks, I was actually glad not to be back with Howard. Even though I'd started doing coke, the weed Howard smoked and the size of his joints was too heavy a buzz for me. Especially in prison.

I met a good-looking guy, who I'm going to call Freddy, who worked for one of the big crime firms in London. Freddy had everything in his cell, including a TV. Nobody had a telly in their cell in those days. Turned out a screw was using his villa in Magaluf.

One day, Freddy had a bit of bother on one of the landings, and a couple of guys started on him. I knocked one out and the other one shit himself. The next day, Freddy somehow arranged for me to be moved to his cell, which was impressive, to say the least.

I told Freddy that Howard Marks talked a lot about a guy with the same name. He confirmed he'd had dealings with Howard. The more I gained his confidence, the more Freddy talked.

It was clear that Freddy and Howard were very well connected. Being moved around cells like that and getting to know these big-time gangster and dealers, and having to gain their confidence, was an education.

I was shocked to hear Howard had died of cancer a few years ago, because Howard was one of the first people I knew who talked about cancer patients or other sufferers using cannabis (or CBD) to ease pain and aid treatment. RIP, mate.

Freddy's actual name was Nigel. But he hated Nigel...said it sounded too gay. By now, he was calling me Basher or Bash. I didn't mind if different people called me various names. A chance to hide my real name in certain circles might be a good thing.

I was only in Brixton another eight weeks. One morning I was told that my bail had been stood... and I was released within a matter of days. Outside the prison waiting for me was Jimmy Tippett and Brian Cox was with him. My bail of £1,000 had been paid, which was amazing.

'Fucking hell, I can't thank you enough.'

I was so pleased to see the guys sat in a nice BMW 320. Jimmy wanted me out as a mate, but also as one of his fighters and enforcers. We went for a nice lunch at a local pub, the three of us, and then I was taken back to Northolt.

Before I left Brixton, I gave Freddy my mum's home phone number, and told him to call if he ever needed help with anything.

'Will do, Basher. Good luck, mate.'

Back in the west London area, it wasn't long before I started knocking around Ladbroke Grove again, and soon hooked up with Chilton. It was good to see him. We quickly picked up from where we'd left off in the '70s, minus illegal drinking clubs and decapitations. A few months later, thankfully, I was informed the outstanding charges against me had been dropped so I kicked on again and managed to keep active and out of trouble for the next year or so.

*****

One day, early 1982, me and Chilton were sat outside Park Royal Hospital, just off Acton Lane, waiting for a pal to get in our car so we could plan some work. I noticed a couple of guys coming out of the bank opposite with bags of cash, and put them in an estate car. No security van, nothing. We followed them for a little bit, and watched them pull into a local factory, we assumed, delivering cash for wages.

We didn't do anything there and then, but came back the following week on the same day. I had a double barrel shotgun, loaded with salt and rice, in home-made cartridges. If it went off it would make a big bang and causes minor cuts and scratches, but it wouldn't blow anybody up. Three or four spare cartridges in my pocket.

We parked up — me, Chilton and our driver in a Ford Consul, wearing gloves but not masks. Sure enough, exactly the same as the week before, two guys put cash bags in the estate car. We followed and they pulled up at the entrance to a well-known double glazing window firm on the Park Royal industrial estate. As one guy got out with the cash bags, Chilton jumped out of our motor and tried to wrestle the money from him. The bank worker put up a real fight so I leapt out and put the shotgun to the head of driver of their car.

'Open the fucking door, give me the fucking bags.'

Their driver shit himself and was about to hand over the cash when, literally like something out of an episode of The Sweeney, a Ford Granada Ghia 2.8 appeared round the bend in the road, rammed into me and pinned me up against the estate car. A fucking have-a-go hero. How's my luck? And, as it transpired, to top it off, this fella was an off-duty police officer. Really bad luck.

My right leg was smashed to pieces and the shotgun flew up in the air. This busy cunt then put his car in reverse. I grabbed the gun and ran towards the Granada, because now I wanted to fucking kill this guy. I fired a shot towards him as a frightener, but he put the car in gear and drove at me again, this time knocking me up in the air. I landed on his bonnet in a heap, as he reversed again. I rolled off the car to the ground, and he came at me a fucking third time. Thankfully, our driver, a laidback Rasta, pulled up with Chilton inside and we managed to drive away. However, matey boy wasn't giving up easily, and followed us through Park Royal as we attempted to navigate the huge area and its various no through roads and dead-ends.

I knew we had problems when we came to a junction, and our

so-called getaway driver indicated left. Fucking idiot...

So we did the left. Then the geezer in the Granada came up behind us again, and smacked us up the arse and bang into the railings of a factory. I came from the backseat, crashing straight through the windscreen, across the bonnet, and on to the pavement again.

I was really smashed to bits now and covered in shards of glass, so I just ran, leaving the gun in the motor with the one bag of money we'd managed to get.

Now on foot, I was able to keep ahead of the smart-arse in the Granada, as I ran in and out of streets and shop units near the Scrubs. But I was smothered in blood, all over my face and clothes. I ran into a builders' yard, grabbed a hard-hat, and rubbed sand and mud all over my face. Now I'd stopped running, the adrenalin was beginning to wear off and the pain of my injuries was heavy. Finally, I'd lost him. Then a 'plain clothes' Hillman Minx pulled up. I knew it was Old Bill. They looked me up and down, and drove off.

I was beginning to think I might get away with this, so decided to try and walk home. I could hardly stand up by the time I got there. Hot bath, cold bath, hot bath. Trying to get the bruising out. I couldn't go to A&E to get my leg and knees stitched up. I kept reminding myself I had to stay away from any hospital, however awful the pain was.

GET YOUR TROUSERS OFF, YOU'RE NICKED

About a week later, I was under the sunbed in the front room at a girlfriend's house in Chiswick Green — an early prototype wooden home sunbed I'd bought her, which cost a fortune back then, and really wasn't very good at all.

As I lay there relaxing, the front door was knocked off its hinges. Loads of Old Bill in the hallway.

'Where's Ray?'

'Dunno...'

'Where's Ray?'

'Haven't seen him, dunno where he is...'

Now, that clearly wasn't going to wash with the police. I had scrambled to turn the lights off, but a quick search found me hanging out of the sunbed, my legs still cut to fuck.

'What happened to you?' asked one officer.

'I fell off some scaffolding?'

'You've been active, haven't you, Ray?'

They started looking around the house. I don't think they had a warrant, and probably didn't need one, or even bother with one much in those days. They weren't even here about the Park Royal job.

I'd lent this girlfriend's brother a sawn-off .410 shotgun. He'd gone on a bit of work, got caught and Old Bill had found it at his house. Silly bollocks had blurted out, 'It's not mine, it's Ray Hill's.'

As the police searched the house, my English Bull Terrier, Bullseye, was going mental, and would have attacked those officers if I'd given him the go ahead.

'Guv, let me move him to the garden,' I said, as I carried him in his basket down the stairs and outside, complete with a loaded handgun under his blanket. That was a close one.

Their search fruitless, I was taken to Ruislip police station and banged up. An hour or so later, some arsehole walked in, and said, 'Take your jeans off.'

'Fuck off.'

'Are you refusing to take your trousers off?'

'Yes.'

'We can do this the easy way or the hard way…'

So I took them off and he looked at my legs,

'Okay, let me look at your head.'

One quick check of my various cuts and bruises, and it was, 'Right, Mr Hill, we're charging you with….'

Fucking hell. He did me there and then…just based on injuries that matched the Park Royal robbery. The .410 shotgun seemingly not a concern to them now.

I was sent to a holding centre in Limehouse in east London, waiting to be allocated, from several large cells housing dozens of prisoners. I asked where I'd be going, and was told Wandsworth, and I thought, fuck it, I don't want to go to Wanno. Then they called out my name and said 'Scrubs'. As I left the cell with some others, I saw Chilton coming out of the another cell, heading to the Scrubs too.

'Fucking hell, Chilt…what you here for?'

'Same thing as you, mate.'

'Fucking hell, Chilt, we must have been grassed up.'

And we must have been. I'm sure it was the driver, because nothing happened to him. Chilton told me he had been nicked too, but he never did any time, the wanker.

Me and Chilt did about 12 months on remand together, but eventually fell out, and had a big fight in there over who grassed us up. I knew it wasn't Chilton, but I held him responsible because he had given us the driver. It all came to a head when a big old nasty fella on the fours Chilton had befriended threatened me with a knife, shouting at me over the railings. I asked Chilton to meet me in the toilets to have a chat, which quickly became a really bad scrap. Chilton's mate appeared and I was lucky it didn't kick off, because I would have come unstuck.

Me and Chilton kept our distance after that, but we did have to get together to talk about the depositions when they arrived. We couldn't be going into court arguing. He'd decided to represent himself, which was a huge gamble.

*****

The day of my trial finally arrived, and as I waited in my cell at the Old Bailey to go up to court for the first day of the proceedings, my QC appeared.

As usual, I had gone not guilty.

'Now, Mr Hill, you are looking at a very heavy sentence, but I know the judge and he may be interested in a deal.'

Here we go again...

'What sort of deal?' I asked, coughing into the sleeve of my shirt.

'Well, this is a very serious offence, Mr Hill, but I think the judge would be prepared to look at a sentence of 15 years.'

'Fifteen fucking years, are you joking?'

'No, Mr Hill — armed robbery, possession of a firearm with the intent to endanger life and assault with intent to rob. And not for the first time, is it?'

I coughed loudly again.

'Are you okay, Mr Hill?'

'Erm, yeah, I'll be fine.'

Minutes later, I was taken up to the court and the charges were read to me and Chilton, as I looked up and nodded to Mum and my sister Diana in the public gallery. Members of the Chilton family were sat there too.

But before the court could get too far into its opening exchanges, my sore throat intensified and I launched into a huge coughing fit. Thankfully, the pills I had been given by a fellow inmate had worked. I can't remember exactly what condition they had been prescribed for now, but my pal assured me they would bring on such a reaction there was a chance the trial may be halted.

As I struggled to stand up, seemingly about to collapse in the dock, the judge said, 'Mr Hill, we're going to suspend proceedings, and bail you to the hospital, so we can get you checked out.'

I didn't expect to be sent to hospital immediately, but within 20 minutes I was handcuffed and sat in an ambulance on my way to Hammersmith hospital, next to the Scrubs. Result. Three Old Bill walked with me through corridors that led to a consultant's room. They took the cuffs off and I was ushered into see a doctor while the officers waited outside for me. Clearly, the consultant was going to give me the all clear, and was then meant to inform the police first, before I left the room. But as he got up to walk towards the door, I leapt up, beat him to it, pushed past the Old Bill and legged it out of the hospital. Thirty seconds later I was out on the pavement. Freedom. Wow.

I managed to run to East Acton station and bunked on the tube to Victoria and again on a train to Brighton.

I called my mate Winston in Wolverhampton from a phone box to sort some Western Union out for me, and plotted up in a hotel on the front for a couple of days. As much as I knew I was bang in trouble, it was lovely to breathe in some sea air and try and get some inspiration for my next move.

Chilton must have been screwing, because he was sent back to the Scrubs and the trial couldn't continue until they'd worked out what was happening with me.

I obviously wasn't thinking straight, but my idea was to do a jewellers in one of the lanes. I knew somebody I could get a thing from down there, so I spent my time working out the best target... which shop could give me the biggest haul of jewellery and watches, which I would take to Birmingham to sell, and then maybe sort out a dodgy passport and leave the country somehow. Realistically, starting a new life abroad was the only way out for me.

Then I decided to phone my mum. Clearly relieved to hear from me, she quickly cut to the chase.

'Me and your sister were called to court, Ray. Your pal Brian Cox came with us too. The judge told us straight. If you don't hand yourself in, he'd lock the three of us up until you did. Please come home, Ray.'

And you can't argue with your old mum, can you? She knew

I was active. I gave her loads of cash all the time, and I often walked in her house strapped up, so she knew the score.

'Ray, this is serious. They're going to put me and Diana in Holloway for perverting the course of justice, and maybe bang Brian up too...because they know you're going to contact us.'

A couple of hours later, I was stood on the platform at Brighton station, reluctantly heading home. That call with my mum did me a massive favour though, because I would have done the job in Brighton, maybe shot someone while on the run...a triple whammy, which would have made things a whole lot worse for all of us.

That evening, I handed myself in at Acton Police Station. A truly horrible feeling.

'Hi, I'm Raymond Hill...they want me for a court case at the Old Bailey.'

The officer on the front desk gave it the old, straight-faced, 'Okay, please, wait a minute, sir. Somebody will be out to speak to you.'

I wasn't fooled.

Within minutes, they were coming at me from all angles. Officers popping out of different doors.

Cuffed.

Straight down to the cells.

Pissy fucking blanket.

It was a Friday too, so a long weekend ahead. I would have loved to have waited until Monday, but I was worried about my mum.

A solicitor visited me the next day, and on the Monday I was taken to the Bailey in front of a horrible old judge called Mishkin, who Howard Marks told me he'd had, and who was now presiding over my absconding. He said, 'You're in a hell of lot of trouble, Mr Hill. You're lucky I won't be doing the actual trial.'

I was taken to an allocation centre in Limehouse, east London, which housed huge cells with up to 50 guys in there at a time, all waiting to be sent to prisons all over the country. No ventilation. Blokes pissing and shitting all the time. Ten hours later, I guess I was lucky to end up at my home from home, the Scrubs.

I had to wait three or four weeks for the original judge to be available to restart the trial, and then I was back at the Bailey. I knew I was fucked. It was like the first day in court all over again. What a waste of time all that was, and now I had to go guilty. No choice. So the rest of the trial was a formality, and over the next day.

I was thinking, hopefully, I'll get ten. I've done a year on remand, so I'll do another five. Chilton went in before me and got nine. Okay, so I'm going to struggle to get less than the 15 I had already been offered, especially because I had the thing. Next my turn.

'Mr Hill, I'm sentencing you to 22 years.'

Fuck...my legs completely went.

'Take him down.'

I called the judge an 'old cunt' and 'a fucking wanker'

A lot of good that did, but it's what you do. That's a big chunk of your life being taken away.

Back in my cell, in the depths of the Bailey, I sat there devastated. My QC came in, insisting we would appeal at the first instance. Blah, blah, blah. Giving me some hope, trying to reassure me that we'd get this thing overturned.

I had neither stolen anything nor killed anyone. Okay, I'd shot at a copper, but I didn't know he was Old Bill. Twenty two fucking years...really?

I was sent to the Scrubs and, of course, I knew so many people there by that point. It was almost like going to the pub.

It helps if, like me, you were in one prison a lot, like the Scrubs, And being a local prisoner, I got to a know the screws on a different level, because they were mostly locals too.

Now another long wait to be allocated. Chilton was put on a different wing to me, and probably asked for that, which was for the best. I only saw him when an occasional exercise session crossed over, so I never really spoke to him again. When there's a grass hanging over a job, it's very hard to ever have the same relationship again with anyone involved. It's the not knowing.

WELCOME BACK

Time to get on with my latest stretch. I was 32 and, at best, looking at doing 15 years, maybe with a few off for good behaviour. I would be well into my 40s by the time I got out. Prime years stuck away again. Fucking hell.

At least the screws at the Scrubs were pleased to see me.

'Fucking hell, Hilly…22 years. Jesus.'

'I know, it's fucking outrageous. Obviously, I've got to appeal it.'

And so I waited patiently for any news of that appeal. My barrister was on the case and I trusted him because he had always been straight up and down and I felt that he was fairly connected and had enough links to the old guard of regular judges and appeal judges. You have to be positive about an appeal, otherwise you have no hope. You'd give up.

I was put on A-wing ahead of allocation, threes up with some arseholes.

I went to the Deputy Governor and said, 'Listen, you know who I am.'

'Yes, Hilly, you've done several bits of bird, we know.'

'In that case, please give me a proper cell and a decent job.'

'You've only been here two days.'

'C'mon, guv, please…look after me?'

So he agreed, and put me working on 'the water' — filling up prisoner's flasks. Hot or cold. It was a decent job that kept me busy. I was also put twos up with a guy who cleaned the landings, so he was out all day too. It worked well.

Everything was sweet — apart from a bully on the fours who thought he ran the wing. Of course, I needed to be the Daddy, and that could only mean one thing. Later in the week, a bruiser of a guy leant over the fourth floor landing holding a makeshift knife, saying he was going to do me. A couple of days later, I went to his cell and we had it. He didn't try and stab me, thankfully, but we really went at it. Neither of us won, but he knew that he didn't want to fight me again, so we left it at that.

I started my shift one morning and there was water everywhere, all over the landings. The tank was empty — what the fuck has gone on here? I mopped it all up, and filled up the tanks again. I came back a bit later and caught one of a group of big cunts, who sold a bit of puff on the wing, letting the water out again.

I went in and bashed this guy up big time. But two of his mates appeared and hit me over the head with a metal bucket. Now I was scrapping with all three of them. We all got bashed up; again no winners, no losers. I didn't know what their problem was, maybe they were just jealous of me getting that job straight away.

At the time I was also doing a few shifts handing out tea and buns in the evening. That night, I was wheeling the trolley through the landings with a screw. He opened up one cell, and the two that joined in the first scrap were both sat there with black eyes. I had a shiner too.

'You alright, guys? Sweet?'

'Yeah, sweet.'

Another cell was opened up at the end of the landing, and there was the guy who started it...who let all the water out.

'Sweet.'

'Sweet.'

Great, all forgotten. The respect was there now, and sometimes things in prison can get sorted out that easily.

Now the four of us joined forces to run the wing together. Because they were banged up most of the time, I helped deliver bits of puff around the wing for them from my trolley. My contribution to our new little firm.

My eyes were always on the bully on the fours, though. He would have loved to stab me up, but at least I had back up now.

*****

A year in to my 22-stretch, I got a bang on my cell door.

'Hilly, you're appeal is up. You'll be going to court.'

Wow, about fucking time.

Often, you don't have to go to court. They come and tell you in your cell if you've been successful or not. But this required a court appearance. I hoped that meant it might be good news. Over the next couple of weeks, I looked forward to a trip out to the Royal Courts of Justice site on the Strand, and specifically the High Court.

Finally the day arrived, Spring 1984, and I was stood in front of three judges, about to give me their verdict.

'Mr Hill, we've read all your papers, and spoken to your barrister, but we need you to go downstairs for a while.'

Half an hour later, my QC appeared in my cell.

'I think we've got a bit of good news for you, Mr Hill. It's still a considerable sentence, but it will be reduced quite significantly.

'The first judge has recommended 14 years.'

'Great.'

'Hold on, Mr Hill, it's even better news, because between the three judges, they have agreed on 11 years.

'Wow, thank fuck for that.'

I couldn't believe it. It was a type of raw emotion I hadn't really experienced before. Sure, I'd had the feeling of being released from jail on several occasions, but this was different. And it meant I could be out by the late '80s. I'd already done a total of two years, including remand, so with good behaviour I was only looking at another four or five years.

I was buzzing. Back at the Scrubs, everybody was saying I'd had a right result. I was quickly informed I was being shipped to Albany in the morning. Wonderful. I'd already done that big stretch at Albany. They don't usually send you back to somewhere you have a lot of history, certainly not the kind I had. I assumed the screws who bashed me up were no longer there...hopefully moved on.

And it was great to be back at Albany. Everything seemed sweet again. B-wing. Single cells, electric doors...click...and my own key. Back training in the gym. Cushty. It felt quite unreal.

About a year in, though, things turned for me again at Albany.

Also returning like me was Dennis, that wanker from Bermondsey, who I clashed with in Chelmsford in the late '70s. Without people like Peter Kelly having my back this time, I feared this could cause problems for me when I was focusing on trying to keep my nose clean as much as possible. I saw Dennis around a bit, and there were no issues. He seemed to be keeping himself to himself too.

But Dennis soon got the hump, and tried to exploit the fact I was keeping my head down. One day at the end of exercise, the bell had gone and as I walked past the allotments, where I could see Dennis chatting to a few others, I was hit over the head with a shovel. I dropped to the floor and was smashed to bits with rakes, spades, pitch-forks. All sorts.

While that little mob fucked off back to the wing, I could just about stand up. Legs and arms battered, cuts all over my body. I was in such a bad way, I was taken to hospital on the mainland. I was treated there for about ten days and then taken to Wandsworth. I wasn't that fussed — it was for the best. If they'd have sent me back to Albany, I'd have badly got nicked for what I would have done to that lot, and been looking at a load more bird.

I got a job on the hotplate and who walked in? Fucking Dennis. I couldn't believe they'd sent him to Wanno too. Nothing happened. He was actually quite sheepish but, a few weeks later, I was taking extra food up to some guys on the ones and I saw Dennis walking into the toilets. I followed him in.

'Alright, mate?'

'Fuck off...'

I hit him so hard his jaw came right through his face, and he was out for the count. I just couldn't let that one go.

Dennis was that disliked, a younger guy came in and said, 'Mate, can I kick him please?' This kid had probably had enough of this bully pinching his tobacco or something like that, so I let him have a go. I lost count of how many times he kicked him.

Dennis was carried out and gone for weeks. When he came back, he was on a liquid diet. He finally knew I was the governor.

* * * * *

But I was soon on the move again. My first time to Maidstone — a new prison for me and a good one. I enjoyed my time there on both Weald and Medway wings.

There were quite a few faces in Maidstone during that period. Billy Blundell, Pat Adams and Bobby Dixie, all of whom I got on well with. It's amazing how quickly you bond with like-minded people inside, but also not surprising, of course. It was the first time I'd met Billy and my second time inside with Pat.

At Maidstone, the local newspaper ran an article about my charity exercise record attempts. I did a thousand press-ups in an hour, and also ran the equivalent of a marathon inside – all 26 miles.

*****

It was now the late-'80s, and I had barely a year left to do. I'd heard fascinating stories from prisoners coming in about a decade of more opportunity, compared to the '70s. Not that I had any ideas of going straight yet.

As I neared my potential release date — maybe just months now — an old mate started visiting me. He was a straight and successful businessman now and, a few times, brought his 19-year-old daughter with him. Let's call her Mandy. Then she started visiting me on her own. My mate and his wife were okay with it, but looking back it was all a bit weird.

Within weeks, I was told I had been awarded some home leave. Mandy picked me up from prison in a brand new maroon convertible Volkswagen Golf. She said we were going to Brighton to stay in a hotel. Fucking hell, okay. And we did, but nothing happened between us. It's my mate's daughter, right? We had a great night, and it was amazing to be out and partying with a gorgeous young lady...but then I had to go back inside again, which was really shit. You almost wonder if it's worth being let out.

During a second home leave from Maidstone, I went to see my mum at the house in Acton, and found out a young child I was closely related to had been sexually abused by some sicko who had managed to get close to them. The horrific details I was told brought back so many terrible memories for me.

I struggled to hold it down, but drove to Ealing police station, which was the last place I wanted to be, but I just felt I had to report this. I couldn't go back inside without doing something about it.

The child in question was later interviewed by the police and, with the use of a doll, asked to describe what they'd experienced and seen. This apparently confirmed exactly the kind of abuse that had taken place.

I was fucking livid when I found out, but somehow I had to keep calm, especially as I had been told who the guy was and knew where he lived. It was so hard not to react. Maybe the hardest thing I've ever had to do.

The suspect was thankfully questioned and charged, and put in the Scrubs. I was back in Maidstone by that point and, through my connections, trying to organise a welcoming party for him.

Shortly after, I was given more home leave for a couple of days and spent most of it waiting outside the Scrubs for prison officers I might know to walk into work. Call in some favours. The screws used me enough for that sort of thing; now they owed me.

*****

In the run up to my release, a bloke had turned up at Mum's door claiming to be our step-dad Bob's son. Because Bob was out, she slammed the door in this geezer's face, and apparently had it out with the old man when he got home.

Two days later, this guy came back with his sister and they waited in his car in our road until Bob came home, and then approached him. Bob went to speak to Mum and had to admit some home truths. And then it all came out, confirming mine and my sister's suspicions. She had tried to change her name to Eastwood by deed poll in 1985 when she had a child with her partner, but they could only find her as Rowlings, not as Hill.

Now, it would seem that Bob hadn't changed our names to Hill when we were kids...because, we reckon, he was still married. Somehow, at some point, I had entered the system as a Hill, probably at my YP, and stayed a Hill. It was horrible for Mum, but they stayed together. A lot of people did.

*****

With just four or fives weeks before my release, my head was all over the place. Mandy began writing letters to me. They were getting more flirty and sexier each time, and I had sent similar letters back.

I was finally released in January 1989, now more determined than ever to make a life of crime pay in the '90s. I also had a lot of unfinished business to deal with, not least the welfare of my kids, which I had obviously neglected massively.

My challenge was to keep active, stay out of prison and be there for my family. Something I'd never managed to do for very long.

On the day of my latest release, Mandy and her dad picked me up and took me to Brighton races. It was such a relief to enjoy that kind of day out, without the thought of going back in again hanging over me.

Mandy's dad fixed me up with a lady he knew down that way. It seemed like he couldn't do enough. He even moved me into his place in west London. Then he and his wife went away for a week and left me in the house with Mandy. One night, we got in bed together...and it happened. I'd only been out a matter of days, and everything was moving so fast. I was powerless to resist. This could only end in tears.

*****

Old Bill tipped me off that the paedo who had abused my young family member was due up at Isleworth Court. I don't know why they were trying to help me, because I'd not been their best friend over the years. Maybe they wanted to keep me updated, so I got this pervert sorted out. Or maybe they were just trying to wind me up, or get me nicked again. Either way, I was happy for the heads up.

I was sat outside the court in my mate's car, and police officers on the case were coming out and telling me what was going on. Somehow, he got off, so now we were both out.

The day after the trial, I went straight round to this guy's house with a shot-gun and waited for him to come out. Bold as brass, stood in the street, pointing the shooter at this gaff. The police turned up and I legged it back to my mum's. The next morning they bashed our front door in and dragged me out of bed and tried to handcuff my hands behind my back. But it was impossible: I was just too big to be forced into their car. So they cuffed me at the front, and instead bundled me in the back of a van, whacking me over the head with truncheons as they did. I was growling at them, and they were shitting themselves.

At Southall police station, I was sat in a room with the same two Old Bill who told me the suspect was in court. They must have taken a liking to me, or were as appalled at the court's decision as me, because they said, 'Do yourself a favour...fuck off. There's no evidence, no gun...just fuck off.'

A few days later, a mate was driving me through Ealing Common. We took a wrong turn and had to reverse back out. It must have been karma, because I saw the nonce walking past us. I jumped out of the car as he ran the other way. I can run, but this wanker was fast. He chucked his holdall so he could run faster and was heading towards Ealing Broadway Station. He jumped the barriers, sped down to the platform and onto the lines, and we lost him. But we found his bag and put it in the back of the car and, when rummaging through it later, I found some kiddie porn mags. The brass neck of it. I was fuming. Let's just say, we were both lucky I never caught up with him again.

* * * * *

A couple of weeks after I was released from Maidstone, I was asked to run the door at a wine bar called Central Park in East Churchfield Road in Acton, just the other side of the railway crossing — barely 50 yards from where I grew up.

It was a great venue, with an upstairs warehouse-type space that had been turned into a club for about 200 punters. It looked amazing up there, with huge figurines of women in stockings and suspenders. Upstairs usually went on until about 2am. Sometimes, we'd shut the door and let it crack on.

My mate Johnny Lawrence and a guy called Willie Waldron had the club, and I ran it on my own for a few weeks because, coming from Acton, most people gave me respect. Regulars like Gary Francis and the Walker brothers were pals. One night, there was trouble upstairs with the Chelsea Headhunters. I knew some of them, but not others. An hour after they arrived, it went off badly — bottles flying everywhere. I started knocking people out and Gary Francis, who had recently been stabbed 26 times in a fight and was still bandaged up, was trying to help me out.

While working on this book, I was having trouble remembering exactly when this happened, so I called Gary and he said, 'Fuck me, Ray, that was a long time ago, but I know it was a Saturday.' Then, somewhere from the depths of his mind, he remembered it was when Frank Bruno first fought Mike Tyson, so that meant it was February 25th, 1989. Thanks, Gal.

What I do remember clearly was the carnage that night. One of the Headhunters had a small baseball bat so Gary started letting off CS gas. Women were fighting like men, and then I got hit with a bottle so my head was pouring with blood. Finally, it calmed down and emptied out. The bar was smashed up and the DJ set-up had been pulled to the floor. Johnny Lawrence had his head in his hands.

I was getting good money, a couple of hundred quid, cash in hand, but to run both floors on my own was becoming impossible. I was getting extras on the door, letting people in, so a lot of it was my fault because those people weren't getting searched.

Johnny said he had another fella he could bring in and the following weekend a massive black guy in a smart suit walked into the venue and introduced himself as Jefferson King. It was a couple of years before Jeff would become a huge star on hit TV series, *Gladiators*, as Shadow.

The next few weeks were sweet, me and Jeff taking a floor each and rotating it through the night. Then one week the Headhunters came back. I was downstairs, but Jefferson let them in and upstairs. I had a word with one of them and said, 'No trouble tonight, lads,' and they tried to claim the main culprits weren't coming, but they did a little later. Then the Acton lot came in.

I sent Jefferson upstairs, while I tried to stabilise the door to the club. But it quickly kicked off again. Even worse than last time. I ran up to the club, and me and Jeff were both right in the middle of it, knocking people out.

Johnny Lawrence wanted to call Old Bill, but I had always insisted, 'Once you call the police, the club will be fucked. They'll be on us and they'll want me out, an armed robber. They'll talk about an attempted murder of a police officer, and they'll want back handers. So leave it to me, I'll sort it.'

But it was mental in there again, and the stakes were about to be upped. I saw Jefferson halfway up the stairs, floored, with two Acton brothers Andy and Johnny, dangerous people, leaning over him. As I got closer, I could see they had a .38 to Jeff's head. The poor guy was shaking like a leaf. Jefferson was ripped and must have been 22-23 stone, but it was the first time that had happened to him.

I pulled the boys off Jeff, with Andy shouting, 'How dare he fucking threaten us, Ray. He's dead.'

'Whoa, whoa...calm down, mate.'

Andy and Johnny left. Jefferson was in a really bad way. He obviously couldn't work at the club anymore. One of the brothers could come back at any point and take a pop at him on the door.

*****

Socially, I was spending a lot of time at The Anchor in Acton. I'd been going to that boozer for almost 20 years now...well, off and on, of course. As usual, always trouble in there, always fights. I think I had at least one scrap there a week. It just happened that way with a pub full of big characters. Dennis Haley, the scrap dealer and demolition guy, was still in there too.

As usual, I didn't really drink— maybe a shandy or a Guinness with blackcurrant and, as always, mainly used pubs and clubs to try to get work...or to pull.

With me and the ex always getting back together and splitting up again, I rented a flat in Goldhawk Road in Bush.

One afternoon, I received a call from the governor at The Crown in Acton.

'Ray, there's a little bit of trouble down here.'

I asked who was involved, and he said, 'Andy (Andy and Johnny, Andy) - and he's saying he's going to kill someone.'

Not him again...

I got down there to find police outside. The governor let me through the side of the pub. Wow, what a mess. Blood everywhere, and I mean everywhere.

'What the fuck has gone on here?'

Someone had said something to Andy about his mother, and he went home, got his .38, came back and threatened this guy who said, 'If you're going to fucking do it, do it...' Boom, he did and blew the whole back of his head off.

Andy went on the run, but was eventually caught. He got life, but I think he's out now.

*****

Mandy came down to Central Park one night, telling me she wanted to make a go of it. I told her, 'I'm your dad's mate, we can't be carrying on like this anymore.'

She wasn't having it, but I insisted it had to stop. She took it really badly, and the next day left all the letters I'd sent her on the side in the house where she lived with her parents. Her mother read them and was furious. Mandy's parents rushed round to my mum's, where I was still based, as usual, and knocked down the door, accusing me of doing all sorts with their daughter. My poor mum, she'd been through more than enough by now.

Me and Mandy's dad fell out big time and he stopped talking to me. His wife went proper gangster, and came looking for me with a carving knife. I never spoke to their daughter again.

It certainly didn't feel like she was a kid, because she helped my mate run his companies. I definitely felt like I'd been set up or, at least, Mandy's parents really hadn't thought it through. Bringing their daughter to me in prison, and then allowing her to visit me on her own? After being away all that time, it was just too much.

I carried on working at Central Park, but I was soon itching for the pavement again.

*****

I always hoped my door work would help keep me out of trouble, but it never seemed to work that way, and often only fuelled more criminality.

At one wine bar in west London where I ran the door, the owner had a sideline with an arms dealer friend, pimping working girls around the world, which he ran from the office above.

I was brought in to clear out the 'yuppies' because the manager felt they weren't spending enough money, nursing a single bottle of wine all night. Other customers were complaining there was too much ice in their cocktails, which was probably true. They actually wanted me to encourage a more straight-up local crowd who'd spend their hard-earned cash more freely.

I must have upset someone, because I was shot in the calf walking home one night. I think it was a local I knew of, who was causing problems, complaining about drinks measures. This fella wouldn't drop it, so I said, 'Look, mate, let's just go outside and sort this out. Just me and you. If you win, I'll leave this job, simple as that.' We went outside and I knocked him out with my first punch. By now, I'd realised that fighting is all about angles. That you can hit someone on chin straight on, and maybe not knock them down, but if you come at the correct angle, they're sparko. Nine times out of ten, assuming I had the right angle, I used my right hand. If I caught someone properly with a right hand, it was all over. Standard. A couple of days later, walking back to Mum's one night, I sensed something behind me. I turned around to see a car driving slowly thirty or forty yards or so away. I could even see something sticking out of the window. Instantly, I heard a loud bang, so dived to the ground, but felt my leg lift up as I fell down. I'd already been shot in the leg. I jumped up and ran for my life across a nearby green, knowing a second shot could finish me off.

Amazingly, looking back, considering I'd been around guns all my life, that was the first time I'd actually been shot, and probably with a .410 shotgun. It was only the adrenalin that allowed me to run home. My poor old mum pulled out the pellets. In situations like this, sometimes it's just best to swallow it for now and move on. I had half a clue who it was, so it would be dealt with another time.

(Right and bottom) The Old Bailey, inside and out.

(Below) Judge Mervyn Griffith-Jones, who was on my first case at The Bailey.

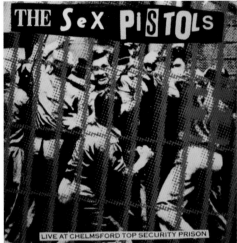

LIVE AT CHELMSFORD TOP SECURITY PRISON

(Above) The LP cover of The Sex Pistols *Live At Chelmsford Top Security Prison* album.

(Right) Deputy Governor Robert Mole at the scene of the Chelmsford Prison fire in 1978.

(Below) A scene from iconic *BBC* comedy *Porridge*, with Ronnie Barker and Richard Beckinsale, filmed at Chelmsford Prison.

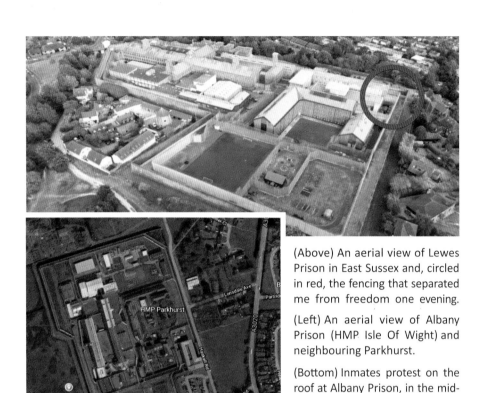

(Above) An aerial view of Lewes Prison in East Sussex and, circled in red, the fencing that separated me from freedom one evening.

(Left) An aerial view of Albany Prison (HMP Isle Of Wight) and neighbouring Parkhurst.

(Bottom) Inmates protest on the roof at Albany Prison, in the mid-1970s.

(Left) A very rare photo of me (second left) in prison, exercising at Chelmsford in 1977.

(Below) In the ring against Colin Cracknell during my own Octopus Promotions event at Acton Town Hall in 1980.

(Above) The seven inch record cover to my ring walk song, *Cool For Cats*, suggested by actor Brian Cox.

(Right) Pictured at my sister's wedding shortly after my release from the Scrubs in 1979.

(Above) Roy Shaw and Lenny McLean at a sparring session in early 1980s.

Right) Actor Brian Cox in an episode of *Minder* in 1982.

(Below) The poster for my bout with Dave Strong at Ilford Palais in 1979.

(Below right) The Venue, Victoria, where I worked as a doorman at the time.

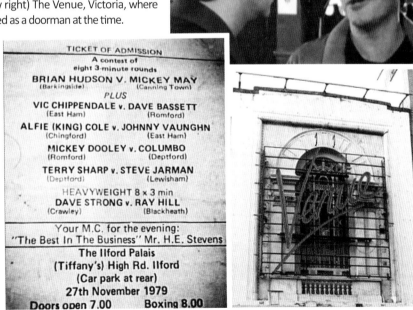

TICKET OF ADMISSION

A contest of
eight 3-minute rounds

BRIAN HUDSON v. MICKEY MAY
(Barkingside)   (Canning Town)

PLUS

VIC CHIPPENDALE v. DAVE BASSETT
(East Ham)   (Romford)

ALFIE (KING) COLE v. JOHNNY VAUGHN
(Chingford)   (East Ham)

MICKEY DOOLEY v. COLUMBO
(Romford)   (Deptford)

TERRY SHARP v. STEVE JARMAN
(Deptford)   (Lewisham)

HEAVYWEIGHT 8 x 3 min
DAVE STRONG v. RAY HILL
(Crawley)   (Blackheath)

Your M.C. for the evening:
"The Best In The Business" Mr. H.E. Stevens

The Ilford Palais
(Tiffany's) High Rd. Ilford
(Car park at rear)
27th November 1979
Doors open 7.00   Boxing 8.00

WARREN SPORTS PROMOTIONS
LICENCED BY THE NATIONAL BOXING COUNCIL

present

BOXING

AT THE RAINBOW THEATRE, FINSBURY PARK

on Monday 10th September 1979

FEATURING A 10 x 3 MIN. CONTEST FOR THE

HEAVYWEIGHT CHAMPIONSHIP OF GREAT BRITAIN

THE HOLDER	THE CHALLENGER
THE IRON MAN WHO HAS NEVER BEEN ON THE FLOOR AND HAS STOPPED ALL HIS CHALLENGERS	FORMERLY ISHAQ HUSSEIN NOW FIGHTING FOR HIS BIG CHANCE AFTER K'O'ING BOBBY POLLARD IN JULY

V

CLIFF FIELD
DUNSTABLE

TSHAKA
ISLINGTON

A 10 x 3 MIN. HEAVYWEIGHT CONTEST

DADDY COOL CONTINUES HIS FIGHT BACK TO THE TOP

LENNIE 'BOY' McLEAN
HOXTON

HAS TWO K'O's TO HIS CREDIT IN TWO FIGHTS

RAY HILL
LEA

A 8 x 3 MIN. HEAVYWEIGHT CONTEST

BOBBY POLLARD
TOTTENHAM

V

BRIAN HALL
ROMFORD

A 6 x 3 MIN. MIDDLEWEIGHT CONTEST

PAUL FITZGERALD
ELTHAM

V

DAVID HAMM
BASILDON

A 8 x 3 MIN. MIDDLEWEIGHT CONTEST

MICKY MAYES
CANNING TOWN

V

MALCOLM RYAN
ISLINGTON

A 6 x 3 MIN. WELTERWEIGHT CONTEST

GARY KNIGHT
CANNING TOWN

V

ROGER FIELD
DUNSTABLE

A 8 x 3 MIN. HEAVYWEIGHT CONTEST

LLOYD WALFORD
BRIXTON

V

JOHN TALBOT
CARDIFF

A 6 x 3 MIN. WELTERWEIGHT CONTEST

☀ THE LOCAL DERBY ☀

REGGIE CHAPMAN v **FREDDIE ROSE**
ISLINGTON   ISLINGTON

DOORS OPEN 7 P.M. – BOXING COMMENCES 8 P.M.
TICKETS: £12.50 . £10.00 . £8.50 . £5.00 . £2.50

available from

RAINBOW THEATRE 01-263 3148   HENRY BROWNE 01-739 7582
RINGSIDE WINE BAR 01-739 1838   THE SOUTHGATE ARMS 01-226 6120

(Above) A Frankie Fraser 'mugshot'.

(Right) Johnny Bindon pictured with Princess Margaret, allegedly on the beach in Mustique.

(Below) An imagined AI image of me aged in my early 30s.

(Bottom right) Eddie Richardson.

(Above) Security Express vans we targeted in the 1970s and '80s.

(Below) The sort of vintage police van I was thrown into many times.

BLAST FROM THE PAST

An old mate hooked me up with a job at a club called Lucky's in Ealing Broadway, and also put me up for a day job, bodyguarding the King of Saudi Arabia and his various family members at a huge house he owned in Ham Gate Avenue in Richmond. A nice little number, paying a £800 a week cash-in-hand retainer, my job was mainly walking the grounds with two huge Dobermans.

These people loved cash. Security Express guards arrived each week and brought money bags into the house. The head house-keeper would oversee the delivery and then gunned-up ex-SAS guys working for the family put the money into safes in the boots of Rolls Royces or Bentleys — and off they went to Harrods.

Our little security team of eight were not allowed in the house, or on the shopping trips to Knightsbridge, but we were often sent to The Dorchester Hotel on Park Lane when the young sheiks, aged in their early 20s, were shagging birds, to be security stood outside hotel rooms. It was murder watching all these fit sorts arrive at the rooms, and having to wave them inside.

I'd see the King's wife — well one of the them, because he was meant to have married 13 times — striding around the grounds of the house in Richmond with dozens of junior housekeepers following her, running on the spot, while she walked in front of them.

The sheer numbers of staff and manpower was incredible. When the King arrived at the house, it was with a huge entourage — 30-40 people in all sorts of motors, the ex-SAS lot, supported by armed Special Forces Old Bill, in and out of the bushes around the property.

The whole family would arrive at Heathrow in one jumbo jet...and go home in two planes because of all the stuff they'd bought.

My cushy role there came to an abrupt end after six months. The young sheiks, back and forth to their Lamborghinis and Ferraris, were fascinated by me and another guard playing penny up the wall. We told them we usually played for a few quid, but they said they didn't carry money and weren't allowed to gamble. They began joining in, and asking to play for high stakes. I said we could play for our watches, knowing full well they were wearing £100k Patek Philippes and we were wearing snide Rolexes.

We'd take their pukka watches off them, but always give them back, because we knew we'd get rumbled. The head housekeeper found out and wasn't amused, sacking us on the spot for encouraging the boys to gamble.

I was heartbroken. Not just at losing decent regular income, but because I'd heard stories of young sheiks or the shaykhahs, the daughters, giving cash bonuses or lavish gifts to their favourite guards. One even got a Lambo.

*****

One night at Lucky's was significant, to say the least. A girl I knew from Ladbroke Grove, who I'd seen at a few after-parties, asked if my name was Basher?

'Yeah, sometimes...'

'I've got a letter for you.'

'Really?'

And it was an actual handwritten letter, from none other than Freddy, who I'd had no contact with for more than a decade...not since I'd left Brixton on bail ten years ago. This sounded interesting.

In the letter, Freddy explained he'd heard I was out, and would like to see me. Later that night at Bootleggers in The City, if possible. The girl was a regular at both venues, so I think that's how my name cropped up.

I knocked off a bit early, around 1am, and headed to Bootleggers. It was easy to find Freddy. Surrounded by dolly birds and with the sleeves on his suit rolled up, he looked like an extra from Miami Vice. Freddy said it was great to see me, that he'd give me a few bob and look after his old mate. I could tell he was doing well for himself. He took me to Browns nightclub in Holborn later that evening, and was splashing the cash.

Freddy explained he was working with a serious firm. He didn't have to tell me how serious, once he mentioned the people involved. I'd come across some of them over the years and, thankfully, had never had any issues.

There was another gangster there that night who had fallen out with this firm. I knew him from inside. He clocked me deep in conversation with Freddy and later dropped a gun in front of me near the dance floor. More to warn me, I'm sure. He tried to make a joke of it, but I knew what he was doing. Fortunately, that little incident didn't boil up the wrong way.

Freddy invited me to his house in east London — a beautiful gaff, done out lovely. I started hanging out with him loads over that side, travelling over there on the tube, going to the gym together. Then Freddy moved further out into Essex, to a bigger place. I asked him for £50 one day and he got a bit funny, and said, 'Basher, if you want money, you need to earn it.'

I knew he was working with major players, and that it was time to try and prove myself. I started doing some enforcement work for Freddy, and was asked to deal with a guy who had grassed on the wrong people. I travelled to Deptford and bashed this geezer up. Job done. But Freddy rang me up fuming, saying this guy had been spotted walking about unharmed. He was furious. I knew I'd done the business, but he was having none of it. An hour later, Freddy rang back and said it was all fine. I was later told the guy had an identical twin.

The next day, Freddy gave me some cash, a couple of grand, and bought me a car, a second hand Rover Vandem Plus.

* * * * *

My relationship with Freddy progressed. We were building a trust. Lots of situations needed to be enforced and there was always loads of cash to be collected.

I'd collect 'parcels' from the boot of an old car like a Skoda. The car keys would be left in the exhaust pipe. Close by there would be another car, insured in my driver's name, because I didn't have a licence still. Everything was always done proper, because nine times out of ten, being uninsured or driving like an idiot was most likely to get you a tug. So with all the paperwork in place, we never drove like idiots.

I'd get the parcel, put it in the boot of the motor. Gone. Up to Manchester, Leeds, Birmingham or wherever.

Two motorbikes in front of our car and two behind. If it got on top with Old Bill, the motorbikes would cause a distraction, which ensured that the police chased them instead of our car.

If it was normal Old Bill, we wouldn't just give ourselves up. We'd be prepared to ram them off the road, if need be, because there would still be a chance we could get away. With parcels in the car, and a thing, it might even be preferable to shoot up the engine of the police car and take our chances.

But if certain specialist police squads are on you, you're fucked, because they know the score.

Nowadays, even if you're masked up and you get away, your journey will be traced back via all the cameras your motor passed through. Back in the day, with much less or hardly any CCTV, it was so much easier. Now with ANPR and Geo Fencing, you're really fucked. Back then, it was rare to get a tug. You just drove. I'd meet the connection at their lock-up, garage or wherever. Usually regular kind of people. We'd try not to talk to them on a mobile phone on the way up. Everything would be pre-planned. Everybody knew where to be and at what time.

My job was simply to collect any money owed previously and give them a new parcel. The top brass wanted their money back in 14 days, but I would give 10 days. I always thought it was best to give people a bit less time, because if I came up after ten days and they hadn't quite got the cash together it gave them some more time before things became unpleasant.

Cash collected, I'd give it to the guys on the bikes and they'd shoot off with it, straight back to London. I never looked at the money. It was accepted it was all correct, and it always was. Never short. The riders were trusted, so they didn't need to look at the cash either. Their job was to get it back in one piece. The only excuse they could have for not delivering the money in tact was if they had got a pull on the way back and were found with cash in their holdall, which could be anything up to six figures. I was paid my wages back in London when everything was squared off.

If, however, the money for the last drop off wasn't ready, then that's when it got really interesting. I hadn't come all the way from London to waste my time. I'm the enforcer so I need to enforce, otherwise my people are not going to be happy. Because I always had a few days to play with I would let them get on the phone and try and call in some favours. I'd pop off to visit another firm in another city. If this lot hadn't got it together by the time I got back, they'd have to suffer the consequences.

It's down to the main man, and that's whoever I gave the parcel to. As far as I'm concerned, he got the parcel, so he has to give me the money.

I heard one guy who couldn't pay up was pinned to a door through the loose skin on his arms and legs with an industrial staple-gun. Another had his hands nailed to a wooden floor with four inch nails. The money suddenly appeared. Those kind of tactics aren't needed again, or very often, because word gets around.

In the early '90s, I was happy to operate as an enforcer because it didn't involve doing armed robberies anymore. It was more individual stuff. Still sometimes strapped, but less need to use that. On one job I was on to collect a debt of twenty grand, it turned out I knew the fella from prison. This guy was a bit naughty, so it put me in a position. When he offered me five grand cash to say I didn't find him, I couldn't say no. It was more than the 10% I would have earned. Result.

I was soon travelling all over the country. Outside of London, pre-internet and camera phones, they usually didn't have a clue who I was, which could be an advantage. However, I like to think I made a name for myself quite quickly.

Enforcing became my game, and I wouldn't stop until I found the person or people in question. Any time, anywhere. I usually sorted things out myself. Straight through the front door. I'd only take someone with me, if necessary. I made a lot of enemies, but I made a lot of friends too, especially in and around the acid house rave scene in the early '90s.

A girlfriend of a mate was a chemist who made sheets and sheets of acid tabs in a discreet drug factory out in the sticks. She converted them into really trippy microdot Es and transported them around the country in her false leg, which was wooden and hollow. I had a few good nights out with that lot. Funny fuckers. I tested one of those pills at a party, and was so fucked, I didn't think the trip was ever going to end.

*****

Towards the end of 1990, I was introduced to the so-called and self-named Billionaire Boys Club — Nigel Benn, Rolex Ray Sullivan, Gary Stretch and a few others. Always known to this lot as Basher or Bash, I became their minder when they were hanging out at central London nightclubs like Browns in Holborn, Pal Joeys, at the site of the legendary La Valbonne on Kingley Street, just off Carnaby Street, and Blondes, behind The Ritz on Piccadilly. Of course, they didn't actually make one billionaire added together, but all were doing very well for themselves and had cash to burn. I'd buy knocked off Hugo Boss suits from a guy in Shepherd's Bush, so I looked the part.

In an interview years later in *The Mirror,* Rolex Ray revealed...

We called ourselves the Billionaire Boys' Club and lived like pop stars, only better. We used to take over front seats, the best tables and we had the biggest cars and best expense accounts. Wherever you have fame and money, you have women and there was a never ending supply of them. We led a charmed life. There was about nine of us. Two are now doing very long prison sentences, one is dead, one I don't talk to and another went off his head.

Blondes was notorious. Football legend George Best had a share in the business, and could always be found propping up the bar. Like a lot of these places, especially in the West End, there was always a gangster element. One night, two Italians got pulled out of Blondes, taken down an alleyway across the road and were shot in the legs.

We'd hang out a lot in the VIP bar upstairs at Browns. It seemed like there was a fight in there every week, probably because everyone was on the toot. There'd be guys hassling my boys and generally causing trouble so my job was to keep that to a minimum.

One Thursday night, three guys had given George Best a load of grief at Blondes and damaged the corner of the bar where the champagne was kept and smashed a couple of magnums — properly taken the piss. I was asked to sort it out, so had a ring round and was told this little mob were now in Pal Joeys. I arrived 15 minutes later, and the doormen waved me through and told me at which bar I'd find this lot, who I was also informed were suited and booted. They looked like lairy office workers to me, with one wearing a Prince Of Wales check suit, very popular at that time. I ordered myself a lemonade, and then turned to one of the guys and said, 'Have you boys been in Blondes?'

'What's it got to do with you?' said one of them, before lunging at my neck with his glass. I swerved out of the way as the drink and ice splashed over me....then I chinned him, and the next one, and the one after. The management called an ambulance, and me and the bouncers dragged these idiots out of the club and dumped them on the street outside.

Three or four days later, I was in Ferdenzies, the old downstairs one in New Burlington Street, with Ray Sullivan and Nigel Benn, when the three guys turned up five or six-handed. They clocked me and it all kicked off. Tables and chairs were flying. I managed to pick off four or five of them again, and the others backed off. Let's just say, Nigel being there definitely helped bring things under control.

At the end of one night with the guys at Pal Joeys, I'd been putting the bottles of champagne they were ordering on top of a piano, but it seemed like some had gone missing. All of a sudden, I saw an arm appear. I looked over and there was a waitress aged 20, 21, absolutely stunning, under the piano with a bottle in her hand.

'What the fuck are you doing?'

'Who the fuck are you?'

The waitress' dad was away on a 10-stretch — a member of a notorious gang of armed robbers — so we connected. I liked how upfront she was, and we started seeing each other.

My new girlfriend's mum welcomed me initially because I treated her daughter well, but when the old man came out a few months later, although he wanted to accept me, he was only a year older than me and because he was a gangster and his wife was also in the game, they didn't really want that for their daughter too.

My girlfriend's mum, let's affectionately call her 'the mother-in-law', arranged a first floor flat in a property in Kingston, a couple of streets away from their home, for us to live in. The family also had a larger house in a leafy private estate in Kingston. I was to give a family friend big lumps of money over a period of time, and then the flat was mine.

There were false drawers in the middle of the island in the kitchen, which I dumped cash in so my girlfriend could help herself when she needed to, or to pay any bills. Nothing was in my name, which suited me fine.

The 'family friend' had one of those metal doors put on the entrance to the downstairs flat, so it looked like it was derelict or had been repossessed, making it a perfect place to stash stuff, which me and him both did under the floorboards. From that perspective, it was a great arrangement.

The 'mother-in-law' was mates with the family friend's girlfriend, whose ex-husband I'd been inside with in the '70s, and who had previously had dealings with Johnny Bindon, so there was a connection there. Having access to the storage was great, but I could see it would eventually cause problems.

Me and my girlfriend also spent time at the other house, which was beautiful and really, really tucked away in a secluded private road on a gated estate in Kingston, and she also spent loads of time at her parents' place. Over the next few months, I transformed the flat, which had potential for a loft extension, into my own personal space where I met people and where I kept my bits and pieces.

The 'father-in-law' knew who I was because he was in Parkhurst when I was in Albany and word travels. We got close for a while. I'd give him stuff to sell on but he wouldn't always pay me, thinking it was easy to knock his so-called son-in-law, and also used that to try and pull rank somehow. He got big on the powder and started running with some very heavy people.

ROLLING WITH THE PUNCHES

A pal, Alan, who the Walker brothers had introduced me to, had some Old Bill on side, who were selling him coke they'd confiscated. These coppers were at it themselves, bang on the gear. It got so bad, a few had to go to rehab.

I started to work with Alan on a few jobs. We began robbing anybody and everybody. We felt so powerful together. We didn't worry about the consequences, because we were dealing with consequences on a daily basis anyway.

Soon after, Alan was the victim of a drive-by. A couple of guys pulled up alongside his BMW, and sprayed him four times with an AK47. He drove straight to A&E in Paddington with blood pissing out of him. I visited him in hospital, which was full of armed police, and in his room. I sat bedside with him for a while, but with all that Old Bill about, I cut the visit short as there wasn't much we could discuss.

When all that had calmed down, Alan and I set up some Welsh guys based in Chiswick. One of our regular stings — taking their cash, without giving them any real drugs. We were sat round the back of the M4, near Brentford Market, in a Toyota Supra 500 — a very powerful car. Fast. I was at the wheel, as usual with no licence, and the motor not registered to either of us, so that went against the strict rules in place working for other firms. Not good practice, but I think working for them made me feel invincible. I already felt that physically, and always had, but now I also felt untouchable, which was dangerous in itself.

Alan got back in the car with 40 large, having given the Welsh guys a parcel they thought was pukka coke, which was actually one pound bags of sugar wrapped up in brown packing tape. They'd already had a kosher sample, but they didn't have time at the meet to unwrap everything. It's a straight in and out, and that's all part of the blag. One of those ones, where we'd built up the trust, and we just had the feeling they'd part with the cash easily. I was doing a fair bit of coke myself now, and regularly charged up, so I wasn't even bothered at the thought of any comebacks. By this point, business was business, however it was done. I think I'd simply been involved in too much crime by now to actually give a fuck.

I drove off, the money in a bag on the floor of Alan's side of the car, when he suddenly took a hand gun from his coat, and put that down by the cash. Shit. I didn't know he had that.

Then suddenly, that fateful sound again...

'Woo, woo...'

I'd just pulled off a big kerb, so maybe, hopefully, they wanted me for parking there. A police car came alongside me, so I stopped and wound the window down.

'Can you pull over there by the car showroom, sir?'

'What's the problem?'

'There's no problem, sir. We just need to ask you a few questions...

'Yeah, right...fuck you...'

Vroom. We were off.

I put my foot down, and headed towards the Chiswick round-about. I did a left by the petrol garage, and then really gave it some welly, but Old Bill were up my arse. I clipped the side of a bus as I chucked a right, and bounced across the road. Fuck, a dead-end. No option, but to drive through the wooden fence in front of me. Wallop. Slap bang into a graveyard. I could see a building site on the far side, backing on to Gunnersbury Park.

Alan got out of the car and ran, with the gun, but without the money. I was shitting myself as Old Bill chased after him, in case he let them have it with the shooter. I started to chase the two coppers, hoping to distract them so Alan could get away, but another officer appeared from behind. I just wanted to try and stop any use of that gun, because it would have been disastrous for all of us. And it worked, because Alan was able to escape. The other two Old Bill now turned their attentions to me, so I chinned one of them, and he was gone. Sparko. Still two coppers chasing me, though, as I ran through the building site. Scaffolders threw pipes down at the police to try and put them off and then the Old Bill I smacked reappeared and was whining like a child. 'Why did you hit me, I only wanted you to stop.'

I was cornered, rounded up and taken to Chiswick police station and thrown in a cell. They didn't have Alan and the gun, thank fuck, but they did have me and probably the cash.

And what were the chances? Treen walked in. The fucking inspector who interviewed me when I bashed up the copper after the Bridstow Place job. Treen! Almost 20 years later. Who I'd thrown up against the wall in the last cell we were in together.

He was worryingly cheerful.

'Hello, Mr Hill, nice to see you again, how you doing?'

'What do you fucking want?'

'You're in big trouble, mate.'

'What do you mean?'

'Well, the money we've got from the Supra. We believe that's 10% of the cash taken earlier in a robbery when someone was shot...and we believe you were the driver.'

'You cunt. You're trying to fit me up.'

A few hours later, I was put on an ID parade, but thankfully wasn't picked out.

I was, though, charged with assault of a police officer (again!) and possession of twenty-five grand in cash. Again, some had gone missing. Standard.

Not for the first time in my life, I was shocked to get bail. I got back home and everything was sweet for a while. I was still working for Freddy but had two crown court cases coming up. First at Kingston for the cash and at Isleworth a bit later for the assault on the copper, which I was fearing the most.

*****

While I waited for my cases, I was hired as part of the security team for Gary Stretch's WBO world middleweight fight with Chris Eubank at Olympia in Kensington. April 18th, 1991. I'd always got on really well with Gary, who was going out with Lionel Blair's daughter at the time.

I was first out on the ring walk, also escorting a little terminally-ill kid, who was part of the entourage as Gary made his way through to the theme tune from the *Rocky* film. It was great to be involved in a world title fight, in what is now regarded as such an iconic era of British middleweight boxing. Six months earlier, in the first of their super-fights, Eubank had taken the WBO middleweight title off bitter rival Nigel Benn, who was working as a pundit for *ITV* at Olympia.

Gary was very unlucky in that fight. The doctor was called at the end of round five to a facial cut on Eubank, which later needed several stitches. The referee was advised to stop the fight, but he gave Eubank's corner the okay for one more round, which ended with a controversial stoppage after Gary was pushed through the ropes, and when all three judges had him ahead on the scorecard.

I've always kept in touch with Gary. He sent me these kind words for the book...

My great friend Mickey Gooch introduced me to Ray in the wild times of central London in the early '90s, and I loved Ray from the first time we met. Goochy and I had a very special relationship, a man I respect greatly. I was having some success with my boxing career and had people from all walks of life trying to pull me in all kinds of directions. Goochy was great fun and a lad to say the least. He loved the excitement of life, but in an amazing way, and was someone I could trust and who protected me always. He let me party but kept me away from the bad influences and temptations that surrounded us. That's where Ray came into the scene.

Ray, a close confidant of Goochy, was hired to keep his eye on me and more importantly on those around me. Ray wasn't a talker, his mere energy and presence screamed loudly. He was often invisible, yet he'd miraculously appear whenever he was needed. Ray was really funny and a true gentleman. However, he didn't suffer fools and he guarded me like his life depended on it.

I was a free spirit but also, believe it or not, a little shy and, I guess, naive. I've lost count of the times people dug me out and tried to fight with me, trying to put a notch on their belt. I remember going into the toilet in Browns nightclub one night and three guys followed me. In the time it took me to take a piss there was a pile of bloodied bodies lying behind me. A grinning Ray stood over them and said, 'Go and have fun, son. I'll clean this mess up.'

Ray has been by my side many times over the years, and I was delighted when he walked me out for the Eubank fight. More importantly, Ray is someone I love being around and can trust implicitly.

Yes, they broke the mould when they made Ray Hill. I'm truly excited about this book's release and look forward to its great success. Knock on champ.

*****

Several months after the graveyard arrest, the Kingston trial for the £25k finally came up. I tried to argue that the money was mine, that I'd collected it for a debt, but the judge was having none of it. He confiscated it and said he'd give it to a police fund, but I did get off. At least that.

A week later, the police officer assault case came up. Banged to rights. Twelve months…in Wandsworth, which was definitely a result, but also a massive blow personally, and for my relationship with my girlfriend which was only just getting going. But, as usual, I knew the risks and had to knuckle down. Fortunately, as ever, there were people I knew, both inmates and screws, so all was good at Wanno. I got a nice job back on the hotplate.

There was no dialogue with Freddy and any of his associates. As far as they were concerned, I'd got a bit of bird, but I'd be out soon. As long they weren't pulled into anything, it was business as usual.

At Wanno, I met Billy Williams — Bill The Bomb — for the second time. He was a great boxer who went to America, but later got bad on heroin. Me and Billy joined forces and took over C-wing and controlled the tobacco. We bashed up any nonces for extra privileges, all that game. Rarely getting pulled in for questioning. The screws wanted it done, because they couldn't do it themselves. We got more perks and got undone more. It worked.

On this bit of bird in 1991, I could tell there were loads more drugs in the prison, compared to when I last came out a few years previously. Drugs became more widely used in prison from the late

'80s onwards, when they did on the outside, because that was the popular culture. People being jailed in that time were selling or used to taking recreational drugs, and so were the people visiting them, and even the screws, so I think it just developed from there.

*****

My girlfriend visited me for the first few weeks, but then I didn't see her for a while and the letters stopped.

Eight months later, at the start of 1992, I was released. I left a silver buckled belt Freddy had given me for Billy as a leaving present.

My girlfriend did at least pick me up, but she wasn't best happy that I'd offered a lift to another guy being released at the same time, or that I gave him the £44 spends I was given in a brown envelope. We dropped the geezer off and we drove straight to her parents in Kingston because my girlfriend said she needed some cash.

'We've got money, darling, we've got money...'

She was pissed off because Winston from Wolverhampton owed me 14 grand for some bits and pieces.

I belled Winston and he said he had something he wanted to talk to me about, and I said, 'Fuck that for now, just sort out the money.'

I quickly hooked up with Wiggy Purdy, an old gangster aged in his 80s, who I'd known since I was a kid, and had been working for me before I went away. He'd drive me about in an old Lada, which was great cover, because it just looked like I was out with my grandad. Wiggy was acting a bit strange and looked like he had something on his mind too.

I was already pissed off with my girlfriend and wanted to know why she hadn't visited for ages — obviously suspecting she'd been fucking someone behind my back. She drove off back to her parents, and within an hour Wiggy and Winston arrived at my house at the same time.

'Right, what's up, you two?'

Wiggy said, 'Well, I noticed loads of bin bags building up in your garden at the back of the flat. One day, I saw your dog Biba had ripped them to pieces. I went to clean it all up and found Durex wrappers.'

Fucking hell. When my girlfriend eventually came home, it all kicked off. Even at that early stage, it felt like that was the beginning of the end for us. I've never really expected anyone to wait for me but, with this being such a short stretch, I really thought she could have held on.

*****

Things got better with my girlfriend but her old man began knocking me more and more. I was working for firms that you just couldn't upset, and stuck between a rock and a hard place. It started to become a problem, but I think the father-in-law wanted that so he could try and slip in with those firms instead.

He had been in some bad situations recently. On a drug deal in Holland, one of his guys was shot dead. He reckoned he picked up the body, put it in the boot of his car and drove it back to the UK. This poor bloke went on to have a proper burial, so they must have found a willing undertaker to take a few quid and organise that on the quiet. The whole thing didn't make sense to me. Why didn't they shoot the old man? They shot his pal eight times. Sounded well fishy to me.

I walked into the parents' front room one day, and was pleasantly surprised to see Johnny Bindon sat in an armchair. I knew he was an acquaintance of the family, but it was the first time I'd person- ally seen or met him since he punched me outside The Cromwellian in the early '70s. He didn't look well, though...and didn't recognise me so I decided not to rake up our scrap 20 years earlier. I'd already heard loads of stories about Johnny's relationship with Princess Margaret from the in-laws and now it was fascinating to hear them from the man himself, and get to know him. Eventually, I did pull him on the The Cromwellian, I had to. But there was no real point going to town on it, because he was an ill man. I was hardly going to settle that score now. And anyway, by then, Johnny was so frail he would have been no match for me.

Johnny died a year or so later aged 50. *The Daily Mail* reported his death was 'from AIDs related illnesses'. Rumour has it, MI5 raided his old flat after Margaret died in 2002, looking for any incriminating evidence hidden in the property, including, I'm told, compromising video footage of her and Bindon together.

*****

Meanwhile, me and Freddy were doing some crazy things together.

In the early days, we worked with phone boxes and pagers. I'd travel as far as ten miles to a phone box we hadn't used before. Most of them are gone now.

One day, Freddy told me we were going on a skiing trip to St Anton in Austria, then heading to Majorca, where he owned a villa. All paid for. I knew this wasn't just a holiday when he told me we'd be away for six weeks. There had to be some work involved along the way.

Freddy being Freddy, he'd gone to Harrods before the trip and bought us all the best ski gear to wear. He even had his own skis, which he brought with him instead of hiring some at the resort.

Freddy was a great skier and really into it. While I was limited to the basic runs at the bottom of the resort, he'd be up the top of the mountain, jumping out of helicopters. I just couldn't get on with it all. Being so big, when I fell over, I couldn't get back up. Young kids would ski past, taking the piss out of me.

Jimmy, a really heavy guy from the Islington area who I knew from Albany, came on the trip too, and brought a couple of other lairy geezers with him. My girlfriend came over with a mate for a little bit while we were skiing.

Freddy and Jimmy were both rolling in at the time and I had a few quid in my pocket, so everything was sweet on the trip, apart from the fucking skiing. We were staying in a really lovely chalet, ate every night in amazing fish restaurants. Everything was laid on.

A couple of weeks into the trip, Freddy explained that we had a meeting with some Columbians. Okay, here we go — this is why we're out here.

We met four of them on the slopes later that day. I don't think any of them had even seen snow before, let alone ever been skiing. One of them, a big lump, decided to go up on the black run with Freddy. Never been up a mountain before, but he did it. No fear, didn't give a fuck.

After about four days of being laughed at and spat on by kids whizzing past me on the beginners slopes, I said, 'Fuck it', and went up to the black runs. It looked so dangerous from up there. If you went over the edge, you'd had it. I took one look at it all, and went straight back down.

Over the next few days, we had meals out with the Columbians and took them to the clubs there. I was never involved in the nuts and bolts of any deal being discussed. That was all down to Freddy.

We were walking back to the chalet in the early hours after a night out and one of Jimmy's guys was giving it to Freddy, the usual stuff about him being so flash. Freddy suddenly stopped and said firmly, 'Enough is enough.' That was my cue to whop him, so I put him down in the snow and we left him there. Freddy couldn't fight, so that was why he had me wrapped around him all the time. He gave a lot of stick out, but he knew I'd sort anything out coming back in his direction, and always back him up 100%. The next morning there was a phone call to Freddy about the incident and my conduct, so he had to sort that one out internally.

At the end of the Austria trip, it was suggested that we all do the bobsleigh, which is nowhere as easy as it looks on the telly. I nearly went over the side of the mountain. If I hadn't been so big and strong I would have rolled into the abyss and probably been eaten by wolves.

Finally, the deal with the Columbians was agreed. There were handshakes all round, and it was time to head to Majorca.

Freddy had good connections there at clubs like BCM in Magaluf and we stayed in his beautiful gaff nearby. Because Freddy was so active at the time, he had loads of meetings in Majorca too. Socially and completely unrelated to any of that stuff, we also met up with Gary Stretch, who was out there with his brother, another good-looking cunt, and Gary Kendall, a former Mr Britain, who ate everyone's leftovers.

A week or so later, we were finally back to London and I was able to resume normal business. My next job was to look after a stock-broker from Surrey with a posh surname, a tall guy, who had trained with the SAS, and who laundered money for a serious firm. Let's call him William Double-Barrelled. This firm had somehow managed to bug the GPO. A guy on the inside, a top BT engineer, had recordings of brokers talking about what shares to buy. I didn't quite understand it all. Don't forget, I was a thug.

*****

In the '90s, I had two children with my girlfriend, a boy and a girl. I was present at the births at a private hospital in west London that we used both times.

*****

Freddy wanted me to collect £30k from an antique dealer in Brighton. As usual, I didn't have a driving licence so I bought an old Mercedes for a monkey to drive down there on the M23. Collect the cash. Bomp. And drive back. I mean, I've never ever had a driving licence because I've never taken a driving test. Up until this point, there had been four or five times when I'd been tugged and been able to either talk my way out of it, or give a false name, which was easier to do back in the day. There had been at least another half a dozen times when I was tugged but just drove off and the police didn't bother chasing me.

One trick was to put one of my Bull Mastiffs in the front with me, and that often made the Old Bill think twice about getting too involved. These days, it's virtually impossible to get away with driving off like that. With the cameras in the police cars now, they know whether you've got a licence or not before they've pulled you over.

On the trip back from Brighton, with the cash in a bag on the passenger seat, bits started to fall off this fucking shit-heap Merc. Suddenly, I heard, 'woo, woo...' I pulled over to the left, and they did too. I got out the car and thought, I'm in trouble, here we go...

They asked my name. I couldn't say Ray Hill, so I said Ray Rawlings. They radioed in, checked, came back and said there was no such person. When they got the handcuffs out, I thought, I'm off and ran up the embankment, leaving the money in the car.

One officer followed, and I was trying to kick him off me, but he wasn't getting the message so, whop, bang on the chin, and he was gone.

I ploughed through the undergrowth on the small grassy hill and when I got to the top, headed for a bridge in the distance. Fortunately, the coppers that did manage to scale the bank, ran the other way. I legged it down a country lane and hid in an old wooden bus shelter. A police BMW 5 Series with flashlights appeared but fortunately fucked off.

I went cross country again, running through brambles. I eventually found a phone box and rang the guy who I collected the cash from to come and get me. I'd already made my mind up, if a car, any car, appeared before him, I'd flag it down and rob it. Fortunately, ten minutes later, he appeared first.

'Get in the car, you cunt, there's Old Bill in boiler suits looking for you.'

He took me back to Brighton and then the next day I took the train back to London.

Freddy didn't believe me, until he rang the guy from Brighton and checked it all out, but he wasn't best pleased.

The police didn't trace the car back to me because I'd paid cash for it. They would have had the £30k, I should imagine, so it was a nice little tickle for them, and why there was no follow-up.

*****

One morning in December 1995, the criminal world woke to news of the so-called Rettendon murders. Tony Tucker, Pat Tate and Craig Wolfe were shot dead in a Range Rover, on a track off a country lane in Essex. Compared to me, it seemed like this lot had only been in 'the business' five minutes, but they'd clearly rubbed some serious people up the wrong way.

I fancy my old mate from Maidstone Prison, Billy Blundell, not the two guys put away for it, helped take those Essex boys out. Billy, who is no longer with us, bless him, had a proper dangerous firm, and lived out that way. He gave interviews claiming he warned Tate three days before the murder. Said he told them straight — if they didn't calm it down, robbing other drug gangs, someone was likely to shoot them all in the back of the head. Either that...or it was the police, because it's strange that all three were found dead in the Range, sat in their seats, apparently without a struggle. There's an argument to say that they'd only be sat there like that if Old Bill approached the vehicle, and then shot them all.

An old pal, Gordon, recently reminded me of an enforcement job we both went on in the early 1980s in the Dartford area, near the site of what is now Bluewater Shopping Centre. It was shortly after I came out of Chelmsford, when I was living in Lewisham. One Eyed Johnny had called for some backup for a job handing over a parcel. I originally asked Jimmy Tippett to come with me, but he was busy on a job with Cliff Field, so I asked Gordon instead. He was a good fighter himself, who got into MMA later, and used to work the doors with Lenny McLean and Micky Theo.

Johnny drove us to the meet in the car park of an orchard. Two guys got out of a Mitsubishi, one in their early 20s, and the other a bit bigger and a bit older. Me and Johnny approached them, leaving Gordon in the car to keep the numbers even. The younger one, about 15, 16 stone, 6ft plus, lunged at Johnny, while the other one, the larger lump, tried to grab the parcel. What the fuck. Wow, this pair had called it on now. They were clearly planning on robbing us. So I chinned the guy who went for Johnny, with a lovely right hand, and he dropped to the ground. Gordon had jumped out of our motor now, and me and him steamed into the other guy and bashed him up. As we left, I grabbed the guy on the floor and gave him another couple of clumps, and then we were out of there, the parcel still with us, of course.

Gordon has since told me the guy I first punched was Pat Tate. It could well have been. Tate was 37 years old when he was shot in 1995, so age-wise it fits. At the time, Johnny told me there might be repercussions, but I just went about my normal business, and heard nothing about it. Of course, Pat Tate's name wouldn't have meant anything to me back then. He became notorious because of those murders, all the *Footsoldier* films and beating up that poor pizza shop kid in the first movie.

THE BUSINESS

Business was good. My money had sky-rocketed. From my earnings of around £25k a week, I was able to buy a lovely two-bed villa in Magaluf overlooking the marina, recommended by Freddy. I paid about £180k for it...in cash, of course. It was all a long way from my humble beginnings. I think I only went out there a couple of times, because I always had commitments, but my girlfriend was   there loads with the kids.

After a meeting at the Hilton Hotel in Olympia, I bumped into a Middle Eastern guy I was in Wandsworth with — Dan, a cocky little character, who I'd looked after inside. He got a big sentence for his part in an arms deal, and always talked about millions of pounds in a Coutts bank account he couldn't access.

Dan had come out and reinvented himself. Delighted to see me, he walked me to his office around the corner and told me about an elaborate fruit export/import blag he had going, involving refriger-ated lorries with water tanks on board. On the way out the tanks would be full up, but on the way back they'd be emptied and filled with puff. He'd work out the weight of the missing water, the petrol and the added puff, to the millilitre, so it meant that when the lorry came back in through UK docks, it was the correct weight to pass through checks successfully, raising the least suspicion.

Never one to learn, I introduced Dan to a mate, who started putting money into these drug deals, and also to a guy I knew called Harold, who forged Indian bank notes and had a huge house and grounds near Hampton Court.

I should have known I couldn't have trusted Dan as far as I could throw him, because he not only cracked on with Harold's daughter — I'm sure with one eye on her inheritance — but he soon owed my mate £30k...and promptly disappeared for three weeks.

Word got to me when Dan resurfaced, so I invited him round to the house. When he strutted in, he was surprised to see my mate sitting there with his missus.

I took Dan upstairs and was trying to reason with him, when I realised he had a new set of brilliant white teeth. They weren't cheap back then, so he'd obviously fucked off somewhere to get them done at great expense. He admitted he'd spent my mate's cash on his new veneers and was laughing, saying, 'Fuck him, the fat cunt.'

But my mate was outside the door and heard him. He suddenly appeared with a baseball bat and smashed Dan to pieces. Fittingly, his new teeth went everywhere. However, there was so much blood on the walls and all over my furniture and ornaments, the corner of my room where Dan had been sitting now looked like an abattoir.

Dan was bashed up badly and barely breathing. We rolled him in one of my big rugs and talked about dumping him in the Thames, not far from my place, but quickly worked out that was a bad idea. So we decided to drive him to Kingston Gate, one of the entrances to Richmond Park. We pulled up, undid the carpet and rolled Dan out into the gutter, and parked across the road. When a few people stopped to help this guy, who looked liked he'd been run over, we drove up and offered to drive him to Kingston Hospital. With the help of these Good Samaritans, who were now witnesses to our offer of help, we put Dan back in the boot of my mate's Range Rover.

We raced to Kingston Hospital, where I ran in and asked for a stretcher for a road accident victim. When I appeared again, this time with Dan on board, I mumbled about having to go and move my car, which allowed us to fuck off, safe in the knowledge Dan was getting the best treatment. Again, no cameras back then.

We hoped Dan would conveniently forget what had happened at the flat. Back there me, my mate and his other half got buckets of hot soapy water to clean the corner of my front room, and petrol to scrub the back of the Range to get rid of any blood or fingerprints.

A few months later, Harold called me, not best pleased. His daughter had fallen for Dan by now, and she wasn't happy when he was delivered to their house in a wheelchair, still unable to speak properly.

Harold had to deal with it for us, but he would have half-known we were involved somehow. I really thought we'd get a visit for that little episode, but thankfully it never came.

*****

Freddy became more and more paranoid about being tapped. If I was at his house, he'd pull the phone line out of its socket, or wrap a towel around the white box on the wall. Unplug the television and put that in another room. He had a mate who worked for BT, who swept his car for him, looking for trackers, which were much bigger than they are these days, and quite easily found underneath the chassis of a vehicle.

Meanwhile, I was still bodyguarding William Double-Barrelled. Suitcases of cash were dropped off at his parent's house in Epsom. I was the security while it was counted and packed up by his mum and dad, and taken in a trailer by their 4 x 4 to a boatyard where their other son worked, and then shipped over to Geneva and banked there. It was a meticulous operation.

William and I became very close. He told me he'd make me a director of one of his companies. He would regularly give me up to £20k as a drink. I bought two six foot high Ming vases, with huge matching saucers, from Freddy for twenty five large and put them in the huge front room at the house on the private estate in Kingston. I also had a pair of 4ft high bronze horses in the front window, which also cost thousands. Crazy. Definitely a far cry from the grubby flat I grew up in Acton. There was so much cash sloshing around at that time, it's unbelievable looking back. I once paid a pal £125k in cash for a diamond-encrusted Cartier Panthére necklace worth £250k.

*****

The 'family friend' asked me to introduce William to him, so I arranged a meeting at the flat in Kingston. For the intro, I was meant to be cut in on any deals they worked on.

The 'family friend' came to me a few months later and said he was finding it hard to get profits back from William. I was pissed off things had progressed this far without me, and they'd started working together on investments behind my back. So I tracked William down to an office above a police station with a dozen traders working there, all connected to the City. I spoke to him on the phone and said we'd be down later that afternoon. William said I was welcome to come down and sort everything out.

William took me upstairs and into his private office. He opened a briefcase and said, 'There's a hundred grand there, Basher.'

The money was in £20 notes in Coutts two-grand bags. I didn't count it, because I didn't think William had the arsehole to mug me over like that face to face.

Now, if the 'family friend' didn't know where I lived, I might well have walked off with that money...told him that William wasn't playing ball, which would have actually made me look weak. Not that I would have cared for a hundred large. But I went back down to the car and handed over the briefcase. I was promised a drink when we got back to the flat, and when we did, I was given ten grand. On one hand, I was very happy with that, but it also made me wonder how much those two had been making on the side. Probably time to slow down the payments on the flat. I'd already paid about £100k and spent another £25k on a loft conversion. The 'family friend' was cako anyway, the boss of a building firm, with a big gaff in Milton Keynes.

*****

As usual, I always tried to have a little door job at the weekends, which gave the impression I had some legit work...something to put through the books. I had stints at some of the big London west end clubs like Hippodrome and Stringfellows over the years too.

One night I was walking back from work at a club in Twickenham, alongside the river at Kingston Bridge. I loved to walk late at night, which was stupid really, given what an easy target that made me. But it was probably all those years of being banged up after 9pm. That night someone pounced on me in an alleyway, and stabbed me from behind with a screwdriver, and legged it. It went through my shirt and I had to pull it out of my back. Agony. I was pissing with blood, and I was so lucky it didn't go as far as my lungs.

I became more and more paranoid about my own safety. It felt like someone was trying to take me out. To be fair, there were any number of people who I'd upset, or who would have loved to have seen me out of the equation by that point.

William Double-Barrelled wasn't having much luck either. The front door of his family home was kicked in and he was taken away to a house nearby. In an upstairs room at the empty property, he was slapped about a bit and tied to a chair. Then left there, ahead of being tortured later that night about his latest missing millions. However, William's kidnappers were surprised when they returned to find he'd jumped out of an upstairs window with the chair still tied to his back — his SAS training obviously underestimated on this occasion. I heard William handed himself in at the local police station, wearing just his pants, cut up to fuck from broken glass.

William apparently grassed up a lot of imaginary people and managed to get himself a two and a half stretch in the process, which was quite clever really, because it got him out of the firing line, without implicating any key faces.

*****

I'd been collecting cash down on the south coast, staying in a caravan in Chichester in between. I was driving a Jeep Laredo 4x4 at the time and was suspicious about unusual motorbikes driving past me on a regular basis. It was the summer of 1996, I believe.

After a few days, I got back to the flat in Kingston about three in the afternoon, parked up on the side road at the back of my property and, as usual, went through the side entrance on that street and along the small alleyway, which led to my patio area via another gate at the back.

I said hello to Biba, the male Bullmastiff, who was sat by the swimming pool as usual. Then walked up a set of stone steps which led to my patio area, where my other Bullmastiff, the bitch, Doughnut, always waited for me. I made a fuss of her, then said 'hi' to my son, who was in the kitchen, and had been staying while I was out working.

I placed a laundry bag on the side, which had £60k cash in it, all wrapped up nicely in bank bags.

My son asked me if I had any cigarettes. I didn't even smoke, and I didn't know he'd started — he was only 15, 16 — but decided to take a walk to the shop about half a mile away to stretch my legs and get a few bits...and him some fags.

When I returned to the flat 20 minutes later...what the fuck! The windscreen of the Laredo had been shot at. All the tyres were blown up too. Fuck me, what's happened here?

I ran in through the side entrance, into the garden and up the stairs, and saw blood all over the patio.

Inside the house, more blood — a long trail.

Oh my God.

'Son, son, fucking hell, son. Where are you? Are you okay?'

No response. Shit.

I crept up the small flight of thick carpeted stairs, also covered in claret, to the next floor.

'Son, are you up there?'

Finally, I could hear him. Shouting down from the loft, where he was hiding.

'Dad, get out of the house, they came to kill you. They were wearing crash helmets. They shot one of the dogs.'

My son appeared and explained that he was in the kitchen and saw two gunmen coming up the stairs of the patio, and then running up to the next floor where the back entrance was.

Doughnut would have jumped up at a stranger, as she always did, so the gunmen panicked and shot her.

I don't know how much my son had picked up about exactly what his dad did for a living, but it was lucky he knew about the loft. Not many dads have a hiding place like that.

The middle level led to the front room and a spare bedroom, where my son slept when visiting. There was a jukebox to the right of huge cast iron gates, which were lowered into the house by a crane when the loft extension was being done. Fortunately, the gates were unlocked, as they mostly were, so my son was able to run through them and up another set of steps into the loft conversion, where the main bedroom was. He knew he could hide in the ornate walk-in wardrobe with mirrored doors I had fitted specially. With architrave all around it, you only knew there was a door there, if you knew. You could push it open easily because it was set on magnets. Inside, a chair, desk, and safe and huge wooden locks, which meant it was impossible for anybody else to get in.

'They came up looking for me, Dad, and then gave up and left.'

We went down to the front room and could hear whimpering from behind the settee. Doughnut had been shot through the chest and stomach. Big wounds.

Seconds later I heard, 'Hello, anybody there?'

Only fucking Old Bill.

Half a dozen officers ran in, screaming, 'Get on the floor, get on the floor.'

They must have thought me and my son were intruders. It was only when my other dog came running up to me, affectionately, they believed I lived there.

'Sir, this is serious. Do you have any idea who would have done something like this?'

'You're right, this is fucking serious. My dog has been shot? I need to get her to a vet as soon as possible.'

The police started to run checks on me, and once they realised how much bird I'd done, and what for, they knew something was up. I worked on the door of a nightclub and lived in a nice gaff with a pool. Thankfully, the police didn't know anything about the hiding place, because I'd closed it all up.

The police decided to leave and, fair play, a couple of coppers helped me carry Doughnut to their van in a bedsheet, all 14 stone of her, tail wagging, bless her. And drove us to an emergency vets. She was just three years old. The vet told me the shots had damaged her vital organs, so the poor thing had to be put down. It broke my heart for her to go that way, but Doughnut putting up a fight probably saved my son's life, because by the time the gunmen came into the house he had been able to lock himself away.

When the police brought me back home in the van, I was fuming about what had happened, and distraught about my dog. Officers that remained at the house had found an automatic and a .22 under another motor. Maybe they were on a bike, and chucked them as they sped off.

I'd been so consumed about Doughnut, and worried about my son, that I forgot I left the laundry bag of cash in the kitchen. Thankfully, the police didn't look in it, and left without arresting me. They'd be back in touch to arrange me making a statement, which we obviously declined to do, and which the Old Bill were not best pleased about.

I called a mate, and we drove around to see if anybody had any information. But it could have been so many people. There would obviously be repercussions and suspects visited. I needed the word to get out that I was taking this very seriously.

A few weeks later, I caught two guys in the middle of the night trying to break into the house through the patio doors. I sensed they must have been known to me, because Biba didn't kick off enough. I ran down the stairs with a big bat, but they disappeared. I did catch a glimpse of one of them and let's just say, he was dealt with internally. My Jeep was being repaired after the last incident, so maybe they thought I wasn't in. Or maybe they were going to try and finish me off, because it was them that fucked up the last attempt.

*****

I drove to visit the 'family friend' in Milton Keynes. He wanted to talk to me about some business and, I'm sure, the payments on the flat. I was sat around his big dining room table. Freddy wasn't involved; he'd have gone mad if he knew I'd even done the introduction to William, because William was his thing. Unfortunately, we weren't alone. Three other guys were sat around the table. I asked who they were, and was told they were builders. One of them took his jacket off to place it on the back of his chair, and a revolver fell out. I don't know if that was deliberate or not, but instinctively, I pulled mine out too. I told them all to stand up. My arsehole was going and I could tell theirs were too. It was well on top. I told the 'family friend' I was leaving, backed out of the room, jumped in the BMW convertible I was using and fucked off.

I had a house party a couple of weeks later at my flat, about 20-odd people there. The missus invited the other half of the 'family friend' and she arrived with him and the clumsy builder. I didn't want to let them in, but was persuaded to.

I was big on the shovel at that point, so there was a large bowl full of coke on the top of the toilet cistern so people could help themselves.

A few hours later, I saw the lorry driver pinch my girlfriend's arse, or I thought I did. Maybe I was being paranoid on all the coke I'd hoovered up? Whatever the case, I smashed this guy in the face and dragged him out of the front room, down one set of stairs, then four small steps, and then another dozen steps to the front door. Bang, bang, all the way down, to the entrance that was boarded up on the other side by the 'repossessed' metal door. I continued giving him a few more kicks and slaps. The 'family friend' was going mental. His guy was in bits. Blood everywhere. Then I went and got Biba and let him have a go on him. He nearly ripped his fucking arm off.

The mother and father-in-law were screaming, 'Let it go, let it go, Ray...' so I told Biba to stop, and their mate took his pal away.

The party continued, as if nothing had happened. Or more like, nobody dared appear like anything had happened. Everyone was off their chops anyway.

What was clear, was that everything was going boss-eyed for me. Fuelled by coke, and all the crazy things that happened in my life, I had become very, very dangerous. Unsurprisingly, it was the end of the road for me and the 'family friend'. Relations with the in-laws would now clearly be extremely difficult too.

*****

My son, now 17, decided to move to Scotland to join his mother, who had already relocated there. After the gunmen raiding my flat, I couldn't blame him for wanting to get out of town. He asked a couple of mates to drive him north of the border. When they reached Scotland, the driver of the vehicle lost it on a corner, mounted the pavement, and drove smack into a brick wall at 60 miles an hour. My boy was in the backseat, but on impact flew through the windscreen. The Air Ambulance crew said he died four times, before they finally brought him back to life at Dundee Royal Infirmary.

As soon as I heard the news, I drove up to Scotland and met my ex at the hospital. Our son looked awful, like he was only being kept alive by the tubes attached all over his body and a bolt in his head to keep his skull together. He'd lost a quarter of his blood and they had to keep sitting him upright to change the tubes. I was crying my eyes out. The doctors feared our son wouldn't make it through the night and started to talk about decisions that needed to be made and papers to be signed to allow him to pass away peacefully. I was beginning to fear the worst and seriously considered if that was the best thing to do.

Then my thoughts turned to the other two in the car. The driver, I was told, had lost one arm and half his face, and the other kid was stable, but in a bad way. They were at a different hospital, but I wanted to know where. I was so angry, I wanted to kill him. I'd asked members of staff where this kid was. I was kicking off so much, the nurses called the police. Suddenly Old Bill came from everywhere. A dozen at least, from an armed response unit, running at me in the ward. Spots all over me. I was arrested and banged up for the night for my own good at the local nick. No point resisting this lot, they'd have shot me.

I was released the next day and given a police escort on the train back to London. I was obviously in bits still about my son and not being able to be with him, but was definitely relieved to have been locked up so I had time to reflect on what could have been.

My son battled for his life over the next days and weeks, despite us being constantly asked to consider what kind of quality of life he may have even if he did pull through. It was touch and go for months. Thankfully, my ex remained so resilient throughout, wouldn't hear of that machine being turned off and was there for him 24-7. Credit where credit's due.

OPEN UP

I got a call from William Double-Barrelled — from the open prison on the Isle of Sheppey on the northern coast of Kent, that he'd blagged his way into — asking if I could lend him 25 grand so he could build up a large stock of phone cards and carry on buying and selling shares.

'Okay...what do you want me to do with it?'

'That's the catch, Basher. I need you to bury it in the grounds of the farm I'm working on, which is attached to the gardens of the prison.'

'Fucking hell...okay...'

William phoned me from his cell and described the exact spot to hide the money in the fields he worked in. A girlfriend drove me to the spot late at night and we reached there in the early hours. Always a big risk, whoever's driving, when there's twenty five grand in cash and a pick and shovel in the motor. We crossed the bridge and parked up at the designated spot, and I got to work. Fifteen minutes later and we were on our way.

William messaged the next day to say, thanks, he'd collected the money. A week later, he called to say a lady would visit with a bag of money. I was to take five grand for myself, and keep the rest until he came out, when he'd give me my 25 back. True to his word, the woman appeared with the delivery, and William was released a few months later and came and sorted everything out.

*****

One night on my way home from the gym, the mother-in-law called.

'Nick nick cocaine.'

'What?'

'You heard, nick nick cocaine.'

I hadn't got a clue what she was talking about, which was often the case. She was probably off her head.

I'd had a bust up with my girlfriend, so she was probably back with her parents — as usual after a barney – and the old woman was probably stirring things up again.

I got back to the house. As expected, no girlfriend...just the German au pair she'd employed to do all the housework. We paid for her education, in return for her being a live-in nanny for our two young children.

The au pair was driving me mad. 'Please, I need to open the gates upstairs. She want things from bedroom. I take to her.'

I just wanted to get rid of the au pair, so I chucked her the keys, let her get on with it and took the dogs for a walk. By now I had replaced Doughnut with Charlie, another Bullmastiff, a big fucking thing I bought from Elephant and Castle after seeing an advert in Loot. When I returned from the walk, the au pair had fucked off. Perfect. Peace and quiet and a night alone hopefully.

Time for a little bugle on my own and to get a little bit fucked up and forget all the usual bollocks going on in my life. I always kept a decent stash of gear in big plastic jars. Usually, I'd hide them in the ruffled curtains by the big patio doors. Tonight, nicely off my canister in the early hours as I turned in, and because of what the mother-in-law had said, I threw the jars into my overgrown back garden. Just in case.

At 3am, after I'd finally dropped off, I woke to a massive noise and Biba and Charlie going mental. Within seconds, Old Bill had bashed through the patio doors and had cable-ties around the dogs' necks. They were armed with electric shields, so the dogs would get shocks if they went for them. They must have cased the property previously because they knew what to expect.

I leapt out of bed and into my secret area. Bang, bang, locked up again. I could hear the police running upstairs, shouting like idiots. Into the bedroom, and one copper said the bed was still warm.

'He's here somewhere...'

Another said, 'Check the window, are there any footprints on the flat roof?'

It felt like a scene out of a film — and not for the first time in my life. About 15 minutes later, I heard the police leave, and car engines starting. Click, click, click, I was out of the cupboard.

Then, I heard some police run back in. They'd only gone out to the cars to make some calls.

Fuck.

Click, click, click. Back in.

But I had been rumbled.

'He's upstairs, he's upstairs…'

I heard what sounded like sledgehammers, starting to smash up the walk-in wardrobe. It was inevitable I'd be found, and I didn't want my hiding place destroyed.

'Alright, alright…I'm coming out.'

Fortunately, the safe was covered with more architrave so they didn't notice it. They just seemed happy to have found me. They checked drawers and hanging space in the walk-in wardrobe, but found nothing, and said no more about where they'd found me.

I was sure the mother-in-law had grassed me up somehow. She must have done, and then felt bad and tried to warn me. Silly cow.

I was led downstairs, and told £500 in Scottish notes had been found hidden in a baseball cap.

'So? I sold a Porsche to a fella and he gave me that as a deposit.'

I could see them looking in and around the curtains. Thank fuck, I'd taken precautions last night. They didn't find the jars…or the few hundred grand in cash stashed in the chimney. I would have had a lot explaining to…and to a lot of serious people.

I was taken to Kingston police station and, unusually, it seemed I'd been arrested by couple of decent Old Bill.

'We don't like grasses, so we'll tell you that it was a close family member who tipped us off. We didn't find anything in your house. All we want you to do is, 'No comment, no comment, no comment,' and you can go.'

They even drove a Mercedes Sport I'd been using round to me, which they'd confiscated. As usual, I had no licence and no insurance, but they handed me the keys and I drove home from the police station. However, when police give you things they shouldn't give you and let you go that easily, it usually means they have an agenda, and they want you out there so they can nick you for bigger things.

Back home and in the loft, I checked the safe. It was empty.

What the fuck! She must have told the au pair the combination. All her jewellery, including the Cartier Panthére necklace, worth £250k…plus £100k in cash. Fucking bitches. Although, if the police had found the safe, at least it would have been empty. But they hadn't, so it was little consolation.

*****

I got involved with another serious firm, who used air stewardesses to take large amounts of cash, often up to a quarter of mil a time, and dodgy passports to the various far-flung destinations they flew to. Then someone would fly out to these places and travel around on the fake IDs and pay suppliers for gear.

Freddy, meanwhile, was getting more paranoid by the day. Unfortunately, that just came with the territory and the sort of business we were deeper and deeper in.

'I think we're under surveillance, Bash, but I need to know for sure.'

So I hooked Freddy up with a mate who supplied surveillance gear to the police. My pal radioed local Old Bill, pretending he was a traffic officer and, using Freddy's real name, said, 'I've just arrested a 'Mr so and so' for speeding, in a Porsche Carrera.'

The voice came back over the radio, 'Please back off…please pull away. Mr 'so and so' is a target.'

Freddy now had the clarification he was looking for. It shouldn't have come as a surprise. He was very, very active.

A week or so later, me and Wiggy pulled up in a Mini Minor three or four hundred yards from an address in west London, where I needed to sort out a regular bit of business.

I could see a couple of guys standing by a car outside the house, looking in the boot at something. As I walked past them, they seemed to be inspecting a vacuum cleaner. The main door of the flat was open, which was also odd. I stepped in and banged on the inside door, which led to a flat on the second floor. The door flew open and two guys hurried down the stairs, as two more came from behind me. 'Her Majesty's Customs and Excise, you're under arrest…' Bang. I was nicked.

Fuck, if Customs were involved, it must be for international import and export, so this was heavy stuff.

I was led up to the flat and into the kitchen. Various hand guns and sawn-offs were laid out on the landing as I walked past. Shit, really heavy.

'What's your name?

'Raymond Hill.'

'I am arresting you as part of Operation 'Blah-Blah' and you will now be taken to Customs House.'

In the car on the way to Customs House, down by the Thames in the City, I could hear the sound of different pagers...bleepers... going off in the boot, so I suspected they'd nabbed a few people. Mine was still in the car with Wiggy, who I hoped had been on the ball, as usual, and had got the fuck out of the area.

I arrived at the Customs HQ and was walked through corridors with huge air tight glass flood doors and taken into a room with a big clock on the wall. I had to hand over my door keys and a gold ring with diamonds in it, that Freddy had got for me through one of his contacts down the Garden.

I was adamant I wanted a brief, particularly with this customs lot. I'd heard these guys were serious people, who virtually lived at this place.

Unbeknown to me, they'd gone round to the flat in Kingston and found nothing. They told my girlfriend I was at Customs House, so when they left she got straight on the phone to her old man, who sent me the best brief he could get me, most probably, because he was trying to protect himself also.

'Try not to breathe, Ray,' the solicitor told me. 'This fucking gaff is bugged to fuck. You can't even fart without them knowing about it. See that big clock, their main camera is inside that.'

I was sat waiting in the interview room, when suddenly one of the top customs officers walked in and introduced himself as, 'Mr Burns.'

'So, Mr Hill, I've got quite a few people in custody today, which means we've got a big puzzle to solve. We're a bit confused, and I'd like to get all the pieces of this puzzle together and then, if we can, we'll let as many people walk out of here as possible. So once the puzzle is complete, then there's a good chance you can go.'

Yeah, right, fuck off. Cut the bullshit.

'Sorry, guv. I don't know anything.'

'Mr Hill, we know that you've done time for various things. Lots of time, in fact. For lots of different things. Look at the size of you, what are you 22, 23 stone? You be must so powerful. You train every day? You box?'

'Yeah, I was an unlicensed fighter.'

'Right, okay, did you have a name? Crasher, Bosher?'

Burns was trying to get me to correct him, and say my name was Basher.

'Nah, mate, my name is Ray Hill. I'm only known as Ray.'

'Do you know what a pager is, Mr Hill?'

'Of course I know what a pager is...'

'Well, we believe you have a pager.'

Then Burns walked out.

My brief was blinding and kept saying, 'Keep it up, Ray, you're doing really good.'

Then Burns came back in again a few minutes later, and said, 'Ray, you might be here a little while. Do you want to use the toilet?'

'Nah, thanks.'

'No, Mr Hill, it's probably best you use the lavatory now, while there's time...'

As I walked towards the gents with the guards, walking towards me was another guy who had been brought in, who I knew well, coming out of the loo. He only knew me as Basher.

In a split second, I realised that Burns had staged this whole trip to the toilet. Fucking clever cunt.

I held my breath, and as the guy walked past me, he casually said, 'Alright, mate.'

I could tell they were sick that no names were exchanged.

I got back in the room and minutes later Burns told me I could go. Lovely. I wasn't expecting that. I went downstairs to the foyer and me and the brief walked towards his car, parked at the back of Customs House. As we pulled away, I suddenly saw Burns out of the corner of my eye.

'Basher!' he shouted, as loud as he could, as he leaned towards us.

I kept my head down and looked straight ahead as we drove through the gates.

'How the fuck did you do that, Ray?' said my shocked solicitor, open-mouthed.

Massively relieved to have been released, because of the other people I knew must be involved — those other pieces of Burn's jigsaw — I was worried what would greet me on the outside.

I received a message from an associate of Freddy, telling me to lay low for the time being. He'd be in touch about any future work in due course. I'd been doing my own thing more and more anyway, so given all the heat recently, I was more than happy to keep my distance for now.

*****

More pressing, I found out that my father-in-law had somehow intercepted 10,000 pills, which were the property of some serious people. I desperately needed to get them back to the rightful owners. The old man also had one of my cars, a Ford Granada 2.8, one of the old square ones. Now, because the mother-in-law had dropped me in it, I need everything sorted including the motor.

The car was dropped off to me but when I looked in the boot, it was empty. I called him back and he said, 'Well, it was all in there when it left here. Someone must have taken it.'

Unbelievable.

My father-in-law called me back and gave me more grief down the phone. I decided to go and have it out with him. I drove to his house, just round the corner. It was a summer afternoon, still pretty warm. I parked just down the road from the house, and walked towards it. I could see through the window of the front room, the old man with two of the Scottish lot from Tottenham — serious people — doing shovel around the front room table. He spotted me, so I called out wanker and gave him the sign. He shouted at me through the window and I gave it back to him. Then

I walked back towards my car.

'Oi.'

I turned round and the old boy was stood out in the street, wearing a three-quarter length jacket, which on a balmy evening was strange. I gave him the finger and then he pulled out a fucking gun, and took a shot at me, which whizzed past my head. I sprinted back to the car, with him running after me. I turned to see him grab a large guy walking out of an Indian takeaway shop, who he mistakenly thought was with me. To my horror, he grabbed the bloke, threw him to the floor and stuck the gun in his mouth.

Now I'd got my thing from the car. The old man, now realising his mistake, clambered off this guy, then ran towards me and fired again. This time, he hit my left arm. The power of the shot knocked me down, but the bullet didn't go in fully. He must have had a .38 or a .45 — a powerful gun. As I tried to get to my feet, he lunged towards me, but I managed to grab my thing up off the floor, and he legged it back down the road and back inside his house.

I phoned my girlfriend, who still wasn't home yet.

'Your old man has just fucking shot me.'

She was going mad on the phone and then met me at the flat, closely followed by her mother, who was screaming at me as she came up the back steps of the patio. You cunt this, you cunt that. Just what I fucking needed.

I was still trying to process the whole thing, when the dad appeared in the back garden holding a fireman's axe, with a big hook on it. He swung the axe wildly, but caught the top of the patio doors, and then fell straight through them. Crash. Bang. Wallop. Glass everywhere. He staggered to his feet, and, bang, I hit him on the chin so hard, he flew backwards into the framework of the patio doors, and the whole thing collapsed on top of him...and me. I shrugged shards of glass off me and pulled the old man up off the ground and smashed the life out of him. The old girl joined in and started throwing some punches at me. It was carnage. The bullet wound in my arm was still pouring with blood, and me and him were both cut to fuck too. It looked liked I'd been stabbed many times.

Eventually it all calmed down for a few seconds. My girlfriend was screaming that we needed to go to the hospital and persuaded me and her dad to go in her car. I was in the back, while he was in the front still raging that he was going to kill me. As usual with me, you couldn't make it up.

In an A&E cubicle at the hospital, a nurse looked at my arm and said, 'You've been shot!', and I was trying to say, 'Nah, nah, I haven't, I've been in a fight,'

'We need to call the police, sir.'

'No, darling, please don't call them.'

Suddenly, to my left, the curtain of my cubicle opened, and the father-in-law was stood there with a scalpel in his hand. He'd been laying in the next bed, being treated, and heard my voice and picked up the nearest thing he could see. I broke free from the nurse and grabbed his arm as he tried to stab me and threw him back into his cubicle. The hospital staff somehow managed to restrain him and I put my trainers on and legged it. I wasn't going to hang around there, waiting for the police. I had so far refused to give my name, so I shuffled out of the hospital, and slowly walked the half a mile or so home. Battered, but still pumped up with adrenalin. Thankfully, when I did finally make it back to the flat, my girlfriend had fucked off back to her parents house...again.

It was time to try and re-group, but my life was only going in one direction...again.

My 50th birthday was only a couple of years away. I wasn't a young man anymore.

It was the shovel that fucked up my father-in-law. Ever since he'd got out of prison, he'd been bang on it, and I think he had started doing crack too. Now, I felt like I was heading in that direction as well.

The gun wound in my arm was a huge concern. I worked on it constantly. Washing and treating it, bandaging and taping it up, with any old rags I could find.

*****

A week or so later, Barbara, the wife of an associate of mine, called me. It was good to hear her voice.

'Ray, you'll never guess what happened.'

'What, Barb?'

'I was on Concorde and that Burns from Customs suddenly appeared in the aisle next to my seat. 'Hello Barbara, how are you?'

'Can you fucking believe it, Ray? On my fucking flight.'

'Wow!'

'I know, Ray. He said, 'I'm Inspector Burns, how are you?' I said, 'What do you want?' And he said, 'Actually, Barbara, it's good that I've bumped into like this. I just wanted to have a quick chat with you?' I tried to shut him down, Ray, and said, 'I'm not answering any of your questions without a solicitor,' but he said, 'It's nothing like that. It's just that I've got Basher's gold ring and his keys, that he left at Customs House.''

'Fucking hell, Barb What did you say?'

'Ray, I said, 'Who's Basher?''

'Fuck me, Barb. Well done, darling.'

*****

Once again, I needed a new opportunity. As usual, something landed in my lap.

I'd been spending time in a pub in Ascot, where there'd been some trouble. Just keeping an eye on it for a friend of a friend. One night, I was having a few lines in the office with the landlord, Lionel, and he asked me if I could get rid of any coke.

'Sure.'

'Kilos?'

'Definitely.'

I arranged to meet Lionel at the flat in Kingston and he brought a key with him. Absolutely top quality. Mustard. He said he'd let me have each kilo for 14 grand, which was silly money, when I could potentially move it on for triple that on the street, or more depending on how cut up it was. I knew people who would easily take them for £30k a pop.

I asked Lionel his source, and he explained that his dad had just retired as one of the senior guys at Customs and Excise, and his former junior officers there were selling him vast amounts of confiscated coke, and the old man was passing it on to him. Crazy. Especially after what I'd gone through at Customs House. But never one to look a gift horse in the mouth, I agreed to his proposal. A nice little blag for a few months.

INSIDE JOBS

The steady supply of coke from the retired customs officer finally dried up, and my future was uncertain again. I ducked and dived for the next year or so. Like various points in my life, it's a bit of a blur looking back, but I kept myself busy with planning and doing small low-key jobs as and when I could, plus any bits and pieces Freddy needed doing.

One day, I was walking through Bush and a Mercedes Sport convertible pulled up.

'Ray, what you up to?'

Fuck me, it was Harrington — one of the most dangerous guys I'd ever met. Usually armed. I first met him inside, can't remember exactly where. Albany or Chelmsford. One of the two.

Harrington was from the Ilford area, but I hadn't seen him for years.

'Jump in Ray, let's have a chat...'

He explained that he'd been driving around in the Merc with a .38, robbing drug dealers and crack houses. He needed some muscle, so I agreed to team up with him. I spent the next few weeks in the car with Harrington, looking for potential targets.

One afternoon, when we were driving to Redbridge, Harrington stopped the car in the Leytonstone area and leant across me to pull his gun out of the glove compartment. He put a scarf around his face, and said he'd be back in a minute. He entered a spill, a card school kind of gaff, and came out five minutes later with a load of cash and coke and said, 'Here, that's yours,' as he divvied it up and gave me a grand and about an ounce of gear (roughly 28 grams).

I arranged a few meets and renewed some old acquaintances in Grove, and was introduced to some Filipinos based in a block of flats in Twickenham. I'd actually had some dealings with them before.

We sat down with the Filipinos and they told us about two Bolivians who had arrived in London with a load of coke they'd nicked back home. They were travelling from hotel to hotel in and around the Bush/Notting Hill Gate/Queensway area with it packed in two suitcases — 20 kilos of the stuff — the finest.

It sounded like an easy hit.

The Filipinos were adamant it was amazing coke, so we took a sample. It was available at £19k a key, still a good price. We had an initial meet with the Bolivians, who offered us five keys. We were like, that's not enough. We want more like the full 20. You guys are literally walking the streets with it all — surely you want to get rid of it?

One of the Grove lot said he knew someone in Covent Garden with a recording studio complex we could use for a meet with the Bolivians. That there were all sorts of music types coming and going morning, noon and night, so we wouldn't get too much attention. Our pal was trying to organise things the right way, even though, because he knew what me and Harrington were up to, he fully expected us to try and take the gear.

The Bolivians were insisting on a safe house to meet at. We suggested the studio and they agreed. It was on two floors, with a concierge type reception at the entrance. And this gaff was the business. Plush. Anyone who walked in was blown away by it. Me and the guy from Grove were waiting upstairs, trying to act like everything was kosher.

The Bolivians phoned up and said, 'We've got the 20 keys, it's got to be cash, and the Filipinos are going to bring it in to you.'

The Filipinos turned up with a proper stunning reem sort. A wannabe singer they brought to make their visit look more legit. She was obsessed with how nice the studio was, and the Filipinos were infatuated by her. It was almost distracting them from their job, which played into our hands perfectly.

I could sense the Bolivians were paranoid as fuck, while the Filipinos didn't seem to have a care in the world. They'd bowled in with a bright pink holdall, with all the gear in it, but were more focussed on trying to impress the girl and even asked our connect if they could hire the place out for a party.

I wasn't actually armed that day, but I reckoned the Filipinos were.

Harrington was definitely holding, as usual, and was on a serious motorbike, which he often used for heavy bits of work.

I said to the Filipinos, 'Harrington is outside with the money. I need to test the coke and take the bag downstairs to him, if that's okay with you guys? And they were like, yeah, cool — definitely more interested in pulling the bird.

On the face of it, there was only one entrance in and out of the building, but we'd already done a recce. So as I took the stairs, I went down, but then through a side door and down another flight of stairs, and on to an outside fire escape, down a dozen or so steps and jumped straight on the back of Harrington's bike, and off we went — speeding through a small archway and out the other side into the Old Covent Garden market area and past the studio again. We actually raced past one of the Bolivians pacing up and down outside in the street, who saw a puff of smoke and what looked like a large pink bag disappear into the distance. What a buzz! We'd just nicked more than half a million pounds worth of gear. If you haven't had a decent blag like that for a while, it's an amazing feeling.

The Bolivians were still all over the girl, none the wiser. My mate, who had booked the studio, had slipped off too, and sped off on his own bike. We met him about a mile up the road and he asked for a key, for his troubles. At this stage and at that time, a kilo could be sold on for £35k-£38k, before it was cut up and distributed in ounces and grams, so there was lots of profit all round. But, fair enough, we gave him one for free, and said we'd meet later in Grove. When we did, he was fucked. He'd done several big lines of the gear and was off his nut. That's how pure that shit was.

On Harrington's bike, we thought we could race anyone, so he said, 'Right, let's get the gear back to Redbridge,' and we sped over east, me hanging onto the bag for dear life. Can you imagine if we'd got a tug? But I like I said, what a buzz.

When we reached Ilford., we unloaded and unpacked and split the 19 keys left, fifty-fifty.

Harrington said, 'I'm going to take some of this gear round to my mate, who is well connected here. Let me take a couple of yours and I'll get you cash for it.'

But Harrington came back and said his mate needed time to get the money together...he'd have it ready in the morning.

'Fuck that, I'm not hanging around here overnight, I'll collect that cash another time.'

I didn't fancy visiting any of my regular haunts over west either, not after the blag we'd just pulled. I wasn't so worried about the Bolivians. I was pretty sure they'd leave London as soon as they possibly could, but I knew those Filipino guys had some serious connections so that situation would have to be handled carefully.

So I took my other six or seven keys to Winston in Wolverhampton. I think I actually got a cab the whole way. I rang ahead to Winston and he didn't believe me. He wanted to see this gear with his own eyes, and help me sell it up there. He put me in a beautiful apartment and gave me a catalogue full of brasses. He took some gear off me and gave me five grand for it and left me hoovering up loads of lines myself and ordering girls by the hour.

One girl, a stunning African babe from Birmingham, turned up, charging £200 an hour.

'Okay, no problem.'

I offered her some coke, and she said she didn't do it. Okay, no problem either.

I went to the toilet and when I got back in the room, she'd fucked off with the first £200 in cash and three or four ounces of coke I'd left on the side, worth about six grand. I went fucking nuts and rang Winston. He made some calls and we got the gear back. The girl was now in big trouble with her pimp but as the coke had been returned we did our best to try and smooth that over for her.

That night I got a call from our pal in Grove. The gear was so good, he wanted another two keys, and even drove up to the Midlands to get them. He had a couple of big guys with him and one pulled a thing on me.

'Nah, nah, put that away, it ain't like that, you won't be able to do that with him.'

Fucking hell, that was all I needed.

When things calmed down, I let him have both keys for a mates' rate of £35k, which was generous, but getting rid of this stuff quickly was always on my mind.

*****

I went back to Redbridge a couple of days later, to see Harrington to get the money owed for the keys he gave his mate, but he only gave me some of the cash.

At the same time, I'd started seeing a bird I knew from Lewisham, Trudy Taylor. A beautiful mixed race sort.

Trudy loved my flat in Kingston and quickly moved herself in. One time my 'girlfriend' came to see if we could make up, and I was in bed with Trudy, who couldn't help herself, and came down to say hello wearing just my T-shirt.

'Who's this, Ray?'

'Erm...it's my son's girlfriend.'

'No, I'm not, I'm your girlfriend.'

Thankfully, my actual 'girlfriend' left without kicking off, which was unusual.

Trudy loved her coke, and took loads of it. This Bolivian gear was obviously right up her street. Wrapped in rice paper, four little blocks to an ounce, I'd smash it up and leave it on the side, so Trudy could help herself. I noticed some of the small rocks were going missing, and that's when I realised Trudy might be on the pipe. Now looking back, and knowing what I know, I think she was seeing someone else, and probably washing those rocks with bi-carb to make hi-grade crack cocaine.

A few weeks later, I asked Trudy if she wanted to go away for a couple of weeks. I just wanted to get out of town again.

'Let's go to Mexico...Cancun,' she said.

So I paid for a pair of business flights, and for an all-inclusive resort, and gave Trudy five grand in cash to buy both of us some new clothes for the trip. Knowing I was cash rich, she also persuaded me to buy her a nearly new Golf Convertible. Trudy could do that, because she was a gorgeous bird. It all set me back about £20k. In a way, I wanted to get rid of the cash and the gear as quickly as possible.

I booked us a hotel at Gatwick so we could stay there the night before our flight. In the room, sorting the cases out, Trudy showed me the stuff she'd brought herself from Gucci and Chanel, and then gave me a carrier bag with the bits she bought me from George at Asda, so that pissed me off from the start. I tried to laugh it off, and we spent the rest of the night getting off our trolleys on a little bit of coke I'd brought with me. We had some great sex, and got smashed all night.

In the morning, we got ourselves together and checked in for our flight, which was lovely. Champagne all the way. Great service.

We arrived in Cancun, which was boiling, but looked like an absolute shit-hole. The villa I'd booked at the hotel was beautiful though. Huge jacuzzi. Amazing view. Stunning.

But now I was starting what felt like a massive comedown, after not wanting to risk bringing any coke with me.

I was desperate to get out in the sun, so I asked Trudy to unpack the bags while I got us some beds sorted on the beach. I nodded off down there in the shade, but when I woke up the sun had moved and my feet were burned to fuck and red-hot. I jumped up and ran in the sea to try and cool my feet down, but a sand-worm got in my Gucci loafers. I tried to pull the fucker out, forgetting the many signs around the hotel, warning guests not to. But I stupidly had, and now the other half was embedded in my foot. The pain was excruciating, so I hobbled back to the room to call reception and sort out a cab to take me to the nearest hospital. Back at the room, me and Trudy had a huge fight over the clothes. I was fuming again. She pushed me, and we started to grapple. I tried to break free and that force sent Trudy flying across the bed. Then she ran out of hotel room, crying. Gone. Fucking hell, what happened there?

Half hour later. Knock, knock on the door. Mexican police. Gunned up to fuck.

'Where is the passport, money and things of Miss Taylor?'

I stood there open-mouthed. How had it come to this? We'd only been here five minutes. Then they suddenly moved Trudy into view from the side, and gestured for her to go into the room, under their supervision. I couldn't argue. I had to play this very carefully.

I couldn't spend a night in one their fucking cells. As she walked past me and started collecting her things, I was thinking, how can you be doing this?

I tried my best to remain calm, and kept my eyes on the police and their weapons at all times. Trudy left the room with her case and bag, and the police went with her. Fucking hell, that was on top. But wait a minute, what exactly had she got? I rushed to the safe and found Trudy had taken everything, including all my cash, my passport and boarding pass for the flight home. Unbelievable. Left me with absolutely nothing.

The only saving grace was that I'd booked all-inclusive and paid the hotel up-front, so drinks and food were all free, but I still had to ring my poor mum up like some stupid cunt on his first lads' holiday and ask her to Western Union some spare money over for me.

I had murders at The British Embassy in Cancun sorting a replacement passport...and had to try and get my foot treated too.

I never saw Trudy again on the trip. I assumed she'd hooked up with another guy out there. Maybe it was pre-planned, and she'd booked his ticket with the cash I gave her, and that's why she couldn't afford to buy me any designer clobber. I visited every other fucking hotel in Cancun to try and find Trudy and whoever she was with. Just as well I couldn't. I'd probably still be doing the time in a Mexican jail now.

When I got back to Gatwick two weeks later, without Trudy on my flight, I went to the long-stay car park and her Golf Convertible was still there, so I smashed the fucking thing up, punching through the windscreen and the soft-top roof. Kicked all the lights out.

A few days later, I got a call from Trudy, crying down the phone. 'What have you done to my car, Ray?' She span me a sob story and the silly cunt I am, I went and collected the Golf and got it fixed for her, costing another couple of grand.

* * * * *

Now back to business. It was time to go and see Harrington because the guy he'd sold my coke to hadn't paid up. I was sure

Harrington had been given more money than he was letting on, but he was adamant we had to go round and sort this geezer out.

'I know where his bird's house is, and that's where he'll be. He's got an XJS convertible.'

Harrington was shouting up at the flat, 'Come down you wanker, we need our money.'

Harrington hadn't told me this guy was a bit of a nutter but I shouldn't have been surprised. It came with the territory.

With no sight of him, Harrington said, 'We'll set his car on fire — it's his pride and joy.'

Harrington had all the necessary paraphernalia in his motor and quickly did the business and the car went up. We went back to his house and suddenly there was a knock on the door.

Harrington asked me to look out of the window. Fuck! The geezer with the XJS was outside with a gun.

'Get a knife out of the drawer,' screamed Harrington.

'No mate, where are your things?'

'They're in the front garden.'

Strategically placed so he could always claim someone had planted them there. But no good now.

So Harrington ran outside with a huge machete instead, and I followed with a knife.

Too late.

The guy pulled the trigger and hit Harrington in the side of the head, who dropped to the floor. I was so shocked, I thought he was fucking about and said, 'Get up mate, what you doing?'

The gunman legged it, so I sat down and put Harrington's head in my lap, but his face was half hanging off. What a mess. Then I heard the guy walking back towards us again. I didn't have enough time to move, and neither could I leave Harrington. The trigger was pulled, and my whole life flashed before me as, thankfully, the gun jammed. Thank fuck. But he tried again. One more go at taking me out, but it jammed again, so he ran off. Lucky it was an automatic and not a revolver, or I'd have been a gonner too.

Old Bill turned up, separated me from Harrington and took his lifeless body away. Even though they knew it wasn't me, because

I was still on the scene and the poor guy's head was in my lap, they arrested me and took me to Ilford police station.

They sent me to Belmarsh and I spent three months on remand — my first bit of bird for eight years, so very hard to take — before they let me go, because they weren't able to charge me.

Court reports later stated that Harrington, aged in his mid-40s at the time, was shot dead in Ilford in the Spring of 2000 by a 36-year-old man 'over an argument about a £150 debt', but it was obviously a lot more money than that.

The report said that the pair had worked together in a criminal drug plot and that the defendant's car was damaged. The judge recommended a minimum sentence of 18 years, which the Lord Chief Justice later reduced to 16.

Harrington's death really hit me hard. Not least because I had witnessed it first hand and had also been involved in the bust on the Bolivians, which had indirectly led to his brutal murder. I was now back out on the street, trying to process exactly what had happened, feeling extremely lucky to have literally dodged the bullets that Harrington couldn't. I didn't go to the funeral because I was in Belmarsh and when I got out, although I wanted to contact the family to send my condolences, I decided it was best to move on, keep my head down.

A ROCKY ROAD

Not for the first time, my life seemed to be spiralling out of control, on whole new levels. I was trying to grieve for my pal, but equally I couldn't dwell on it. I was another £40k out of pocket for the coke that Harrington's killer owed me, and which was obviously now written off. Winston was still getting rid of the rest, but any profits were slow coming.

Worse still, while I was in Belmarsh, Freddy was arrested in a major sting, which involved a few of his associates. I was probably lucky I was away for something else at the time. But this wasn't looking good for Freddy and even if I didn't end up implicated too, I could obviously lose out on a lot of work if he went down for a lengthy stretch.

It later came out in court that Customs and Excise were already doing surveillance on Freddy when our guy radioed in to the police. So when they heard a so-called 'officer' on the radio saying Freddy had been arrested for speeding, they knew he was actually in a property they were watching. They also now knew Freddy somehow had someone on the inside, as such. The police had also managed to tap a phone box Freddy was using, after putting a tracker on his car. All his worst fears.

*****

There was more and more trouble at home as well. My on-off relationship with my girlfriend was in free fall. I was sure she was seeing someone else when I was away, so I was always up to no good too.

I struggled to juggle my commitments to my girlfriend and our young kids, paying their £5,000 private school fees to the headmistress in cash one day. Her husband, an SO19 (Specialist Firearms

Command) police officer, told her not to accept it. I really think that made them look at me more. But I didn't have a bank account. I was just trying to get back in the missus' good books.

Then the in-laws died within months of each other. Clearly, the complex and volatile situation between me and the mum and dad hadn't helped any of our relationships. I couldn't get past her old man shooting me, nicking loads of goods from me, nor her mum grassing me to the police. Not your usual in-laws, for sure.

Before they both passed, I'd see the old man in Richmond Park with my son, and it would really wind me up. He used to sneer at me, which was the final straw considering what a wanker he'd been.

Me and his daughter hadn't lived together for some time — me at the flat, and she either at his place or at the bigger house tucked away on the private estate.

She would allow me to see our kids for only four hours at a time. One weekend, I took our little boy to Covent Garden to have a portrait drawn of him in a Chelsea kit by a street artist. It was pissing down with rain and really windy. The big umbrella he was sat under blew up in the air and came down 50 yards away, right at the feet of my girlfriend and a new fella she'd been seeing. What were the chances? I looked up at this geezer, an old flame of hers, and he was holding my daughter. I just saw red. Grabbed our little girl, gave her to my girlfriend, then bashed the geezer all over the place. I left the scene with our son, and rang up my girlfriend later that night to tell her I was fucking off somewhere with him and wouldn't be coming back. In the end I gave myself up, handed our son back, and was eventually let go.

Not surprisingly, my access to the kids was stopped. I was so incensed and taking so much coke every day that there was just no way I was going to take that lightly, but what I did next was inexcusable.

My girlfriend had paid for a bench by a tree in Richmond Park and had spread the old man and woman's ashes there barely 24 hours earlier. Not knowing when or if I'd be able to see my kids any time soon, I headed to the park and the memorial bench. With a plastic bag, I marched through the park collecting dear shit, and walked back and threw it all over the bench and the surrounding area. Then I drove round to the family home, where my girlfriend was staying and banged on the door, shouting and screaming about what I'd done. She came to the upstairs window and told me to fuck off. I was off my head, but there's no excuse for what I did in the park, or the dramas I caused at the house.

Understandably, a restraining order was placed on me, with loads of conditions and restrictions meaning I mustn't go near the kids or their mother.

A week or so later, I was stabbed in the back walking home from working the door of a club, late on a Saturday night. Jumped from behind. As usual, it could have been any number of people, not least a friend of the in-laws.

I rang my girlfriend and accused her of having something to do with it. She laughed and told me not to visit her as she was at the house with a well-known crime boss — something that only added fuel to my fire, and ensured I would visit her.

I arrived at the house and banged on the door. Her mate answered it and kept repeating that this big shot gangster was inside with my missus. Then she appeared at the top window again, in just underwear, repeating the same thing. I was going crazy, and then she said, 'Of course, I'm winding you up, Ray.'

She said she didn't believe I'd been stabbed and as I took my jacket off to show her...splosh...I was covered in white paint, from a large pot she'd thrown at me. What a bitch. And it was gloss, not emulsion!

As I staggered off, several police cars pulled up. Nicked. For breaching the order...and probably for looking a complete mess too.

They threw me in a cell at Kingston Police Station, and because everyone there was scared of me, they wouldn't help me clean the paint off. An emergency Sunday morning hearing was held at the Family Court at the High Court in the Strand hours later, and when I was wheeled in the court, still covered in paint, the judge went mad due to the condition I was in. I was granted bail immediately, then the whole thing thankfully got chucked out.

Clearly, me and my girlfriend were done, if we weren't already. My behaviour had been unacceptable, but aside from anything else going on in my life during the '90s, the in-laws had been a pressure cooker waiting to explode the day the old man was released from prison. It was always going to be a shit-show.

It was time to leave Kingston. I rented a flat at Brentford Docks so I could lay low. It probably suited a lot of people.

I spoke to Lionel, my partner in the Customs and Excise coke blag, and he agreed to store my Ming vases and silk paintings in the cellar of his pub in Ascot. I arranged for them to be collected from the house on the private estate in Kingston, as I couldn't count on those ever been returned to me.

*****

I was keeping my head down at the flat in Brentford Docks, having to rely on other forms of income now news had reached me that Freddy had been sentenced to 11 years. Time to forget about him for a while, move on from all that work and try to develop both new and old contacts.

My personal life was in tatters. There was no way back for me and my girlfriend. Not after the last few months and how I'd desecrated her parents' memorial bench.

One day sat in the flat at the docks, bored, I flicked through the escort section of the local newspaper and booked a brass. An hour or so later, I watched a Mercedes sports car pull up outside my block and a decent looking sort got out. I opened the door to a pretty light-skinned black girl, aged in her late 20s, who introduced herself as Rhian. We had a good bit of fun for a few hours and some lines of coke from a little stash I had, and then she said, 'Are you up for a game?'

'A what?'

'A game, you know...with some of my friends?'

'Really?'

'Yes, Ray, we can make a call...'

'Erm, yeah, course...'

Rhian told me to ring a number and a girl with a harsh south American-like accent answered. She sounded really stern — moody almost. We chatted for a while and then Rhian left the apartment and said she'd be back soon.

An hour or so later, she was back and on her way up in the lift again. I opened the door and Rhian introduced an absolutely stunning black girl, Sandi, and they both slipped into the flat. Then Rhian said, 'Ray, we've got a little surprise for you.'

And then another girl appeared. Wow! She was the prettiest of them all. When she said hello, I instantly knew it was the girl with the south American accent on the end of the phone earlier. She told me her name was Monica.

Wow, wow, wow, I've had a right little touch here.

The three girls were all over me, as I racked up more lines. Amazing. I didn't even know that Sandi and Monica were sisters at that point.

And then suddenly Monica said, 'Ray, this isn't quite working. I need to pay someone a visit, I'll be back.'

'Okay, no worries.' So off she went, and I continued to muck about with Rhian and Sandi.

When Monica reappeared about an hour later, she asked if I had an empty coke bottle. Because I'd been enforcing for Harrington, I had half a clue what she wanted it for, but still wasn't completely sure. I emptied out a plastic bottle and gave it to her. I watched intently as she poured water into the bottle, put foil over the top of it, and an elastic band round that. Then with a cigarette she burned a hole in the side of the bottle, put an empty pen case in the hole, and used bubblegum to seal around it. Then she put some small white rocks on top of the foil and said, 'Have a go on that...'

Yes...as I suspected...crack cocaine.

I took a drag through the pen and it was like, fucking hell, what is happening here? The most amazing feeling I'd ever experienced. And that was it. The four of us smoked all the crack Monica had, and then it was straight on the phone ordering some more. Downstairs to collect it. Back upstairs to smoke it, and then put another order in. Still having a game with the girls the whole time and the sex just feeling completely off the scale on the crack.

The four us were in bed now, for what seemed like hours. Through to the next morning, but I really liked Monica the most.

She hadn't told me at the time, and quite understandably so, but Monica had tasted fame back in the day as a TV actress. Her time in the spotlight had been and gone now, and Monica had got on the crack and the game to fill the void after a whirlwind couple of years of success. She had become a celebrity in her own little community just outside central London so, when that showbiz lifestyle ended, it was hard for her to take.

I became obsessed with Monica...and with crack...and so the two went hand in hand. Now, I was on a mission to do as much crack as I could get my hands on, and pay for Monica's too, so we could hang out — and so I could get further and further away from my troubled life, and the trouble I'd caused. It helped deal with all the pain I had endured and built up over the years. After decent spells out of prison for most of the '90s, now Freddy, the amazing money I earned each week and my girlfriend had all gone, my two new addictions were a very welcome distraction.

I'd have periods around the early 2000s when I could knock the crack on the head, but if I did, I'd still be doing loads of coke, and existing in that frazzled state, which really isn't that much better. You can function slightly more, but you're still fucked a lot of the time. But not doing crack, meant not seeing Monica, and I couldn't seem to do that for very long.

*****

A pal got a tip off that there was a hundred grand in cash stashed in the loft of a gangster's brother's place in Hove. I straightened myself up for a day or two and we drove down to the main guy's house, and knocked at the door, suited and booted, pretending to be TV licence officers, before barging our way into the gaff. We tied this guy up, filled his bath and then waterboarded him until he told us his brother's address. We drove the gangster there, me in the back, keeping him quiet, and made him tell us exactly how and where the cash was hidden. We split the £110k with the tip-off, so three ways, because that was a nice little heads up. I now had another 30 grand in my pocket to help with cashflow.

A month or so later, me and the same pal were invited to a house party in Eastbourne, where we came face to face with the gangster we'd robbed. How was our luck? That was an awkward one but, probably because he wanted to save face and was still fucked from our last visit, nothing was said before we made a quick exit.

*****

It was never long before Monica and I were hanging out solidly again for a few weeks, getting up to no good. Smoking our sorrows away.

One day, she came to the flat to say her old management had got her a small part in a movie being shot in LA with some serious A-listers. It was a bit of a shock, to say the least. So off she went to America, and I didn't see her for months. I assumed this relationship was going nowhere.

Soon, I was back on the pavement.

As I walked along Hammersmith Grove one day, I bumped into a pal's sister. I didn't recognise her at first; I hadn't seen her since the '70s.

'You got a smoke,' she asked, not realising it was me either.

'Fucking, hell, darling, what you up to?' When to me, it was clear she was on the game.

'Hi Ray, what you doing round here?'

'I'm going to find a room to have a smoke, you know what I mean...fancy coming?'

I mean, she was hardly going to say no. Sat in a grubby hotel room, we got on the pipe for the next few hours.

I'd begun smoking crack on such a serious level that I needed and wanted to do it all day, and for that, back then, I needed between £500 to a grand in my pocket, because £50 of crack would only last me about 15-20 minutes, especially if I had company. Meanwhile, a hundred quid's worth of coke could last most of the day.

Funds were running low again now. I was still doing little robberies, mainly drug dealers, trying to carry on the stuff I had been doing with Harrington on a lower scale.

A pal, Billy, called me and said he needed to speak to me. He wouldn't tell me on the phone, so I went to visit him in Perivale. We went for a walk along an alleyway near his house. I wondered if I was being set up, but Billy explained that a serious firm I had links to had paid him a visit. The message they delivered was that they weren't happy with me.

By this point, I wanted to try and front out anything like this. Dependant on crack, I didn't have any filter…or fear.

'Okay, sure, I'll meet them.'

I suggested the car park at Homebase in East Acton on the A40.

I was about 12-handed. I had to bring some back-up. They wouldn't be on their own, would they?

Billy turned up in a black Mercedes Jeep. I still worried he was setting me up, but he said, 'Don't worry, Ray, they'll be here.'

But they didn't turn up.

'Fuck it, Billy. I'll meet them on their manor, instead.'

So we agreed a meeting point in east London and, again, I went mob-handed. When I got there, instinctively, I didn't trust the situation, so I climbed a fire escape at the back of an old cinema, close to the meeting point. As I stood on the flat roof, strapped up and fucked on crack, looking through a pair of binoculars, I'd completely forgotten I was no good with heights. I kept seeing the same motorbikes, two-handed, flying about down below. Something wasn't right. I knew it was that lot, but for some reason, they no-showed again.

*****

Out of the blue, I got a call from Monica. She was at Heathrow Airport. Could I go and pick her up? Of course, I said yes. I had missed her massively.

Monica looked awful when she walked through arrivals. Bobbles in her hair, gaunt…a right state. She'd partied hard in LA. It sounded hardcore. Within days, we were very close again. Monica needed looking after, and I was just so happy she was back.

It was time to celebrate, using the relatively small amount of cash I had tucked away. I booked a large suite at the Radisson Edwardian at Heathrow, with a jacuzzi and a huge bath. I ordered half a dozen magnums of champagne and spent three or four days there with Monica, Sandi and three of their mates. The whole stay cost me £14,000, and most of that was spent on the girls and crack.

By now, to smoke crack, the girls were using a small Martell brandy bottle, which they'd drink first. Then they'd use a screw and a small hammer to smash the bottom of the bottle, so it created a hole through the glass — carefully pouring any small shards out of the neck of the bottle. Then push wire wool in top of the bottle, so it was sticking out slightly, and use the tip of a metal coat hanger to poke at the wire wool to make it as compact as possible. Then put the crack on top of that and burn it. Then they'd suck at the hole in the bottle and smoked the crack that way. This created a different much more powerful buzz altogether. Wow, next level.

I'm sure the more fucked they got me, the more money and gear they pinched. But I didn't give a shit, I was in ecstasy. After all the girls had finally fucked off, I paid the bill in cash at reception. I literally just had enough left to pay that hotel bill, and had to walk back home to Brentford Docks along the A4. At least it sobered me up a bit. I think I slept solidly for the next 48 hours.

*****

Around this time I was interviewed for *Streetfighters: Real Fighting Men Tell Their Stories* by Julian Davies, published in 2002 by Milo Books. I'm featured alongside two dozen guys, including Richard 'Crazy Horse' Horsely, 'the toughest man in the north east' and Malcolm Price, 'the legend of the Welsh valleys'. It was great to be asked by Julian, who must have caught me on a good day when he interviewed me. Thanks again, Julian.

*****

Monica continued to cause me all sorts of problems or, more like, my obsession with her did. I loved crack and Monica in equal measures. It and she got hold of me in such a way that the two went hand in hand. There were days on end when we were with each other 24/7.

I was doing some work for an antiques dealer friend, who had worked on TV shows. We were having breakfast in a cafe with his mate, Mo, who had an antiques shop nearby. I made a call in a phone box outside and overheard Mo bragging he had been with Monica too.

I wanted to smash him up there and then, but because I needed this bit of work, I couldn't. I did confront him, though.

'You've been fucking my bird.'

'No, I haven't, Ray.'

'Yeah, right, you'll pay for this, it will cost you.'

For once, I actually reasoned with myself, and came up with a solution that I thought would make me feel better, and cause Mo no physical harm. So the next day, I turned up at his antiques shop unannounced and bowled in. His sister was running the place.

'Can I help you, sir?', even though she knew exactly who I was.

'Yes, you can. I want that silver clock.'

As she started telling me the price, I said, 'No, this is mine, so I'm taking it,' and then walked out. I did the same thing with various other items every day for a couple of weeks. Sometime a few times a day. Mo didn't say anything because he was too scared to.

Often, I'd take the item back to another mate's shop, and sell it to him. I think they both knew what was going on.

Mo was never at his shop. One time as I left with another antique, he was driving past, but he shit himself and carried on. I saw him turn right and I knew he was now heading down a one-way street. He got stuck in a small traffic jam so I was able to run round and catch him up. Like a lunatic, I punched through the driver's window of his van and glass shattered all over him. I grabbed Mo by the neck and tried to pull him out of the vehicle and in doing so had the huge gold chain he wore in my hands. The cross at the end of it snapped off, but the chain was now in my possession.

I leant across him and opened the glove compartment and pinched some cash I found in there. I needed crack, so I didn't give a fuck. I threw Mo back across the inside of the van and fucked off. In my mind, I was still not letting this go.

I got hold of some gear, called Monica and we met up and got back on the pipe — the whole time arguing about who she had and hadn't slept with. She was adamant she hadn't gone with Mo, when he'd actually been with both her and Sandi.

*****

My next targets were the Walker brothers, who had a second-hand car showroom in Slough. The old man had a big construction firm and there was a load of sisters knocking about too. I can't even remember why now, but the Walkers had fucked me off.

I drove up there with Alan and a pal of his.

I said to the salesman, 'Where are they?'

'They're not here.'

'Oh, okay. Well, see that Range Rover? That's mine, I'm having that. And see that Audi? That's mine too.'

'No, Ray, you can't take them.'

I pulled out a hatchet from inside my jacket and slammed it through this guy's desk. Bosh.

'I want the keys and the log books to the Range Rover and the Audi. And I want any money you've got in the safe too, and while you're at it, you can empty your pockets.'

The guy was petrified and gave me £500 in cash, some shrapnel, the keys and paperwork.

I was so tunnel-visioned at that point, that I could only think about the next hour and the next hit.

When I did that Walkers job, I crossed the line. I was in the car outside, on the pipe. Alan, sitting next to me, was really shocked. The first time he'd seen me do it.

Crack is such a dangerous buzz. It gives you too much power. A couple of lines of decent coke, and you're feeling nice. And then you can have it every now and then as a top up. But with crack, you've got to have it all the time. A deep puff, a five minute buzz, and it's gone...you've got to start preparing another one. You just want that buzz back. The good one, not the bad one. But you've got to have money all the time, and you don't care how you get the money, because you need that good buzz. I'd be awake for six days at a time, 24-7...with dirty people and naughty women. Difficult to sleep.

Nine times out of ten on coke I couldn't perform sexually, but those crack sessions, with the girls fucking around with each other, well, more often than not it just clicked.

You don't know how you'll get the money, you just get it. It got to the point that I'd rob anything or anyone. It's an unforgiving drug so there is no room for sentiment. Crack is a filthy, nasty money drug. You're not interested in what you look like, what you're wearing, and you stink. It's a 24-hour thing. All you're eating and drinking is sweets and cheap energy drinks.

It's a real shock for your old pal to see you casually doing crack in what is already an extreme situation.

At the Walkers showroom that day, I told Alan he could take the Range, so he drove off in that, and got away from me as quickly as he could, I think. I took the Audi to Monica's place to pick her up. I was bibbing the horn outside, making a right old racket. Nothing. Fuck, I need her to go and get us more crack. As I drove back through Monica's estate, I could see at the end of the road the now familiar sight of a police cordon. I slowed down and an officer with a megaphone told me to get out and put my hands on top of the car. On the back seat was the car's price stickers, which I'd ripped off from inside the windscreen and tossed over my shoulder as I drove off...and the axe. They were treating me like an armed robber and, of course, that's exactly what I was. I was taken to Ealing police station and refused to make a statement.

'You're well nicked here, Hilly.'

'Whatever, fuck off...'

'The car, the axe. You're in proper trouble.'

'Mate, let me tell you something. In the morning, I'll be out of here.'

I knew the Walkers wouldn't press charges, and the gear I had on me would only amount to a caution for possession.

And the next morning, I was right. 'Mr Hill, you are free to leave.'

(Top) With Mum at brother Bobby's wedding.

(Middle) My favourite photo of Mum.

(Above) In my garden in Kingston in the 1990s.

(Left) My brother Keith today.

(Above) Gary Stretch fighting Chris Eubank for the middleweight world title in 1991 and (inset) as handsome as ever in one of his movie PR photos.

(Below) and (bottom) Me on the ring walk at the fight.

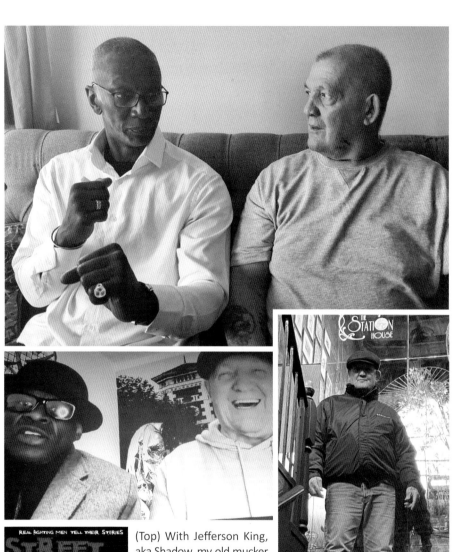

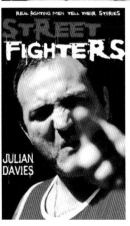

(Top) With Jefferson King, aka Shadow, my old mucker from the door at Central Park, Acton.

(Right) The stairs at Central Park (now Station House) at the spot Jefferson was held at gunpoint.

(Above) Doing a podcast with my crazy pal, Fish.

(Left) The *'Streetfighters'* book by Julian Davies I'm featured in.

(Top) Police officers wearing the sort of uniform (Specialist Crime & Operations/SCO19) I wore for my crazy raid on a Carphone Warehouse depot in 2004.

(Left) Outside the tower block in Ladbroke Grove in 2024 where I lived during the time of the raid, and where I was arrested by armed police using a shredder to cut through my door.

(Above) With Mum, also during that period, when I was hooked on crack, which you can tell in this photo, by the glazed look on my face.

Pete Doherty back on heroin in prison, inmate claims

By DAILY MAIL REPORTER
UPDATED: 12:24, 16 April 2008

 View comments

The Ministry of Justice was poised to launch an inquiry today after pictures of Pete Doherty in his prison cell were smuggled out of a London jail.

The images show the singer inside Wormwood Scrubs, where he is being held after repeatedly breaching bail conditions imposed for drugs possession convictions.

Doherty's cell is in the wing of the London prison used to detoxify drug-addicted prisoners.

(Clockwise) The media coverage of my photos of Pete Doherty in the *Daily Mail, The Sun,* — who ran the original article — and the *New Musical Express (NME).* I was really shocked at all the coverage photos on a little camera phone produced.

The Sun newspaper has published pictures of Babyshambles frontman Pete Doherty in **Wormwood Scrubs** prison in **London**.

The newspaper claims that **Doherty**, incarcerated for on a 14 week sentence after breaching parole last Tuesday (April 9), has been using heroin in jail on top of a methadone programme he is on.

It is claimed that **Doherty** has been gaining drugs by writing I.O.U. notes to inmates.

The report also says the singer has befriended an inmate named **Ray**, who has been acting as the singer/guitarist's protector in jail, where he is receiving a lot of attention from both inmates and guards because of his celebrity status.

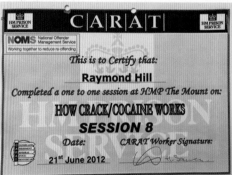

CARAT

HM PRISON SERVICE · HM PRISON SERVICE

NOMS National Offender Management Service
Working together to reduce re-offending

This is to Certify that:

Raymond Hill

Completed a one to one session at HMP The Mount on:

HOW CRACK/COCAINE WORKS

SESSION 8

Date: *CARAT Worker Signature:*

21ˢᵗ June 2012

(Above) Outside the Scrubs in 2024. I helped rebuild the inner wall seen in the distance during my time there.

(Left and bottom) Some of the certificates from my stint at the Scrubs on my IPP sentence.

PRISON FELLOWSHIP

SYCAMORE TREE

Victim Awareness – Restorative Justice

This certificate is awarded to

Raymond Hill

for actively participating in this Prison Fellowship programme
that included the following:

The impact of crime   Awareness of Victim's needs   Taking Responsibility
Reconciliation   Saying Sorry, Showing Remorse   Act of Restitution

This is to certify that

Ray Hill

completed the

Enhanced Thinking Skills (ETS)
Programme

at

HMP Wormwood Scrubs

April 2008

Resettlement Manager Signature: *Treatment Managers Signature:*

(Top) With my good pal Shaun Attwood during an interview for his top-rating podcast. I was so happy Shaun wrote the foreword for this book.

(Above/right) Mucking around with pal Ronnie Sweet in a police uniform and a vintage Rover R6 police car owned by Terry Haley.

(Above right) With Chris Lambrianou during our podcast interview for LADBible.

(Top left) With Jordan, who tattooed my 'BANG BANG' knuckles.

(Above) That's me in the suit of armour at Terry Haley's house in 2024 with him and our pal Alan Dean and (left) with my old pal Gary Stretch.

(Below) Me and Terry on a night out.

CLOSING IN

Now I knew I really was a target.

The police gave the Audi back to the Walkers, but Alan still had the Range Rover, which Old Bill didn't know about. It was parked in a garage off the A4, but we couldn't start it because it had been disabled. It also had a tracker on it, so the Walkers traced it. In the end we just gave it back to them at an organised meet. Nothing much was said, really. It's crazy looking back, but it was like these sorts of scrapes happened all the time.

I still had my old Rover — a red 350 — so I drove to see my pal to get some crack. When I arrived at the meet in Gunnersbury Park, I could see yellow fucking jackets. For me again. How did they know I was going to be there?

The Old Bill had dots all over me. Armed police everywhere.

'Get out the car, get out the car.' Blah, blah, blah.

I refused, so an officer leaned in the driver's window and tried to cuff me but he was so nervous that he handcuffed me to my seatbelt, so now I couldn't, 'Get out of the car, get out of the car.' What a shambles.

They eventually dragged me out and took me to Greenford police station where the desk sergeant told me I'd be spoken to about a few things, and then I was thrown in a cell.

Later in an interview room, I pulled my T-shirt over my face as they tried to talk to me and kept telling them to fuck off. A usual tactic of mine. See if they eventually get bored and let me go. Instead, they charged me with the antiques shop robberies and attack on its owner. I was taken to Isleworth Crown Court in the morning and remanded in custody to the Scrubs. At least that.

I was taken back to court three weeks later, hoping to get some good news. Thankfully, Mo had dropped all the charges. Good man, but no surprise.

This wasn't the end of this little episode, though. Far worse was to come. There was a flurry of activity in the court, and I saw a police officer talk to the prosecution's QC. Then a member of the CPS stood up to join in the hush-hush chat going on. Next the judge informed me that I was also on an attempted murder charge. For what? Who? I was told it was someone I'd scrapped with recently, during some enforcement work. Serious head injuries and it was touch and go. Fuck, this must be a fit up.

I was taken back to the Scrubs, where I no-commented my police interview, held via video link, probably because I was deemed a risk, and then I was actually charged with attempted murder. I'd been charged before with grievous bodily harm (GBH) or wounding with intent (under section 18) but this new charge, involving the 'M' word, carried a maximum term of life imprisonment. Fuck.

Back at court a few weeks later, I was offered a deal.

A fucking deal? There hadn't been a trial yet?

'Life, recommended nine.'

'Are you mad? Do you think I've never been in prison before. You're not able to promise me I'll only do nine years.'

One minute I was about to walk, the next I was looking at some serious bird again. Fucking hell, I wasn't having that. I went mad. I thought I was about to go home, and now I was looking at a deal for nine fucking years minimum. I picked up a chair and threw it across the court. And then ripped the wooden door on the dock off its hinges. It took four screws to restrain me and put me in a cell downstairs, which I smashed to pieces too. Then I was dragged kicking and screaming back to the Scrubs.

Two months later, I was brought back to court and stood in front of a horrible judge, who gave me a big old lecture about smashing up the court last time, and then told me investigations were still on-going. So back to the Scrubs, where I'd spent so much of my life by now.

Once again, I decided not to do drugs in prison, which was fairly easy for me, even though I was a crackhead...simply, I think, because I'd never done drugs in prison before. For me, it just never seemed worth it in such controlled conditions as prison. It's always been all or nothing for me, I guess, and being in prison was like a default setting again. I even bashed up the guy I was twos-up with, because he started smoking brown in our cell. In the morning, I told the screws we'd had a fight and I wanted him out.

They put a new geezer in the cell called Ricky, who was from Harrow, who was in for importing cannabis, on very flimsy evidence. A nice guy. On his way to court, the prison van was involved in a road accident. He went crashing into a wooden partition and later received fifteen grand in compensation...and got off the charge. He later asked me to be godfather to his little girl. He's kept out of trouble ever since and has now got a really good job in the motor business.

I'd been chatting to Monica quite a bit on the prison phone and she also came to visit me once. It was great to see her, and catch up. I could tell she was still on the gear because of the burns on her fingers, but Monica always looked beautiful to me, whether she was using or not.

Saying goodbye to Monica was really hard, the hardest. I couldn't wait to be able to call her later that evening.

Back down to earth again with a bang, it was eleven months before I was brought back. A long nasty bit of remand bird, with a potential murder charge hanging over me.

Finally back at court, I was put in a room with a nice young barrister who said, 'Mr Hill, the reason this has been held back so long, is that now they want you to plead guilty to this,' ... and then he handed me a piece of paper, which just said, 'ABH' on it. Actual Bodily Harm.

Wow...

'Yes, Mr Hill, there is insufficient evidence to prosecute on a charge of attempted murder.'

Minutes later, I was in the dock, pleading guilty to ABH and being sentenced to six months by an apologetic female judge, who was quick to point out that because my time already served, I was free to go. I was ecstatic.

Old Bill gave me daggers as I walked out of court with my barrister, who told me straight, 'Ray, you've got off this one, but they are really after you now. They want you bad. You really need to keep your head down and your nose clean.'

'Okay, mate, okay, mate…sure.'

When in reality, that was going to be impossible because, now I was out, all I wanted to do was smoke crack, and that's exactly what I was going to do. As usual, crime would have to pay for it.

*****

Back out and once again I had enough on my plate — obsessed with hanging out on the pipe with Monica.

I answered a phone call from a number I didn't recognise and, fuck me — it was Freddy. He'd escaped. What a boy. I already knew Freddy had used his influence to secure a place in a D-Cat open prison, years before he was entitled to. He was on an outside working party, where he walked off, so technically he'd absconded, because he didn't break out or jump over a wall.

It was great to hear from Freddy. He explained he was on the run in Paris and wanted me to arrange a meet with some import/export contacts. Freddy also asked me if I could borrow him £100k. I told him I didn't have that kind of money anymore. Things hadn't been easy recently.

I had, though, been talking to a firm from Basingstoke, who needed hooking up. Freddy was a man who could help. People like him, whatever their circumstance — inside, outside or absconding — often carry on doing whatever it is they do. They can't give it up. It becomes all they know. So I took two of the Basey boys on the Eurostar to meet him.

We met Freddy in a club in Paris city centre and he was with someone I recognised — a motorbike security guy who had worked with us. An average-sized fella who was a top hitman. Serious.

'Look at the fucking state of you, Ray. You look like you're bang on the heavy stuff, mate?'

I denied it, but, he could tell. I was a mess. Usually suited and booted for this kind of thing, I was wearing jeans and an old leather jacket with a button missing. I wasn't even aware that the Basingstoke boys gave Freddy a parcel of money and did a deal on the side. I had always been Freddy's enforcer, but it was like he only needed me for a connection now, and I was being told less and less about the job.

Back in London a few weeks later, Freddy called up and said, 'My mate is delivering gear in his ice cream van. Meet him and he'll give you 50 key of Thai grass, which has got wet at the bottom of a boat. You can have it…see if you can do anything with it.'

I think it was Freddy trying to offer me a lifeline. Something that might help sort me out, but what was I going to do with a load of soggy hash? I called Winston in Wolverhampton and he told me he was coming down to sort it out. He drove me to a big cash and carry and bought a dozen cases of rum, which we poured into a bath and one by one soaked the keys of gear in. Then we laid it all out on bed sheets and it all dried back normal. Proper Thai grass again. Amazing. What a useful trick.

Now, I had 50 key of the stuff. Each one was about the size of a laptop computer, but thicker, and back then could be sold on for around £1800 a pop, so about £90k in total. My crack addiction was so bad I let Winston have the lot for ten grand. Which really only amounted to two or three weeks of crack at best for me. Especially if I had ten large in my pocket, because then I'd really smash it, and get a few girls involved too. Silly cunt.

And then I became greedy. I had Freddy's friend's number and, to him, what I said went, so I went over the top greedy. I called him up and said I needed another 30 key, which thankfully didn't need to be washed up. I sold that on to whoever would take it the quickest. I gave the geezer some of the money, and then took another 30 key, and repeat. To the point where I'd taken about 100 key and still owed the guy £70k. All this was against my principals as an enforcer, and would never have happened on my 'clean' or, even just 'coked-up' watch. Yet here I was, a greedy crackhead, exploiting my own rules and the people around me. But I was being exploited too. That's the thing, when crack is involved, anyone around you taking it with you is usually on the blag as well.

One day, I was at a flat in Fulham I was using as a safe house, smoking some crack in the bedroom with Monica, while Sandi was on her phone in the kitchen. I heard Sandi shout that she was popping out and then the front door slam. Half an hour later, I staggered into the living area and saw that the window was wide open. Strange. But when I opened the fridge door, instead of six keys of Thai grass I'd put there, only two were inside. That fucker Sandi must have thrown the other four down to the hedges below. She denied it, of course, but while I might have been fucked, I wasn't fucking stupid.

When you're on crack you have no friends. You're not even a friend to yourself. You just don't give a fuck. And neither do the people you smoke crack with. You're not thinking what's right or wrong. You smoke more crack and then you just want more. It's all about the next hit.

I needed a lot of money, a decent piece of work, to help get me out of this hole. Lots and lots of cash to feed this awful habit. And crime was the only way I could fund it. The same as any crackhead.

*****

I had been speaking to some farmers in Bedfordshire about a cannabis grow. I'd taken Sandi down there one time with me to show off the amazing gaff there. Unbeknown to me, while I was talking business with one of the guys, she'd slipped off and flirted with his mate, got his phone number and a few days later rang them up to organise a game with a few of them at the farm. Fucking cheek.

Sandi told me about it, because she wanted me to be security for the day. I agreed because I felt responsible, and because I knew Monica wouldn't be involved in that sort of thing anymore. I stood outside the house, peering through the windows, watching Sandi off her head on crack and five of her pals fucking three or four burly farmers all afternoon. It's was like one big orgy in there. Sandi came out to speak to me and asked if I was missing Monica so I nodded. She replied, 'I asked her to come, but she was busy.'

'Monica wouldn't do this sort of thing now.'

'Ray, don't be stupid, Monica does this stuff with me all the time.'

And that really fucked me off. When I questioned Monica on the phone the next day she admitted Sandi had asked her, and couldn't explain why she was still being asked if, like she'd told me, she had given all that sort of thing up.

I was fuming, so in the middle of the night, early hours, drove straight round to the sisters' family home with a knife and cut the roof of Monica's beautiful old convertible to shreds. I was out of control. I could see Sandi looking out of the window so I legged it, but she ran out the house and into the street and almost caught up with me.

I was later arrested at the apartment in Brentford, but Monica didn't want to press charges so, thankfully, I was free to go. Our 'relationship' was on hold again, though.

A CRACKPOT IDEA

Slowly running out of cash, I headed to Ladbroke Grove, a place I always went when I was looking for a leg-up. I spoke to a contact, a well-known villain and fixer, and asked him if he had any work for me. He said he'd try and sort something out.

I bumped into another mate, who told me he'd just done a job at a Carphone Warehouse depot in Park Royal. His little gang had knocked through a wall and got away with about £20k of Motorola Razr handsets.

'When we were in there, Ray, we saw a lorry container full of phones, but we had to get out quickly with what we already had. There's a great bit of work still in there, Ray.'

My pal drove me down there to see the site and to have a recce around the outside of the huge building. He really shouldn't have been back in that area, so soon after his job, but he explained from the outside looking in how they pulled it off. The whole site looked imposing, so I needed to think of a plan of how we could get in. I was sure my crack-addled mind would come up with something. It had to.

I remembered a friend of mine in Ealing, who had nicked a load of legit police and HM Customs and Excise uniforms from a 'plain clothes' police van, parked outside a nick in south London. I was particularly fascinated by the SO19 (Specialist Operations) outfits, with padding on the legs and the arms, and the mask, the helmet and the big gloves with lead in them. There were Customs bomber jackets and baseball caps too. Kosher gear. I just loved it. I negotiated a deal where I paid for the uniforms after the piece of work.

I couldn't afford the Brentford Docks flat anymore, so that had to go. Through a contact in Grove, I moved into a flat in a tower block on the Edward Woods Estate, across the road from Grenfell Tower. I was so hooked on crack, I'd lost all the money and gear I had stashed in the properties in Kingston. Me and 'her' couldn't stay together for more than a few days at a time, and while I missed my children, I was just in no state to be a parent to any of them. For the time being, it was again all about survival.

*****

Monica and I had been meeting up again, but during a period when she went AWOL, I hooked up with Sandi and a mate of hers at The Hilton in Ealing Common. I took about a monkey's worth of crack with me that I'd blagged off some poor sod. We were having a right old game in there when, unbeknown to me, I was given a snowball (a mix of crack cocaine and heroin). I took a puff on the pipe and, wow, I thought I was going to die. It was the strongest hit I'd ever had. Looking back, I think it was payback for what I'd done to Monica's car. I reckon their plan was to leave me for dead in that hotel room, and just let it go down as an overdose.

But I was very much alive, and ran out of the hotel in the early hours, leaving the girls in the room. I was hallucinating so much, I thought Sandi had called some guys and they were chasing me all the way home.

I went home to my mum's, and woke her up.

'Mum, I'm in a bad way.'

But she didn't understand or know what to do, poor thing.

She said I needed to go to the hospital, which I was always reluctant to do, but I walked down to the local mini-cab firm, and pleaded with them to take me. I didn't have any money, but they agreed, and drove me to the Hammersmith Hospital on Ducane Road, near the Scrubs.

At the hospital, they checked me out, and confirmed I'd OD'd. I said I'd drunk something and thought I'd been spiked, but they knew. They put me on a bed and jabbed me two times up my arse, and within half an hour I felt myself coming round again. The hospital staff wanted to call the police so I said, 'Listen, I'm a bit of a bad boy, please don't.' Thankfully they didn't, and let it go.

*****

A blast from the past, One Eyed Johnny, got in touch and said he had a bit of work for me — visiting a traveller family called the Smiths. So I went to their house near John's in Lingfield and asked for the old man. They said he wasn't in, and I said, 'Well, he owes the money, he needs to be pay up.'

I pulled a thing out and shot it in to the air, just to shit them up, and then left.

I went back to John's and shortly after a traveller van pulled up. It was the guy who we were trying to help out.

'Thank you so much, they've paid up. Come out here. I've got a present for you.'

I wasn't sure what he was up to, but went outside, and he gave me three cooking apples in a bag. Three fucking cooking apples!

'What's that, then?'

'Go and see John and he'll tell you.'

And then he fucked off.

I was furious, because I was supposed to be getting paid extra by the guy, if the other family paid up, which they now had.

'Fucking robbing cunts.'

John explained that the apples meant that I was now on-side with this guy, and we could do other business with his family.

I said, 'Never mind other business. I want to get paid out fully for this job first.'

Inside the house was this guy's son, a big coke dealer. I tried to see if I could strike a mates rates deal for a kilo, but he would only do half a key. We arranged a meet a couple of days later in Clerkenwell, near Mount Pleasant...out that way. I got a little team together. A pal who could drive us there in his Range Rover and two others. Then the other motor turned up. The guy had the half a key, but wanted me to buy a few thousand double doves for £15 a pop, which was way over the odds, and not part of the original deal. It really fucked me off. First the apples, now this. I decided we were going to take the lot without paying anything. Within a few minutes, we had fucked off with the coke and the pills in a couple of carrier bags.

Word got back to John and he rang me up to tell me the names of people who were going to sort me out. That I was dead. By this point in my life, I really couldn't give a fuck who he was threatening me with.

The next day I got a call from a guy who was selling the brown stuff. This guy had got my number from a Greek guy John had introduced me to the previous week. If they were calling me wanting a meet so soon after yesterday's blag, they mustn't have spoken to John in between. Or was this a set-up? It was a gamble, but I agreed to the meet. I was so fucked by now, robbing people left right and centre, so it was what it was.

The other lot pulled up in a Land Cruiser and as I approached the vehicle, about ten yards away, I pulled out a police ID card from my mate in Ealing...just to mix things up a bit. Now, Mr Brown thought I was Old Bill, and Mr Greek was wondering if I'd been Old Bill all along. The pair of them leapt out of their motor, pushed past me and legged it. Perfect, I could now find the gear in their car and drive off in it. Except one of them had central locked the car with the key fob as they ran off and silly bollocks here, hadn't grabbed the keys off them. I picked up a nearby brick and threw it at the windscreen, but it bounced back and the fucker nearly hit me. One of them looked back and clocked me doing that, and then realised I probably wasn't Old Bill after all. Now they both ran back and started chasing me.

I ran into a convenience shop and showed my police badge again.

'Police, police...I'm being chased by dangerous criminals, I need to hide in here.'

'Yes sir, yes sir.'

Thankfully, they ran the other way, and I'd somehow got away with my latest hairbrained scheme...for now.

*****

Despite everything, I kept seeing Monica. Even at my mum's, when I'd stay there to try and get clean. Climbing the walls, desperate for a hit, I'd end up calling Monica. To avoid my mum, she'd shinny up a big tree in the back garden and clamber through my bedroom window to deliver a few much-needed rocks. My poor mum. I'm sure she could smell us smoking it. Of course she could.

Back at the tower block I'd have crazy sex on crack with Monica and she'd make some weird and wonderful noises. When she left, I'd suffer awful psychosis and paranoia. I'd hear those sex noises Monica made, long after she'd gone. I'd go out of my mind and think she was downstairs, fucking someone else. I'd run down to the floor below, opening letterboxes to see if I could hear which flat she was in.

Those were desperate, desperate times. Once I'd finished any stash of crack I'd managed to get my grubby hands on, it usually meant I had no money left, not a penny. I'd walk from my tower block to the entrance of Westfield looking for fag butts, just to get some kind of hit. If I found half a cigarette, I thought I'd had a right result. I could see other crackheads doing the same. If there was one in front of me, all the best butts had gone, so I needed to find a different route. Later, I'd get back to the flat and smoke all the butts I had left. How had it come to this? I used to be a chap, a gangster earning thousands of pounds a week.

I'd regularly walk the length of Edgware Road or roam around Kings Cross, robbing street dealers...just to get enough cash together for more crack.

In the early hours one morning, as I trawled the streets looking for butts or someone to rob, I caught Monica on Goldhawk Road, punting a geezer who had just got out of his car to get a kebab. Bold as brass, literally — turning tricks on a busy late-night patch of Shepherd's Bush. I ran over, knocked the fella out, took the one and a half in cash he had on him, and me and Monica spent it on crack.

One day, Monica visited me and asked me about the police uniforms laying around. Looking back, I appreciate now I had reached rock bottom, because any sense of confidentiality or discretion had gone out of the window. Sat in the front room of a grubby flat, off my nut, smoking crack, casually saying, 'Ah, I'm going to do a bit of work. It's that Carphone Warehouse job I was telling you about.'

'Fucking hell, be careful, Ray.'

I didn't know she cared. It would certainly seem I didn't.

*****

Two days later, summer 2004, I was dressed head to toe in an SO19 police officer's uniform, tugging on a crack pipe, trying to plot a hugely ambitious 'raid' on a Carphone Warehouse depot.

I'd sourced a seven and a half tonne box lorry and a pal, Dave, who I pulled in on the job, drove us into the area. But we had a problem. The two guys I'd found to wear the Custom and Excise jackets and caps hadn't shown up. They'd obviously had second thoughts, and who could blame them?

I had to frantically ring round a few old contacts to see if anyone else was available…albeit at very short notice. Me and Dave just couldn't do this on our own. This was supposed to be a Customs and Excise raid / official inspection — checking that all the phones in the warehouse had passed through the correct clearance channels.

Thankfully, somebody called me back. They'd found a couple of guys. Well, they were kids, really — 20-21 years old, maybe. A couple of shoplifters, at best, completely out of their depth. Not that I was anywhere within mine.

While I'd waited anxiously for these numpties to arrive, I was sat in the back of the van, on the pipe, off my canister. I just wanted to get in there and get started. I had a clipboard with sheets of A4 paperwork that looked like sales dockets.

Then a big lorry drove past us and into the depot.

When my pal pulled up with those two fuckwits, 20 minutes later, at around 4.30pm, I went mental. Shouting and screaming. I was really off my nut off by now. My head was ready to explode. I calmed down, and tried to tell everybody how it was going to be. The two kids were looking at me like I was fucking mad, which, of course, I was. I mean, you don't see a police officer doing crack every day. I got the boys in the back of van, and kitted them out in their jackets and caps.

'Right, we're going to walk in there, and I want you two to run upstairs where the offices are. I'll shout, 'Everybody, stop what you're doing. This is HM Customs and Excise. We have reason to believe there are counterfeit phones being processed in here.' I'll ask everybody to get on the floor and with the hands behind their backs…and then Dave will cuff them with these cable ties. Upstairs boys, what you're really looking for is the hard-drive to the CCTV. If you can't find it, ask where it is and then unplug it, disable it, smash it up…whatever you need to do.

As we tried to gather ourselves, we watched the same lorry drive out. I gave the signal and the four of us walked through the gates and into the Carphone Warehouse compound. What was I thinking? Me dressed as SO19, with kosher ID, Dave wearing a police sergeant uniform and two very junior Customs officers.

Because we'd been hanging around for so long, and the lorry had just left, the warehouse staff had sent down the shutters. Just as they were reaching the bottom, I banged on them loudly.

'Police, police. We have reason to believe there has been a serious fraud taking place at this depot.'

The door in the shutter opened, and we rushed through. The kids shot upstairs to the mezzanine level, as instructed, while I barked orders to everyone on the shop floor.

'Listen everybody, I'm SO19, I am assisting the Customs and Excise officers here to make sure there are no problems. Everyone has to be cable-tied, and then my officers outside will also come in and check every phone.'

A Paddy/Irish manager quite rightly smelt a rat and said, 'I don't know anything about this.'

'Please, sir, can you get on the floor, and do as I say.'

Upstairs, the shoplifters had cable-tied everybody, as instructed, but instead of moving onto their next step of looking for the hard-drive, had started taking watches, rings and other bits of jewellery from the various members of staff now under their control. They were standing at the top of the stairs, dangling a shitty Tudor watch, with big grins on their faces. Like I said, fuckwits.

Meanwhile, Dave helped me cable-tie the shop floor staff, around eight or nine people, including the big Paddy. Now I felt comfortable to have a look around. I spotted the container full of thousands of phones and I could see a huge brand new black van with its back doors open to our left, waiting to be filled with phones for deliveries to Carphone Warehouse stores all over the UK.

I explained that all the staff need to get inside the black van. Now they knew it was all bollocks. Silly cunt.

The big Paddy had had enough. He ripped the cable-ties off his wrists, and ran towards me, but I hit him so hard with a big leaded glove, he dropped to the floor, sparko. The rest of the staff decided to do as they were being told, but they now knew exactly what was going on.

We pulled up the shutters, and Dave reversed our lorry in. We quickly started to fill it with boxes and boxes of phones from the container. Mostly Motorola Razr and Blackberrys.

I was still shouting at the kids.

'Where is the hard-drive. The fucking hard-drive...'

'We can't find it.'

'Right, just get in the van, get in the van.'

Fifteen minutes later we had managed to load around 100 boxes into the lorry, which filled it up. In the end, more than 5,000 phones with a street value of more than £1m. I drove the lorry out of the compound, with Dave in the front with me and the kids in the back in and among the boxes, with some staff laptops they'd also nicked, the fucking idiots.

As we pulled out of the depot and drove towards the main gate, suddenly, the familiar sight of flashing blue lights came into view. A row of police vehicles and vans lined the street outside. As I drove out of the gate, I floored it. I wasn't stopping for any fucker, so I kept going, smashing through a police car and a van, parked alongside each other.

As we sped off, Dave was crying to get out of the motor. He wanted me to stop, but I carried on, struggling to control the lorry with its battered front. I managed to get on the A406 at Hanger Lane, where we let the boys out, and they got the tube back to Grove. I said we'd sort them out later, but they'd be lucky to get anything, although they did have the laptops and a few crap watches. Dave then took over the driving, and drove the lorry to the A40, heading to his house in the Slough area.

I now know that somebody on the top floor at the depot raised the alarm, while the kids were fucking around. The police didn't follow us, which was strange. Why, I don't know? Maybe, because driving like that, I was deemed a danger to the public — which clearly I was. And they didn't want to add to it.

We parked the lorry up on Dave's estate, and a contact came up with another van. We switched all the phones over, and he fucked off with them. We'd work everything out later, but he gave me a couple of grand up front. Because Dave was skint, he insisted on taking four boxes and dropped me back to the tower block in his car.

Just like the raid itself, there was no clear plan as to exactly how we would get rid of the phones or even the lorry. I was just glad to have got home, without getting nicked, so I could think again about getting some more crack, and maybe have a steady income for a while from the sale of phones to help feed my addiction.

The next morning, the contact called.

'We need those boxes back from Dave. We're getting good money for these.'

I phoned Dave and he said he'd sold his lot to an Indian phone shop, so I told him to go and get them. He had murders sorting it out, but managed to retrieve most of them from the shopkeeper.

*****

Meanwhile, I was on the 9th floor of my tower block, ploughing through rocks of crack. Like a proper nut-nut, I'd tied a thick rope around the balcony. In my frazzled mind, if it ever got on top, I was going over the side, through someone else's flat, and would escape that way.

Monica came round for a go on the pipe, and was looking more shifty than usual. She didn't hang around long, which was odd, given how much crack I had.

Next Dave appeared with the phones he'd managed to get back from the shopkeeper. He stood in my flat telling me everything was sweet, had a cup of tea, and then fucked off too. I decided to have a little lay down.

Buzzing nicely off my head now, I was spaced out on my bed when there was a loud knock on the door. Who the fuck is that?

I saw two women through the spy-hole, so opened up.

'Hello, sir. Would you be interested in a new television?'

'Nah, nah, not today, girls,' and slammed the door.

A few minutes later there was a huge crashing sound. Armed Old Bill trying to get in, but the piece of wood I had fitted across the inside width of the door was making it difficult. Not when they got a shredder out, though. Wow, it literally took layers off the door in a matter of seconds. I froze in bed. Then I realised they were in the flat now, shouting, 'Come out, come out,' towards the bedroom door.

They wanted me to walk out of the room backwards, but I came out normally, to more infra-red dots all over me. As I was walked out of the flat, cuffed, I passed the two 'TV saleswomen' — plain clothes who had simply being confirming that I was in the flat.

I was taken down the stairs by four or five Old Bill, cuffed to two of them, one in front, one behind. There were two armed officers on each landing.

The affects of my last go on the pipe were still there. Weirdly, I still felt strong from it. That I had a force of power. I still had hope I could escape, which, the more Old Bill I saw, the more I realised I couldn't.

I was taken to Wembley Police Station and put in a cell. As usual, I took my T-shirt off, and whacked it over my head.

An inspector was in my face, asking me what I'd done. Telling me I needed to go with him to be interviewed.

'No comment, fuck off. No comment.'

'C'mon, Ray, let's go and have a chat. We've got some cigarettes for you in the interview room.'

Which is the hardest thing to turn down, because I always smoked when doing crack or coke...standard. But I refused to give in. I just wanted to go to the Scrubs, and start doing my time. I knew I wasn't getting off this. I knew I was bang in trouble.

Friends have told me that various people grassed me up for the Carphone Warehouse job, because they simply wanted me out of the way. That because I'd been terrorising so many poor fuckers, there were plenty of people terrified of me. It's not for me to say, really, but lots of people have since told me how feared I was, even though I was ravaged by crack addiction.

Now banged up yet again, keeping away from crack in prison would be so much tougher this time because drugs were now so easy to get hold of inside. There was no point even thinking about crack now, or any drugs. Just keep reminding myself that prison is the worst place to do drugs. And try and turn this latest negative into some kind of positive.

And so the massive comedown began.

Forty eight hours later, I had a pre-hearing at Willesden Magistrates Court, and was finally sent to the Scrubs.

As fate would have it, as I was walked up the stairs into the reception, to be allocated a cell, coming towards me was a familiar face, and for once he wasn't trying to attack me. Only my old childhood enemy from The Priory youth club, who I hadn't seen since the 1970s when we were kids. He'd done a massive stretch for shooting up the pub (and the police), and years later had been recalled for various breaches. As we met on that staircase, despite all the fights back then and the things we'd been through since, we hugged and both welled up. In that moment, it was like we were mates and everything was forgotten.

'Fucking hell, Ray.'

'Do you know what I mean, mate?'

Other times I came across someone like that, a so-called enemy, it might have kicked off. Maybe, me and this guy, coming from the same area, growing up as kids, scrapping like that as young adults... well, it was just different. Best that we stuck together now. Which is strange, because we had never ever got on.

The thing with prison is...you never know who you're going to bump into from one day to the next, and what dealings you've had with them in the past. I came across lots of people I've robbed before.

*****

I was put on A-wing, where Dave was, so we were able to catch up about everything. Some of what he was saying just didn't add up, so I had my suspicions that he might be a grass.

The guy I was in a cell with let me use a phone he'd smuggled in to call Monica. No answer, but the sister Sandi called back.

'What's it like, cunt...being banged up again? You're going away for a long time, you fucking wanker.'

Soul-destroying when I was at my lowest point again, but it was hard to argue with that comment.

On a lighter note, a few weeks later, I was shown an article from a local newspaper in Kent, the *News Shopper*, about an old mucker who had managed to turn their life around, and help others. I had to chuckle at Harry's one-liners. Maybe there was hope for me yet?

AN EX-CON, who turned away from a life of crime, has scooped £295,000 of lottery cash to rescue a community centre for hard-up pensioners in Deptford.

Harry Haward, 70, of Brockley Rise, Forest Hill, admits he has "more form than Red Rum", but this has not stopped him trying to give something back to the community.

The only thing Harry could remember about his Deptford childhood, was "the walls were so thin in my house, we could dip our bread in next door's gravy".

The father-of-five has rescued Deptford Action Group for the Elderly (DAGE) from the ashes and it now offers advice and information for pensioners. But it doesn't stop there.

A successful £295,000 application for lottery funding to re-open the old charity shop was the result.

Harry said: "The building was so dirty when we bought it, even the mice were wearing overalls."

INDETERMINATE

Three months in to this latest remand, I was moved to C-wing. Dave was also shifted…to a cushier wing.

But I had a touch because I was put twos-up with an old pal, Gary, who I knew from my doorman days. He owned four or five clubs at one point but got caught with a load of guns and got a ten-stretch.

'You okay, you got money, Ray?'

'No, mate.'

'Give me your mum's address, I'll get something over to her.'

And then he arranged for a postal order to be sent to her for a couple of grand, which was so good of him.

I managed to get a job in the laundry, sometimes 15/16 hours a day, getting locked up late, around 8.30/9pm. I worked in a big cell with loads of washing machines, making sure the boys got their correct clothes. Every day was hard work, which was great because it made the time go.

Just my luck, I bumped into one of the guys in the Land Cruiser, who I tried to rob pretending to be Old Bill a few weeks earlier. Quite understandably, he was calling me everything under the sun, and was really pissed with me. So now I knew I had to fight him, because I had to be strong in there from the start again. But I wasn't getting any younger, mid-50s now, and, fucking hell, he was a big guy in his late 20s. And even though I was still a lump, at my age, I had to get it right. I landed a great first shot and he went down like a sack of spuds. If you get that first punch right, it's usually all over.

*****

Despite the harsh words her sister had for me on the phone, I'd stayed in touch with Monica as much as possible, and was thrilled when she requested to come and visit me. And she had some big news — she was pregnant. Thankfully, it meant she'd cleaned herself up. I loved the girl, so I was happy she seemed healthier, but with the big bit of bird I was surely looking at, deep down I knew it was over for us and I'd likely never see her again. That was the toughest visit. Monica just being round the corner in Acton made it even worse, and even if she did request another visit, I was fairly sure I'd turn it down to save myself any more heartache.

*****

I was always trying to get to see Dave at the Scrubs, so I could question him more, but I just couldn't get it sorted. I did as much as I could to keep myself busy. Mopping and scrubbing the landings constantly. Going to the gym whenever I could. The screws could see that I was working my bollocks off and working out loads too. Someone doing hundreds of press-ups and sit-ups each day can't be doing drugs. Ironically, I was rewarded with a job on the Conibeere — the drugs unit at the Scrubs, for prisoners who require a substance misuse stabilisation regime. Of course, there was a risk they were fighting fire with fire, but the trust those screws placed in me spurred me on, to keep clean. Those Conibeere screws were proper screws, the best.

My job meant that I had my own cell on the Conibeere unit too, like the 'patients', which was mostly unlocked. I ran that wing with two other prisoners working there. It wasn't always a pretty job, though — cleaning up all the vomit and shit from smack-heads coming off heroin or whatever.

The Conibeere screws began letting me go to see Dave, which they weren't meant to do. Now I could see for myself that he was definitely getting benefits. And he was never pleased to see me.

Twelve months in, I received my deps, and it confirmed my suspicions. In not so many words, it explained that when Dave left my flat the night I was arrested, the police took him away and he accepted a deal — the fucking dirty grass. The Indian shopkeeper had called the Old Bill on him.

While I was on the Conibeere, a year or so in, I bumped into a familiar face one day. Only one of the fuckwits from the Carphone Warehouse job.

'Hello, Ray?'

'Do I know you?'

'I was one of the lads your mate brought up to Carphone Warehouse for that job.'

'Of course, mate...what happened to you?'

'I never got a tug, nothing, mate.'

This kid was in his early 20s now and fucked up himself on crack. He was on the wing for a few weeks, but I didn't have much more to do with him. I certainly didn't want to talk to him about the job. I didn't want to give him any ammunition, because he might try to get a deal for himself for whatever he was in for. Or it could even be a set-up and part of a deal he'd already worked out.

Two and a half long years later, I was still on remand at the Scrubs.

*****

Finally...the court case, in early 2007. Two weeks earlier on a visit, my barrister offered me a deal for 'a nine' in return for a guilty plea. He also explained the defence would be using new facial-mapping evidence from CCTV-footage they'd been able to obtain, which could navigate around my SO19 balaclava. I didn't believe it had got through my mask, so, as usual, I said, 'No deal, I'll take my chances.' Again, my world had been turned upside down, but at least I was clean, keeping out of trouble and once more removed from the disruptive life that had put me away again.

The case started at Harrow Crown Court. I had a big hunch my co-defendant/fucking grass, Dave, was on my prison bus, either getting on first or last, and they were keeping us apart in different boxes at each end of the wagon. I saw him out of the corner of my eye on the first day. I was put in a cell, and told by one of the screws that Dave had been taken upstairs to get a coffee and a sandwich.

Dave had gone guilty because he had to as part of his deal. When I heard the prosecution's opening statement about the facial mapping and how much it appeared Dave had cooperated, I thought, fuck it and changed my plea. When there's a grass on the firm, you've got no chance. Now no need for a jury if both defendants go guilty.

Dave wasn't in the big holding cell underneath the court with the rest of us standing trial for similar charges that day, which said it all. I did see him with a couple of screws in the large square room that leads into the courts, and I said, 'What's going on, mate?' But he just kept his head down.

Dave was then led into the court, and I asked one of the four or five screws with me if I could look through the small piece of glass in the door, and he said, 'Go on then...' I peaked through and could see Dave talking to the judge, the fucking grass.

Half an hour later, Dave was led back out, with his head bowed, and I said, 'What the fuck you done, Dave, what's going on?'

The screws quickly led him away. Us not standing side by side together to be sentenced, really told me all I needed to know. I was told that wanker got five years. I would have loved five years. We'd both already done two and half years on remand. So he'd be out very soon...and so would I.

Now my turn. The judge said to me, 'I am not going to sentence to you today, Mr Hill, but I will in the near future and you will be receiving a custodial sentence.'

Which I already knew, of course.

Then a female court clerk jumped up and said, 'Your honour, I just want to bring to your attention that Mr Hill is eligible for an indeterminate sentence, under the new IPP model. He's in that range and that is now a sentence available to the court.' The judge replied, 'Yes, thank you for the further clarification, we are looking into that.'

I didn't have a clue what they were on about, but it didn't sound good. I desperately wanted to find out where Dave had been taken, so I could get a message to someone.

I was taken back to the holding cell in the basement, and I went mad, ripping a bench from the wall and smashing it all over the place. The screws, fair play, let me try and get it all out, and when I'd calmed down a bit, came in and took me back to the Scrubs.

Two weeks later, I was taken back to court for sentencing. The judge did his recap — attempted murder, smashing up the police cars, endangering life...blah, blah, blah, and then said, 'We are giving you an Indeterminate Sentence Of Imprisonment for Public Protection, also known as an IPP...for a minimum term of 30 months.'

An IPP...and a minimum term of two and half a years. What does that fucking mean?

The judge was also quick to inform me that my time on remand would not be taken into consideration — a real kick in the bollocks.

I eventually lost my place in Kingston and my villa in Magaluf. Fuck knows how they even knew that was anything to do with me, but they find these things out. They'd already done a lot of homework along the way.

There was also always a considerable amount of cash in the chimney at the flat in Kingston, which I hadn't visited for ages. With hindsight, it would have been easier to rob my own flat than that Carphone Warehouse depot, but I wouldn't have done that to my ex and kids after all the grief I'd given her. Would it have still even been there? I know if I'd been left alone with it, it wouldn't.

The judge gave me a load more shit about what I'd done, and then I was taken back to the Scrubs...back to the same wing.

One of the screws said, 'What'dya get Hilly?'

'An IPP.'

He didn't really know what it was either, and then another screw said, 'It stands for 'indeterminate'. I think it means a life sentence, Hilly. Sorry, mate.'

'Life? Don't be stupid...it can't be.'

Another screw said, 'It can be up to 99 years. An indeterminate prison sentence is worse than a life sentence.'

Fucking hell, these screws were no help at all.

I was gutted on many levels. If I'd taken the nine years deal, I could be out in another two or three. But I'd never taken a deal in my life. I just didn't trust those fuckers.

Two days later I was sat in front of a psychologist.

'Mr Hill, do you know what an IPP is?'

'No.'

'It's an Indeterminate Public Protection (IPP) order...which means the public need to be protected from you.'

Well, I'd understood that by now, and there were certainly many people who needed to be protected from me...not least myself.

The psychologist continued, 'It's an indefinite sentence which means you are on licence for 99 years. Any breaches mean you can

be kept in or, when released, recalled anytime over the next 99 years.'
Just to clarify, here's an official explanation of an IPP...

The IPP was introduced in 2005 through the Criminal Justice Act 2003 and was intended to apply to dangerous people convicted of violent and sexual offences who did not merit a life sentence. People would serve a minimum term in prison (their tariff), during which time they would undertake work to reduce the risk they posed.

It became clear that I needed to take and pass several dedicated courses if I was ever to be allowed out again. But these would only be available to me once I had been allocated.

During this time, as I tried to wait patiently for my courses, I actually got 'on the board' — i.e a parole hearing. I think because I'd served two and half years on remand, and my IPP had a minimum term of 30 months, they had to at least put me in front of the panel. I didn't know it was an actual parole hearing until I sat in the room. I wasn't dreaming of being released yet anyway, but there was a small chance I could have been allocated to a Cat-C prison, for my good behaviour and work on the Conibeere.

I wasn't surprised when it was firm 'no'.

Now I'd been convicted, I was able to enrol on some general courses at the Scrubs. In 2007 that included Social Development, Level 1 Food Hygiene, the Crack Awareness Group and Victim Awareness — Restorative Justice.

I continued to pass any drugs tests through to early 2008 and then received a certificate for the PASRO (Prison-Addressing Substance Related Offending) programme, which focused on things like 'enhanced motivation to change', 'relapse prevention' and 'lifestyle change'.

For ETS (Enhanced Thinking Skills), a Christian group brought some victims of robbery into the prison, who described how their lives had changed, how scared they were now and the precautions they now take on a daily basis. One of the church ladies sat us in a circle. She had a bowl of water and was talking about 'the ripple effect'. She took out a huge potato and threw it aggressively into the water, which went everywhere. When I went back to my cell, I looked at the work sheet they gave us, which had wavy lines on it, like ripples, which explained how a victim's life could change from the way they lived before the job, and then after. It's not rocket science, when you think about it. And it did make me think about it and all the distress I'd caused.

I continued to work out in the gym as much as possible. Getting big again. One of my mates was getting 'roids' sent in, so I got on those too for a while. Apart from that, I was healthy and sober, and drug free. I felt great.

*****

Eighteen months or so into my IPP, I received a letter from Monica, which began 'To my white ape'. It was nice of her to take the time to find out I was still at the Scrubs. She explained that she had been 'off the scene', clean for six months and was loving motherhood. She said she had tried to write a letter to me many times, but couldn't find the right words. She claimed she had moved on from our relationship and said she would love to know that I had moved on too.

In reality, I had to move on. Of course, I had no option while inside, but if and when I got out again, I was finally getting my head around having to drastically change my life on the outside too. Monica and I didn't know another way of existing together. We'd done crack that first day we met, and our whole relationship revolved around it. Despite everything we'd been through, I was happy to hear she was doing well. I missed her badly and I also missed that destructive lifestyle and chaos too. But I knew I couldn't go back to it.

*****

I got my mate Gary a job on the Conibeere, and they put him two cells down from me. He had managed to hide a mobile phone in the lid of a washing liquid bottle.

One night, around February/March time, 2008, I had to help a screw at the first night centre give some methadone to a grubby new inmate, with tobacco stains all over his fingers and on his face.

I said to the screw, 'Who is this fucking geezer?'

'It's the music star, Pete Doherty.'

Which didn't mean a lot to me. I'd never heard of him, but I knew it was an opportunity, all the same.

Doherty was in the first night centre for a couple of weeks, buying drugs off whoever he could. I said to one of the screws, 'Shouldn't we get Pete over to the Conibeere, and he said, 'He's coming over anyway,' and I thought, 'That's handy.'

When he arrived, I decided to step in, selling him little bits of extra methadone and other pills I blagged from the unit, plus some other bits and pieces from the guys at the gym.

Some of the junkies in the drugs unit, if they were prescribed liquid methadone, they'd spit it into their mugs instead of swallowing it, over a period of a few days, and then sell it, so they could buy the proper stuff — heroin. Fucking disgusting.

Doherty was now two cells away from me. Result.

I'd get up at 6am, as usual, each morning and get all the medication ready for the prisoners on the unit.

'Pete, do you want anything extra?'

'Yes please, Ray.'

Me and Doherty became pals, and I supplied him every day — whatever I could get my hands on. He started telling me about his relationship with supermodel, Kate Moss.

A mate I was in touch with on the outside suggested we try and phone the papers up. Ask them if they needed anything from us?

By now Gary had been released, and had left me his phone, a Nokia I think. A little silver flip handset, one of the first camera phones that did multi-media messaging. My mate outside kept it topped up by texting me a code which I punched into the keypad. Only a few centimetres long, the phone fitted neatly in the lid of a large bottle of Comfort.

Then I got word from my pal. *The Sun* had bitten our hands off. He reckons he was told anything from Kate Moss, a letter or a card that she'd signed, would be worth five figures plus. But we couldn't find anything from Kate. Maybe the screws weren't giving Doherty all his mail. I gave my mate loads of details over the phone, and then sent photos I'd managed to take of Pete in a text.

Amazingly, a deal was done with *The Sun*, and a few days later, in April, 2008, we heard we'd made the front page. Wow. And fucking hell, my pal must have got a fair few quid for it, because the same day he put five grand in my mum's bank account.

Here are excerpts from *The Sun*'s front page story and double spread inside from April 16th, 2008, by Anthony France.

PETE STILL DOES HEROIN...HE'S CLUCKING FOR IT

PASTY Pete Doherty's manic craving for heroin has shocked fellow lags, The Sun can reveal.

The jailed Babyshambles rocker is shooting up with drugs smuggled into the detox unit of London's Wormwood Scrubs prison.

The heroin revelations came as The Sun obtained photos of 29 year-old Doherty behind bars, wearing prison-issue blue T-shirt and grey tracksuit bottoms.

The pictures, taken with a phone camera, show him gawping listlessly in his cell, brushing his teeth and talking to other lags on a landing.

Doherty was banged up for 3 1/2 months last week for failing to take drug tests ordered by a court after he admitted possessing heroin, crack, cannabis and the horse tranquiliser ketamine.

He is sharing a cell in the Scrubs' Conibeere detox wing with a 28-year-old drug dealer.

Doherty has struck up a friendship with a burly ex-streetfighter named Ray, who is protecting him after lags started a rumour the singer brought a stash of drugs with him from the outside.

The national press were all over *The Sun*'s scoop. *The Daily Mail/MailOnline* reported later that day...

The Ministry of Justice was poised to launch an inquiry today after pictures of Pete Doherty in his prison cell were smuggled out of a London jail.

The images show the singer inside Wormwood Scrubs, where he is being held after repeatedly breaching bail conditions imposed for drugs possession convictions.

The pictures are the most high-profile breach of prison security of their type since an image of Soham murderer Ian Huntley in his cell at Woodhill Prison, near Milton Keynes, was taken by an under-cover reporter.

Music magazine *NME* even ran a story. Fantastic, but not the kind of attention I needed. I couldn't believe my mate had given my first name to *The Sun*. Within a couple of hours of story breaking, the head of security at the prison came crashing through my cell door, clearly about to launch his own version of the Ministry of Justice's inquiry.

'Get your fucking gear together. You're going down the block, you're nicked.'

'What you talking about?'

'You're nicked, Hilly, you wanker. You've put us all in the shit.'

What could I say? I knew I was going down the block, anyway.

I'd love to speak to Pete Doherty to explain my side of the story and why I did it. It would be great if he did a podcast with me, because I did protect him, and we got on really well. It was so hard to turn down the money, especially as I knew it could go straight to my mum, and help her out.

Pete talked about the experience in his own autobiography, *A Likely Lad*. Here's what he said...

The Scrubs was another Category B prison, but it had a terrible reputation. It was old, Victorian, dirty, rat-infested and rundown, full of murderers, rapists and terrorists. While I was inside The Sun ran a picture on their front page with the headline about me smoking heroin in my cell. That was a load of bollocks. There was no way I was smoking heroin in the cell on the detox wing where they put me after induction. Someone took a picture of me brushing my teeth, which was the photo on the front page of The Sun. I remember distinctly someone saying 'Smile' and I turned round to the cell door brushing my teeth, and this other prisoner had a camera phone. He said, 'So, if we get money for this, how do you want to split it?' 'No, you do what you like, I'm not getting involved. I don't want their money.' Then the next day they got the photo out and it was in the papers.

There were all sort of threats while I was in Scrubs, people saying they're going to knock me out just because I'd got a name in the papers. I was intrigued to meet the people supposed to be doing the knocking out — they normally turned out to be all right, if slightly warped. Ray, an old bare-knuckle fighter, made himself busy on my behalf. There was all kinds going on in that place.

(The prison governor) she actually had me sent to the segregation unit after that Sun story, thought I was undermining all her good work.

I did feel bad for Pete, and for the screws, because they had looked after me and they were good people. They got in trouble because there was a phone on the unit, which they never found, and then photos appeared on the front of the biggest-selling newspaper in the country. Back in those days, probably the worst thing that could happened for them. But, as I have always maintained, it's dog eat dog in prison, and that includes the screws. I had a trusted position on the Conibeere, but when Doherty came in I just saw pound signs.

REBEL WITH A CAUSE

After a couple of weeks on the block, I was shipped out from the Scrubs to The Mount, in Bovington in Hertfordshire, complete with the same mobile phone up my arse. Fortunately, it was still before they installed x-ray chair machines on entry for prisoners that could detect that sort of thing, and known in the trade as a 'body orifice security scanner'. They'd spun my cell at the Scrubs and found nothing, but for some reason didn't carry out a physical inspection while I was on the block.

Meeting Pete Doherty had ruined any chance of me getting early parole. It seemed like it had put me back a few years. I still didn't know enough about the IPP at this stage or how it would affect me. But on the other hand, it did me a favour in a roundabout way, because I needed to be allocated and that's when I started doing my psychology courses.

On arrival at HMP Mount, a Cat-C, I realised this was another unique prison. The inmates there seemed to have a lot more responsibility. It was deliberate, because The Mount was not just a working prison, it was a learning prison too. I was met by a couple of inmates, who acted like they were almost checking me in to the place, like a hotel.

The were single cells throughout The Mount. Touch. Everything there was about 'the board' on the wall at the start of any wing. It informed each prisoner what they were doing every day.

Very quickly, I was taken to a room and finally told all aspects of the IPP: what was required and expected, if I was to eventually get released. It was like my card had suddenly been marked. I'd been in the Scrubs for two or three years, and I'd hardly been told anything. It was a real shock.

In a way, I was lucky because I was one of the first prisoners to get an IPP, so I was able to enrol on the initial courses available. But it does what it says on the tin. Indeterminate means 'not exactly known, established, or defined.' It's indefinite, and if you don't do the courses and you don't try and understand why you've done what you've done, you don't get out. Simple.

It's a mixture of group classes, a dozen or so people, and also one-to-ones. In the first week, I had to role-play a robbery in front of my class...get up and go through the whole routine. 'Get on the floor you fucking cunt...' Etc, etc.

I told the class about a girlfriend I had in the early '90s called Ellen, who managed a local branch of Barclays Bank. I'd met her at Lucky's in Ealing when I was doing the door. Ellen really shouldn't have had anything to do with me, but we clicked...and she also loved a bit of shovel. I'd been seeing Ellen on and off for a month. We had some wild nights on the gear and then she asked me to go to a dinner party with some of her bank friends at a house in Perivale. Suited and booted, I looked so smart, and got coked up in the toilet after the meal. When a lady asked me what I did for a living, I told her I was a bank robber, so she said, 'Are you one of those people who put guns in people's faces?' When I said, 'Yes,' she went mad, and rushed straight over to the host. Turned out she had been held up in her bank recently. Me and Ellen never saw eye to eye after that. But for the first time, in that moment, it made me think about the victims, and what other people go through. I'd never come face to face before with someone who experienced the sort of trauma I was so often responsible for.

There was never any room for sentiment in my line of work. I never set out to harm anybody; I just wanted the money or goods I was trying to rob. Security guards and bank workers were just obstacles in my way. So many times, a guard with a gun in their face refuses to hand over a bag of money that isn't theirs. I guess it's a natural instinct that kicks in. In that split second, they completely forget that the companies they work for, anything that handles cash over the pavement, are fully insured.

Up until some of the basic courses I first took on remand at the Scrubs, like ETS (Enhanced Thinking Skills), I hadn't ever officially been involved with the psychology side of it all. Nobody had ever sat me down to look at that aspect of it. It's crazy to think that on the many occasions I was locked up and released, there was so little support.

Early on at The Mount, I managed to pass a gym instructor course and more regular voluntary drug tests, plus an initial course in CALM (Controlling Anger and Learning to Manage It), which had a total of 12 modules.

As time went on, I knew people on IPPs who had been on the waiting list for modules to begin for three or four years, which is tough because the actual course takes two years anyway.

Even when you manage to get on the right course, the sessions might be once or twice a month at best. But I think that was all part of it. The inconsistency, the system — trying to break you down to see how you react. It's a challenge to take the course on in the first place, and there are so many individual battles during the process too.

My problem was that I kept failing courses, because nines times out of ten, most prisoners did. And that's because we're not the kind of people who take courses, let alone pass them. It sounds easy. Ticking some boxes and saying the right things, but it's really hard...for us, at least.

I had to try and look at the positives. Being on crack meant that I carried out that crazy job dressed as a policeman. Then getting the IPP might just save my life.

*****

Looking back, I must have been paranoid, but at the start it seemed to me that all the psychologists were young women in their 20s. I felt that they dressed provocatively, to see if we could handle it. I felt like, if I said the wrong thing, I'd be in trouble. But like I said, maybe I was being paranoid.

The screws would come into my cell and tell me when my next appointment was, and I'd need to make a note of it in an exercise book. If I missed an appointment, they wouldn't come and remind me. In a world where every day is the same, you have to be ready at the right time on the right day, or get a black mark. Even making the necessary notes in my textbook was difficult for me. But I steadily made progress. They wanted me to complete all the CALM modules, but Christina Rowe, my Offending Manager, argued that wasn't necessary, that I'd kept out of trouble long enough.

My 30 month IPP tariff had expired six months earlier so that, coupled with all the good behaviour, meant my first parole board at The Mount came in May 2010. Including my two and a half years on remand at the Scrubs, I'd been banged up for six years now. When Christina told me there was a former police officer on the panel, I knew it was going to be really difficult. At the hearing, as I sat there nervously awaiting the outcome, Christina put a big word in for me, as she repeated in an official letter...

On the basis of the information currently available to me and following my contact with Mr Hill, I am inclined to support a move to open conditions. He has engaged well with appropriate offending behaviour interventions and I am of the opinion that, in this respect, there is little more which could be offered or gained by the continued detention of Mr Hill within closed conditions.

The Offending Supervisor added...

I would recommend open conditions for Mr Hill as this would help with his reintegration into society and he could put into practice the skills he has gained from his courses.

However, an intervention from the authorities put a kibosh on any hopes I had off a lower category or being released. The letter stated...

The Secretary Of State would like to invite the panel to ascertain what Mr Hill's plans are if released. The Secretary is also aware that Mr Hill committed the index crime for financial gain to buy crack cocaine and considers that if he is released and unable to take up employment immediately, he may revert back to drug misuse as he will be unable to fund his habit.

The Secretary Of State considers that Mr Hill should not be transferred to open conditions or released on licence. Mr Hill needs to prove that he is able to abstain from drugs in closed conditions for a long period of time. Once he has managed this successfully, he should then be given the opportunity to be sufficiently tested in open conditions and develop his vocational skills and have home visits to form part of a considered release plan.

That coupled with the copper on the panel putting his foot down meant I wasn't going home any day soon.

A month later, CARAT (Counselling Assessment Referral Advice Thoroughcare) tried to push my case further by writing a letter to 'Parole Services' that included this paragraph...

Having completed the 'Crack Awareness' and PASRO (Prisons Addressing Substance Related Offending) courses before his transfer to The Mount, and taking into account his presenting a lack of any further substance concerns, we decided to keep Mr Hill's file suspended. Since that time we have had no referrals from the Testing Department or any other information which might lead us to believe he was in need of any further work. Given that there is no other substance related concerns and no evidence of any alcohol misuse history we are satisfied to keep his file suspended until nearer to release. Raymond is open to working with drug services on release, with which we will be able to assist him.

I was then advised that I could appeal the decision and so, with the help of legal aid, solicitors wrote to The Parole Board, and explained...

The experts appearing before the panel were supportive of Mr Hill. [Because] The Parole Board declined to release Mr Hill or to recommend his transfer to open conditions, Mr Hill seeks to challenge this decision by way of Judicial Review. The Parole Board gave no reasons why the professional opinion of the probation officers was ignored and their recommendation rejected.

Then nothing. So that was that...as usual. However, maybe, just maybe, I was actually getting closer to being released. I certainly had some good people at the prison pushing my case.

Over the next seven or eight months, I kept up the pressure by completing courses on Healthy Balanced Living, How Crack Cocaine

Works, Relapse Prevention and Managing Relapses.

Most of the courses are like psychology for beginners, so there are lots of silly drawings and then it's all about triggers, which are the most important thing to try and understand. Once you've got your head around them, then they say to you, 'Well, if you had challenged your thoughts along the way, you wouldn't be in here again. If you had thoughts about possibly hurting someone, killing someone, getting caught, getting locked up, and doing loads more time…if you had seriously thought about that, Mr Hill, then you might not be here now. You must always weigh up the pros and cons.'

So when I finally understood that every crime I'd committed came from a trigger, and that I could examine the triggers that would potentially get me in trouble, and then work through the possible consequences, then things began to fall into place.

When I spoke to a psychologist, there was also another prison staff member listening in and watching me throughout. I had to make sure I had good references from the screws and the gym. So in the run up to those course results, I had to behave. No violence, no getting involved in stuff I got involved in previously. They started pulling me up on things like, 'When you were mopping out the showers this morning, people came in and you shouted at them to get out.' When previously, the screws were asking me to bash certain people up in the showers, and that was no problem. Now they wanted me to conform, but my instinct had always been not to conform.

I got in trouble along the way, mostly I think, for talking too honestly. Like about the ducks, of which there were hundreds waddling about The Mount. I used to throw scraps of chicken out of my cell window to the ducks, and they'd gobble it up, when I was sure ducks shouldn't really be eating chicken. I likened it in one of my counsellor sessions to prehistoric man's dog eat dog mentality to survive. Apparently, that was not the right thing to say, because that was me trying to excuse my crimes.

Another counsellor I had, her boyfriend was a gym screw, a PTI. I'm sure he was feeding her information about me being too aggressive in the gym, where I worked, shouting at other lags to put their weights away at the end of their session, and keep the place tidy. She mentioned it a few times. How else would she have known?

So it felt like there were still always obstacles in my way. It was so much to get my head around. I saw a couple of people go crazy and smash the room up. I came close to doing that myself, because I've always felt predisposed to do that.

When you sit back and think about it, the courses are just common sense, and then the drawings suddenly all make sense. Especially when you're out of the game...and sober. If I go down a certain street, or take a certain path, that's a trigger. I should turn around and go the other way. If I went down that road, I might see a crack dealer, or meet another criminal who will try and tempt me into doing something I shouldn't. And because I have a history of violence, it's even more important to make the right decisions to cross over or walk the other way. But it's fucking hard.

The final process was sitting with the head counsellor, Wendy. She helped me so much. She really understood where I was coming from and in turn she unlocked cells in my head, that had never been opened before. It took six months, but it was six months well spent. When I explained my backstory, what had happened to me as a child, at my aunty and uncle's house and then at the kids' home in Wales, we were both crying. It was an emotional moment and one which I think was a real turning point in my life. For once, I was humble, vulnerable and everything just poured out. It was the first time in more than 50 years that I'd spoken to anybody, let alone professionally, about what I had endured as a child. In fact, I'd never told anybody the whole story — just bits and pieces to a few close friends and cell-mates.

*****

I knew things were looking better for me when I was moved to a special wing where people are sent after good behaviour, or if they are close to release. The cells are open all day, so you can come and go as you please, until lock-up, which itself is later than normal. There's a kitchen where you cook for yourself. There's little or no screws knocking about, and I still had my nice job in the gym. I earned extra spends from personal training sessions in the gym with various cons – helping to build them up before they got out.

I'd spend the extra cash on whole chickens, which I'd cook up every day and enjoy with a large portion of roast potatoes. Things were cushy, and I was convinced my release might finally happen. But I had a setback...it was inevitable.

I'd been looking after an rich old Iranian guy from Edgware Road for a mate of mine called Fish, who was also on an IPP, but had not progressed to our 'good behaviour' wing. Fish had minded this fella previously, and appeared on our wing one day, when he really shouldn't have been there. I made the mistake of telling Fish that the Iranian crime boss had said he was only interested in him for his money, which we all were, of course. Fish lost it, and ran up to the TV room, and bashed this old boy up in front of all of his little mob, and then managed to fuck off.

Suddenly, I was locked up, and I hadn't been banged up during the day since I'd been on that wing. Then I was dragged off to the block, for instigating the whole thing. Fuck, this was the last thing I needed. Down in segregation, Fish was in the next cell. 'Stop whinging, you silly cunt,' he told me, unsympathetically.

After a few days, I was told I couldn't go back to the good behaviour wing, but I wasn't getting nicked either. I was being put on the Bristow wing on the ground floor, which still had a lot of the same privileges, and that I should keep out of trouble. A pal of the Iranian guy, also Muslim, who ran the wing there was giving it the large one, so I offered him out in his cell. He told me to keep my head down, and everything would be sweet. Thankfully it was, but not for my old ticker...

One night I was dreaming I was in the gym, asking the guy I was working out with to put more and more weights on my chest. When I woke up in the early hours, I was having what I can only describe as a heart attack. I sat doubled-over at the end of my bed until daylight. I didn't ring my bell, I just tried to ride it out.

A few weeks later, I was sitting on my bed and started seeing so many colours, all over the cell. Then I collapsed on the floor. I managed to drag myself to the toilet and was violently sick in the pan for what seemed like ages. The guy next door heard me and got on his bell to the screws. A couple appeared and were talking to themselves rather than attending to me.

'Is he soaking wet with sweat?'

'Yeah, I think he is...'

And then they left me there.

The next morning, I was taken to hospital for a check-up and was told I may have had a heart attack — a second one, I believe — but that was it. I was just sent back to my cell. It shook me up, because I could have died at any point over the previous 36 hours, and I don't think anyone would have really cared. Prison isn't the best place to have a heart attack. You really just have to suck it all up and get on with it.

However, there was another ray of light. It seemed my daughter and son from my marriage, now both adults, were intrigued enough to see how their old man was getting on, because they paid me their first and only visit in prison when I was on the Bristow wing at The Mount. That nutter, Fish, was still on the block, because he was escorted past us to a closed visit, and was bantering with me and shouting the odds, as he was ushered through. The visit with the kids went really well, and it gave me hope that we could have some kind of relationship if and when I ever came out.

*****

Meanwhile, Wendy did everything she could to help get me released. She also fought hard against me doing an extra C.S.C.P (Cognitive Self-Changing Programme) course, arguing that I had already jumped through enough hoops.

I also had a case officer, a screw assigned to me and other inmates. Other screws reported to him on how I behaved in various situations each day. So he would play a massive part in me eventually getting released (or not) and worked with Christina in probation to write up any reports needed for any possible parole hearings coming up.

I saw Wendy twice a week, an hour at a time. For the first time in my life, I started to make real progress in the way that I processed recollections of certain events and the way that I actually processed my own thoughts. Wendy said something in my mind had been trapped. Like it had a large cobweb in it. A cell that was clogged and needed to be cleared out. And this blockage had continued to make me be the person I was, and act the way I had.

Finally, in the summer of 2012, another parole hearing came up. My case officer tried to argue I hadn't completed all the courses and processes, but, based on Wendy and Christina's verdicts, the parole board were satisfied that I'd finally ticked all their boxes.

It took a long three months before I was informed that I was actually being released, and another six weeks before I was eventually free to go, which felt like six years. I'd served just over eight years in total, my longest and, maybe, just maybe, my last ever bit of bird.

I was obviously looking forward to getting out, but this time it was going to be completely different from any other release. Finally, I knew I couldn't go back to my old life. I was heading to a hostel, not back to a life of crime and privilege. Armed finally with the right things — loads of life skills which might help me become a straight-goer.

LAST CHANCE SALOON

I wasn't exactly thrilled at the prospect of this new life. It was the first time I'd come out of prison to nothing. No money, no relationship, no prospects. This time it had to be different.

Like any time I'd got out over the years, getting the date a month or so before release was so exciting, but as the days drew nearer I began to appreciate exactly what I'd signed up for this time. I didn't have any decent clothes for my release, so a guy who had just come in gave me the jeans and sweatshirt he was wearing. The jeans were so tight, and I was so big, I spent my final weeks doing as much cardio in the gym as possible. Bike, rowing machine, cross trainer… and watched what I ate. No carbs.

My mate Gary Francis picked me up in his Mercedes. I hadn't been in a car for years, and I can remember being frightened as Gary put his foot down on a country lane. He might have only been going 50mph, but it felt double that. Gary drove me straight to the parole hostel in the leafy suburbs off Ealing Broadway, where I met Christina, and was shown to my room, which was a bit bigger than a cell, with a bed that wasn't that much better. I met some other recently released cons, but I kept myself to myself.

The next day, I had an appointment at the job centre in Ealing Broadway to explain my personal situation, which I'd never needed to take seriously before. For all those years away this time, I was due a one-off payment of £400 or something silly like that, but to add insult to injury they didn't have me on the system as Hill. They had me down as Rowlings.

I was in that hostel for six months. Cameras everywhere. Every day, police running up and down the stairs, recalling people. Younger guys with their whole lives ahead of them, who didn't give a fuck. But this was my last chance. One wrong move with this IPP and I was back inside. Possibly forever.

I was signed up to the local doctor's surgery, and had to go for regular check-ups. The hostel was in such a posh area of Ealing the patients and staff looked at me like I was a piece of shit. I could just feel it.

It's not easy being an old ex-convict. It feels like every person you deal with, in any position of authority, knows they have the power to put you back where you came from. I had to dig deep and try remember and use the skills I was taught in prison to deal with these people in the correct and proper way, so as not to offend anybody, and get myself in trouble. And always make sure I was back by 6pm, or too many of those and I'd definitely be looking at a recall.

Even though I'd been keeping my head down and sticking to the rules, any time the police pulled up outside the hostel and ran up the stairs to nick someone, I feared the recall was for me. I guess it's just natural for me to think the system is against me.

It's all the same thing. Being institutionalised. I could be holed up in a palace, but if I couldn't come and go when I wanted, it would feel like a prison sentence. Being banged up is being banged up.

One day they said to me, 'Right, you need to go and see a housing officer in Kingston.' They told me they'd found me somewhere to live permanently, but it felt like an old people's home. I thought, are they sure? It was warden-controlled. I could imagine getting woken up throughout the night and checked up on. Or nutty old residents badgering me all the time. We all have to get old, but there were some really old people in there. Sitting at tables, playing cards and dominoes...and dribbling. Everyone smelt like death. I said, 'I'm sorry, this is not a bit of me.' So they said, 'You can only refuse three places you're offered, or you'll go back inside. Recalled.'

So I had two more chances.

As usual, I spent a lot of time at Mum's house in Mill Hill Road. When I first got out, I was sat in the kitchen there, and my sister, Diana, came in on a zimmer frame, all buckled up, with septicaemia, from treading on a rusty nail. It broke my heart to see her like that.

A couple of weeks later, my housing officer took me to some flats opposite Ikea in Wembley. That was awful too. One room, with a shower, sink, cupboard and bed, and a shared kitchen. There were so many different nationalities in there, the combined smell of all the different food was awful. They showed me a room over-looking the north circular, but I couldn't open the window, because it was so caked in grime from the pollution. I could only imagine what is what like at night, with everyone running around, loads of different types of music. I said, 'Nah, this ain't for me either.'

My probation officer at Hendon gave me a good talking to. 'Mr Hill, if you can't or won't conform, you will go back to prison.'

'But you can't throw me to the wolves like that. And if I go back, and get in a bit of trouble, I might never come out.'

I'd started using a gym in Ealing Broadway. A proper place called Eden's, in a basement.

I was drug-tested weekly after my release, and had to report to a centre in Hendon, which was a pain to travel to. The counsellors kept saying the same thing, week after week. If I get back on drugs, I'd be recalled immediately. I'd had more than 200 negative tests during my IPP by the time I got out. I still had all the slips, so I was annoyed they were still testing me on the outside, but obviously it's different. There's temptation everywhere.

In February, 2013, I received a letter from the Ministry of Justice (MOJ) telling me I had been at Ealing Hostel for four months now and *'you have fulfilled your condition of residence...'*

It added...

There are offenders being released from custody that the service must accommodate and your bed is required for others. You will no longer have a place at the hostel after April 1st, 2013 and you must leave on or before that date.

Fucking hell, I needed to find somewhere...sharpish.

A couple of days later, I came out of the gym and heard 'beep, beep'...a pal of mine I'd been in The Mount with.

'Alright Ray, how are things?'

'Alright, mate, I'm at a hostel. I've just refused two places and now they're about to chuck me out.'

'Fucking hell, do you want a flat?'

Just like that.

My pal took me to Harrow and showed me a one-bedroomed flat. Which was great, so kind of him, but this would have to be approved. I explained to my housing officer it was a guy I was in prison with, because there's no point in lying to them, they find out. So they went down and inspected it. Thankfully, and very fortunately, in March 2013 I received a letter from the MOJ giving me permission to move into the flat.

It was like a gift from God. My own front room, my own bedroom. Going to the gym regularly. Everything seemed good.

I was now free, but I wasn't really free. This flat was better than where I could have ended up, but it still wasn't anything like what I was used to over the years. I always kept that flat clean, because prison makes you like that. The rent was paid for by the council, and then I had £120 a week benefits to live on.

Probation said they could get me a job in Asda or Iceland, but that definitely ain't a bit of me either. I was worried I'd start watching the patterns of the cash collections and end up plotting to rob the gaff. In the end, they actually advised me not to get a job, because then I'd have to pay my own rent. It felt like they wanted me to reoffend. Almost leaving me with no option.

I had another heart scare, just after I moved to Harrow. I had an indigestion pain, which started giving me jip in bed one night. In the morning, the pain was still there. I struggled to walk up the hill to my mum's place later that day. She called an ambulance and I was taken to Hammersmith Hospital. Kept overnight for tests, I had three stents inserted to unclog my arteries. Another close shave.

A counsellor at the drugs unit I visited as a condition of my IPP release told me I was 'lucky' to be 'given' a flat in Harrow by my pal.

'Lucky?' I screamed. 'You're fucking joking, aren't you? I've lost my kids, my wife, my girlfriend, my homes and millions of pounds. I've come out to nothing.'

I was fuming and I think he shit himself a little bit because a week later I was told he'd recommended I didn't need to see him anymore. I'd done so much talking at The Mount, I'd had enough of all that anyway.

*****

Back out in the big bad world, I nearly got a recall thanks to MAPPA (Multi-Agency Public Protection Arrangements). MAPPA is various agencies such as the police, the Prison Service and probation work together to protect the public by managing the risks posed by offenders living in the community. It's an agency of ex-policemen, shop-keepers, postmen, members of the public...whoever wants to get involved. Anyone can be a member of MAPPA and help keep an eye on ex-convicts.

As I walked home from a probation visit, a car pulled up. It was a mate, who had only ever done six months in prison, for driving offences.

'Where you going, Ray?'

'Chiswick.'

'Jump in, I'll give you a lift.'

So he dropped me to Chiswick. I got out of the car, and my phone rang.

'Mr Hill, this is your probation officer.'

'What's up?'

'Can you come to the office please?'

'What now, is there a problem?

'Yes, now. Yes, there is a problem.'

Fucking hell, I'm going to get recalled here.

On the way back to the probation office, on the bus and walking along the road, I was looking for undercover police, any car that was two or three handed.

I went in, and my probation officer said, 'You were in a car with a man (called so and so), is that correct?

'Yeah, he gave me a lift. I was going to Chiswick, he was going to Chiswick.'

'So you arranged to meet him?'

'No, not at all.'

'You're sure you didn't make a meet with him, Mr Hill?'

'Yes, if I was making a meet with him, the car would have been parked outside.'

'But, Mr Hill, this gentleman is a known criminal.'

'He's done six months for something minor, yes.'

'He's a gangster, Mr Hill.'

'A gangster? He's just a kid.'

'You must not be involved with any criminality...at all.'

'But I've been in prison most of my life, the only people I know are criminals.'

Apparently, someone saw me get into my pal's car and by the time I got to Chiswick, they'd done a check on the car and found out who he was. Luckily, the car was in his name and he had a licence and insurance. They had checkpoints and a MAPPA man spotted us, or maybe they let the local MAPPA man know I was coming out of the probation office at that time. By the time I got back to the probation office, via MAPPA, they had a photo of me in the car that somebody took on their phone. They want you to feel, wherever you go, they are on you and, to be fair, I probably needed that early doors.

There were a couple of times, at the hostel, where I was suspicious of people hanging around. One guy took a load of photos of me from the street. I wondered if he was working for any of my old connections, but he could have easily been from probation or MAPPA.

For a while, I worked for a jeweller in the Garden, minding him. There's so much gear in the safes in the shops down there, it's frightening, but even being around those sort of high-net-worth areas just wasn't good for me. I got ideas.

My Ming vases and some rare paintings were out there somewhere. I found out Lionel didn't have that pub where he had stored them for me anymore, and it was impossible for me to try and find him or the pots and pieces of art, which were off the back of a lorry anyway, without contacting the wrong kind of people and even if I did find them, handling that sort of shit would have breached my probation.

I received a letter during that period, telling me to stay away from a named person, who I'd worked with in the past, and who I hadn't even met up with yet since being out.

Over the next months and years, contact with my probation office dramatically reduced. I had the odd meeting, but I could tell getting the IPP officially removed from my record wasn't going to be easy.

A SENTENCE OUTSIDE

When I was last released, so much had changed again. It was the story of my life. A common thread. I spent a big chunk of the so-called Swinging Sixties in Borstal and then lost most of the '70s because of my two-year YP for the wine store robbery and the five I did for Bridstow Place. When I was released at the end of the '70s, I couldn't stay out of trouble long enough and spent most of the '80s banged up as well. The '90s were the first decade since the '50s as a kid, when I felt like I was out more than I was in. It just seemed I was always being released to new eras. Mods and rockers, yuppies, acid house, mobile phones, the internet — and CCTV every fucking where!

And that's the thing. Today, there are cameras all over the place. That's why I reckon most police stations have shut, because they don't need police stations anymore. If it's not captured on CCTV, it's on people's mobile phones and then uploaded on social media. People can't wait to put things up on *Twitter* or *Facebook*. Buses have cameras and cyclists love recording stuff. Anyone wearing a body-cam or a Go-Pro is a police officer now. Even me, if I've got a camera phone.

There was those supposedly encrypted phones that tricked thousands of criminals all over the world into thinking they were on a network that couldn't be accessed, but it was largely set up by the police themselves.

In prison, they could stop mobile phones in a heartbeat, but they don't want to, because mobile phones inside actually grass up loads of people. So the prisoners are becoming police too, without even realising it.

Aside from the enforcement work, I was caught and convicted for a handful of biggish jobs, but I've probably done another 30 or so decent-sized ones over the years successfully, so that's a pretty good success rate. On top of that, I reckon only around 20% of planned jobs actually happened. So that's a lot of jobs being researched, discussed and, if we were lucky, actually completed. When I wasn't banged up, it became my life.

Now, I just wanted to be left alone to get on with doing my time, because that's what I was looking at now — a sentence on the outside.

It took a long time to get used to not wanting to be active anymore, but not talking to old mates, contacts or villains is difficult — when that's all I've ever known. I had to become reclusive, keep myself to myself. But it's so hard when all I associated being outside with, was being active.

It is virtually impossible when you get out not to talk to people you've been away with. When I was a YP, I knew 15 or 20 people from my Borstal. Then in adult prison, I knew 30+ odd from my YP, and it went on and on, the more I was in and out. Then the more friends you make inside, the more like-minded people you get to know on the outside. On the other hand, you can come out after a long stretch and go back to your manor, and most people you know have moved out of that area to better themselves. Unfortunately, over the years, there have always been a few people left knocking around to tempt me back into trouble.

As I got older, there were also more and more people I knew when I was younger who hadn't been in prison then, but had now. So I don't always know when I'm talking to someone if they have or haven't been inside. That's just the way things are for me.

*****

Towards the end of 2019, I was given some hope by the probation office that my IPP might finally be cancelled. I went through extra assessments over the next few months, and all the paperwork was completed. Then Covid hit, stunning the world. Of course, mentally, I was fully equipped for a lockdown. Close friends were great and dropped food and supplies round me to regularly, but I'm sure I coped better than most during the pandemic. A lot of the time, it felt no different to being in prison. Then, as things slowly got back to normal, I was told that my application to have my IPP revoked had not been processed, due to Covid, and actually hadn't even been submitted yet. It was a kick in the teeth.

* * * * *

In 2021, through podcasts I was asked to do, I was so fortunate to reconnect with the son of scrap dealer Dennis Haley, the well-known regular at The Anchor, our infamous local in Acton back in the day. Terry Haley messaged me offering me a set of weights. We met up and only then did I realise who he was. I hadn't seen him since he was a teenager, more than 50 years earlier. Dennis' scrap business went into liquidation in the mid-'70s. Years later, Terry set up his own business, now a hugely successful metals operation called BFA Recycling based in Uxbridge, so fair play to him.

Terry helped get me out of the flat in Harrow, and moved me into one of his properties nearby, and has helped me put this book together, which I'm eternally grateful for. Terry has been amazing. He's a proper decent person, a Godsend and true gentleman, who I'm so lucky to have looking out for me, and who has been a massive part of keeping me out of trouble. I'm overwhelmed by the fantastic support I have around me.

When I was last released the new big thing, of course, was social media, which in recent years I've embraced by recording regular videos for my *YouTube* channel *'Bang Bang' Ray Hill*, a name given to me by Christian Morgan and Marvin Herbert, the people I did my first podcast with. I've put out hundreds now and (at the time of going to print) have almost 20,000 subscribers and millions of views logged of the online content I've been involved in. I film myself on my phone, attached to a stick, tied to a weight-lifting bar. I sit on a stall, with a huge photo of Wormwood Scrubs on the wall behind me, and chat away about various times and incidents during my life of crime and being inside. For some reason, people love to hear about violence. Most of these types of channels are run by people who interview old gangsters, and there aren't many of us left. I've also done podcasts for the likes of LADbible and my pal Shaun Attwood, which has been great, but there are not many old-timers like me, who chat directly to camera about themselves. I find it helps to talk, and it also gives me something to do.

I'd love to finally apply for a driving licence, so I could get about a bit more, but they'll never give me one now. I sit in my flat at night sometimes without the TV on, in the dark, and I suddenly realise five or six hours have passed, and I've been sat in the same spot, haven't moved an inch. Just sitting there thinking about prison and everything that's happened to me. Everything I've done. The hurt I've caused. Like Harry Haward, with the prison cell he created in the basement of his pub, if I ever have any criminal thoughts I go into my office and stare at that huge print of the Scrubs, and that's the only deterrent I need.

I still try and look after myself and work out with weights in a gym that Terry Haley built for me at the top of the plot where I live, but I have to be careful with my stents. I'm lucky that keeping fit in prison throughout my life and from such a young life, despite my drug addictions, has stood me in good stead and given me that discipline.

My dream is to set up a programme at our gym so we could train young offenders to become personal trainers. It would be great to get some of my old friends from boxing or, who I've trained with in the past, involved. It would be amazing to give something back, especially to kids who find it hard to get an opportunity when they are released from prison.

I do miss boxing, though. I had 42 unlicensed fights in total. Twice a week, most weeks. Won 38, drew two and lost two. Proper scraps. Not like this *YouTube* scene now, where there is less actual boxing and consequences, and even more rules than the professional game we were never a part of. Fair play to them, though, they're earning fortunes.

*****

I've been out over ten years now, and my life has completely changed. It had to. It would be very hard for me to take now if I got a recall. Impossible, in fact. I wouldn't be able to do the bird. I really think I'd die in prison if I ever went back.

If I went in again, and touch wood that never happens, nobody would know who I was. I'm too old now to be anybody inside. Standard. Eventually, I had to realise and appreciate that I just couldn't do crime any more. Thank God I got an IPP, though, because otherwise,

I wouldn't have the tools to stop me going back in again.

Others go back to prison to survive, because there's nothing out here for them. If they can't exist taking drugs out here, they think they're better off inside. A pal's kid came out of prison recently and wanted to go back in, because he said he could get as much puff, crack or whatever as he wanted, and had also been pulling some of the female screws too. I know of a female inmate who had relations with her prison's governor to get early release. Which doesn't surprise me, because I read that more than 80 prison staff, mostly female, have been sacked or reprimanded since 2013 for having affairs with inmates.

Just before we published this book, a video of a female screw having sex with an inmate in a cell in Wandsworth, filmed by another guy smoking what looked like a joint, went viral. It was also featured in *The Sun*, this time online, 16 years after my photos of Pete Doherty appeared in the printed version.

The screw pleaded guilty and was convicted awaiting sentencing. I read that the prisoners weren't being investigated, which wouldn't surprise me, because that would open up a whole other can of worms. And then they'd have to investigate the whole nick, and the authorities would worry what else they might find, at what is supposed to be their toughest prison. I should imagine the inmates were moved on, like I was so many times. Out of sight, out of mind. And they probably shifted all the screws somewhere too, and shipped a new lot in. Yes, the governor and prison service had been massively mugged off, but it's all about damage limitation.

It was a crazy graphic video, which went viral so quickly. What were they all thinking? Apart from anything else, I couldn't believe how many trainers those two guys had in their cells. Racks of them. We were only allowed two pairs, maximum.

*****

A life of 'old school crime' is virtually impossible now. The Proceeds Of Crime Act (POCA) was a big turning point. It fucked a lot of people. The days of getting a ten stretch, doing your time and coming out to your money have gone...but that's the fucking point.

You go into prison as a big-time Charlie potato, used to earning £20k a week, and now you're fighting over a £15 week job in the kitchen. Some well-off cons are so used to living like kings outside, they're desperate to live the best life they can inside. They don't want to work in prison, so they use other people's 'canteen' money to buy their own stuff. Then they use their cash on the outside to help those con's family and friends. So every time that prisoner spends £50 for them in jail, they'll spend a few hundred for them on the outside. We've all done it, on both sides, but it's obviously got harder over the years to have any cash outside.

Although prison in the '60s and '70s didn't ever deter me from committing more crime, I reckon that type of tough regime would sort out a lot of young criminals today, who are spoiled in comparison. It's all about human rights now. We didn't have rights.

Take that recent *Channel 4* programme, *Banged Up*, where they put celebrities in a prison with a bunch of old cons. They should have put the celebs in a proper fucked up old jail. Now that would have been a TV show.

Most prisons are just too cushy now. The cells have actual phones in them. You give the screws a list of your favourite numbers, they check them out and then you can have long calls with your loved ones. I've been told screws are listening into the calls, perving over birds talking dirty to their partners.

Other screws are earning fortunes bringing gear in. They say it's coming in on drones, but c'mon, if you're a young screw and you can earn a couple of grand a week on top of your basic salary, which might only be that a month? It's actually quite a straightforward piece of work — certainly compared to what most of us did, to get put away.

Back in the day, if you sold drugs inside, you'd get slaughtered — it just wasn't allowed. Now, it's almost encouraged. Sex offenders are even allowed to buy drugs, because if they spend money, the dealers and the screws let it go. It's business. In recent times, Wandsworth was put on 'special measures' by the chief inspector of prisons when tests revealed 44% of prisoners tested positive for drugs.

People do what they need to do. A lot of people ran me down for selling the Doherty photos to *The Sun* — inmates and people on the outside — but most of them would have done the same. I knew I could raise some funds for my mum, so it was a great opportunity for me. Pound signs never leave you, especially inside. When a rock star came in, even though he looked fucked, I had to make the most of it. In the end, me and Pete both sorted ourselves out. I saw a photo of him in the paper, living in France. He'd put on a bit of weight, and looked so much healthier than he was in prison, so I'm really pleased for him.

*****

When I came out of prison for the last time, I was sat with my mum at her house, and something came on the news about historical abuse at children's homes in Wales, and we both looked at each other and started crying. It was finally an understanding between us of what had happened to me. I sat there and discussed it properly for the first time with Mum as an adult. And we just sobbed. It was so hard after all those years trying to explain exactly what kind of abuse I'd suffered — the gruesome details — but it felt like she finally believed me. Maybe Mum didn't always put two and two together, or didn't want to. She just didn't realise the full scale of it, bless her. She was widowed with four kids and three jobs, just trying to do her best.

Mum said we should do something about it, but we never did. I was approached by some guys in Scotland, who had been in homes in Wales too, but there are no computer records. And the people involved won't even be alive now. And even if they were, it would be so hard to prosecute any of them now, without DNA, etc.

I've even read that leading lawyers are calling for an investigation into the treatment of Borstal inmates around the time I was there, now describing our treatment as verging on torture. They're arguing we should receive compensation, but that would take some sorting out. They don't tend to like giving compo to people who have gone on to be career criminals, and many of us have.

Despite all the fights and the beatings I took from my brother Keith, I'm closer to him now, and love him to bits. He told me in later life what happened in the attic. He admitted that he knew all along, but didn't want to tell me as I grew through my teens because he could tell how powerful I was becoming, and he was sure I'd find my uncle and kill him. And it's true, maybe I would have devoted my life to killing paedophiles, and ended up doing even more time.

On one hand, it's so hard to work out the effect of the sexual abuse when I was a child because I try my hardest to bury it in the back of my mind, but if I really think about it, I can remember it as clear as day. Like it was yesterday. More than 60 years later, I often wake up with mental images of what happened to me in the attic or at the care home.

I read too much into every day situations. I'm aware of an adult holding a kid's hand too tightly. I can tell if a child is uncomfortable, as if something has already happened, or is about to happen. It's not difficult to bribe a child.

How much the awful things that happened to me in my childhood influenced my life of crime, I'll never be able to really say. Was it the sexual abuse that made me the person I became, and created the life I've led. Or was I born that way?

Just before I came out from the IPP, a guy called Dominic, aged in his early 20s, came to my mum's house in Mill Hill Road and announced he was the son of my uncle Raymond, my dad's brother. Because his surname was Rowlings and we were all Hills, Dominic had been trying to find us for ages. He was training to be a priest at university, and is qualified now.

Dominic explained that my dad, Patrick, was one of five brothers born in Ireland, along with Raymond, Roy, Stephen and John. All armed robbers. Turns out my dad and this little mob were always in trouble with the police for hold-ups and fighting in local pubs, and Raymond was the worst of them all. When my mum told me all about it, it got me wondering whether I simply had criminal genes. Maybe it wasn't the sexual abuse. I don't believe I was born to be a gangster or hurt people, but maybe I just came out a powerful, dangerous child.

I often wonder why I did not choose a path other than crime. All my family are straight-goers. Have had decent jobs. Never got into trouble. So why me?

My younger brother Bobby is a top chef, Keith is an electrical engineer, Diana had her own stables in Lingfield and Jackie was a school teacher. I'm also close with Diana, and she's been really helpful filling in a lot of gaps for this book.

If things were different for me back then, would I have got into less trouble? Surely the abuse didn't help. I've met so many guys in prison who were abused as kids or had abusive childhoods, who have been in trouble ever since, and fighting all their lives. It's impossible to know, and I should imagine the majority of people who have been abused probably don't commit any crime.

I also believe being able to handle doing my time was part of my downfall. It meant I continued to play the numbers game, and commit more crime, despite the continued consequences.

One thing is for sure, without the psychology courses during my IPP, I wouldn't have got out of prison. But what if I'd had a better education as a kid? So many ifs and buts.

*****

My family live normal lives. Some of them might be intrigued by my former gangster side, like many people are, but maybe not always the human side. It's that side I need to concentrate on now.

I was never around long enough, or at the right times when I was out, to build any normal relationships with my kids, and by always getting banged up I'm sure they feel I let them down again and again and again, which I fully accept.

Since his car accident, my eldest son has been through so much and spent many years in a wheelchair, cared for devotedly throughout by my ex-wife. He's been through so much and is a real survivor. He keeps in touch with his dad and we meet up, which I really appreciate.

My son and daughter with my girlfriend from Kingston live with their own families in Australia and America respectively, and have done well for themselves, so good luck to them.

I have another son, Ricky, from a previous relationship, who I'm in regular contact with and who visits me a lot, which I'm grateful for.

Mum died in 2018, aged 94. A tough life, which I didn't make any easier, I'm sure. I happily spent four or five days a week at her house in Mill Hill Road when I lived at the hostel in Ealing and then at the flat in Harrow. After being away for so much of both of our lives, the best part of three decades in total, being able to spend time with Mum in those final years was so precious. As ever, she was always there for me. The only person in my life really there for me, unconditionally.

When she passed, I believe it was easier for me to take than my brothers and sisters, because I was so used to being apart from Mum. I tried to deal with the trauma of her going in my own way and didn't go to the funeral. I felt it was time for the rest of my family to feel their own pain, without me as a distraction.

*****

I am in contact with some old friends, mostly the ones who are keeping out of trouble themselves now, but I have no contact at all with a lot of the key players and close pals I worked with, which is for the best. Those old days were crazy for everybody involved. All of us had to do our time along the way, but nine times out of ten, after it all goes tits up, there's not much left to say.

Lots of old mates have driven past me, put their hands over the side of the faces, and kept going. I've got used to it...comes with the territory.

I heard that Freddy was finally re-arrested after being on the run for 20-odd years. The authorities had been watching him for a long time and knew exactly when he was about to re-enter the UK for the first time, and nabbed him.

By the mid-2000s, the 'family friend' was starting a large sentence for major offences. A couple of years later, so I'm reliably informed, he had his sentence cut to just six years because of his 'generosity' with certain information.

Very recently, I found out that someone mentioned in this book tried to arrange a hit on me worth thirty grand. I was sent a copy of a police interview transcript from the early 2000s, in which that person told the police he had discussed the hit with an associate, who agreed to do it.

I'm sure there were enough people who wanted to take me out over the years. I am genuinely surprised that I wasn't removed.

I spent enough time working for people who based their lives on that of mafia don John Gotti — i.e getting rid of people who know too much. The amount of times I was called to a house at three in the morning for a pick-up, and it rarely occurred to me that I might get topped. If you think about the mafia movies, that's usually how they do it.

When I last came out, I met a beautiful lady, who has been an absolute rock to me. She was someone I could talk to who wasn't involved in my life of crime. All these years later, we're still close. Having that constant in my life has been so important. She knows who she is and how special she is to me.

Alan, who I worked together with loads, he's gone straight and sorted himself out and I'm really pleased for him. He's very much a family man, and we're still in touch, which is great.

A mate told me he'd bumped into an ex-girlfriend of mine, who had moved out of London to get away from the whole scene she was involved in. I said I'd love to see her and he said, 'Ray, you wouldn't. She's been doing crack ever since. She's in a bad way, no teeth, thin as a rake.' I meant it when I said I'd love to meet up with her again, and it pains me to think she is still in that rut, but I just can't be hanging out with people who are still involved in all that stuff.

Friends invite me out for dinners with their families. I rarely go because I find it hard and uncomfortable sitting in normal social situations — being around people talking about everyday things, which I can't always relate to. There are so many cameras in pubs and restaurants these days, I worry I'd get caught up in something.

*****

In 2023, I received a letter from the probation service asking for me to attend my first meeting in months, which ended with, 'Failure to attend this appointment will result in enforcement action,' which, after all that time, was a bit strong. Someone at probation services then told me I was one of the first IPPs to be released, and the only one they knew of that had been out as long as me, and had not reoffended or been recalled. That might explain why they didn't know what to do with me, and why nobody wanted to officially take me off the IPP.

Next I was given a probation officer, a new recruit, who didn't even know what an IPP was.

In April 2024, I was asked to attend a meeting with probation in Uxbridge. I fully expected the usual, 'I'm afraid, we don't have an update on your situation, Mr Hill...'

My probation officer, probably my tenth since my last release, was looking at her computer, going through my file, and then asked me to go back to reception, while she went upstairs.

I was sat there for about 45 minutes, before she came back down. In those moments, the longer I waited, the more I worried I was going to get a recall. What were they up to up there? I knew I'd kept out of trouble, but the paranoia has never left me...or the suspicions that the authorities are trying to fuck with my head.

Eventually, my probation officer appeared, holding an envelope. We went back into her office, and he handed it to me. I opened up the letter inside, on Parole Board-headed paper, and quickly scanned through to the last paragraph. As usual, it took me a while to read it and understand it but, fuck me, I honestly thought it was a wind up.

The panel concludes that it is no longer necessary for the protection of the public for Mr Hill to be subject to licence conditions. The IPP Licence is therefore terminated.

Wow. I was in shock. Both happy and relieved. Sure, it was so satisfying the IPP had been quashed, but when it had sunk in a few days later, it felt like I almost had to be extra careful. If I got caught up in something now, what would be the difference? Yes, I couldn't get recalled at the drop of a hat, but I wouldn't get bail either, so I'd be banged up on remand, which is basically the same thing. Pals asked me to come to pub to celebrate but, as usual, I kept my head down, and out of the spotlight.

I now realise I was spoiled as a gangster. For so long, I always had whatever I wanted, when I wanted. Because I was so feared, as an enforcer, my day-to-day business was getting a few grand, for just going to see someone and, most of the time, just having a word with them.

*****

As we finished writing this book, I was keen to track down Brian Cox, but it's almost 40 years since I've seen him, and he's become a huge star now.

I'd love to speak to Brian and thank him for all his support during the late '70s and early '80s.

I found some quotes online from an interview Brian gave to *Cheshire Live*, which I can now admit are quite fitting...

This world of gangsters and hard men is interesting territory, but I don't particularly like it as a culture. I find no glamour in these people. In Russia, they have a wonderful phrase about these sorts of men that goes, 'Little mice who blow off their own tail and become elephants' — which describes how they come to think they're bigger than they are. These criminal characters are dramatically interesting, but only in terms of their idiocy.

Brian, me old mate, you might just have hit the nail on the head there. I was an elephant who blew his own tusks off.

ACKNOWLEDGEMENTS

Ray would like to thank...

To my brothers and sisters. Keith and Diana — thanks for looking after me when we were younger, and being there for me. And a special mention for my younger sister and brother, Jackie and Bobby.

To Jamie, Jay, Ricky, Sonny and Ruby-Ray. I'm sorry I wasn't there for you.

A special shout out to Jay for the way you've battled through life. It's been great to see you recently. And to Ricky for also keeping in touch and for your visits.

Of course, the biggest thanks and respect to my darling Mum. And to the Nelhams (Nell and Alf and their children, my cousins, Terry, Roger, Pam, Christine and Dennis).

Many thanks to Christine for your support over the years. To Cherry and Harmony for being like family to me. To Danni for being an important part of my life. To Miracle for your loving friendship.

A massive shout out to these great friends and characters or big influences on my life (past and present)...

Lesley McIntyre, Nicky Smith, The Jakemans (Gary, Keith and Philip), Colin Cracknell, George Whelan, Harry Holland, The Collins family (Bobby, Philip, Whacker and Janet), Ray and Johnny Wells, Dennis Haley, Willy Waldron, Brian Cox, Cliff Field, Lenny McLean, Roy Shaw, Columbo, Steve Riches, Gary Francis, John Downing, Matty Howard, Terry Combes, Terry Sharpe, Frank Warren, Mickey Green, Eddie and Charlie Richardson, John Bindon, Jimmy Tippett Snr, Jimmy Tippett Jnr, Jefferson King, Danny Williams, Alec Jones, Mickey Gooch, Gary Stretch, Ray Sullivan, Nigel Benn, Nobby Griffiths, Ario, Junior Jospeh, Ken Edwards, Ernie Wise, Terry Oatway, the McCoys from Fulham, Matty Howard, Gordon Monaghan, Ronnie Sweet, Ian Bennett, Barry Henley, Raj Raj Armit, John Adair, Jamie Bennett, Fish and Ricky Masoero.

To Milo for introducing me to Christian Morgan and Marvin Herbert and a big thanks to Christian and Marvin for all your friendship and help too.

A huge thanks to my Offending Manager Christina Rowe for helping with my release on licence from The Mount ...and to my probation officer Bose Davies for all your help with the termination of my IPP. Thank you both so much.

To Shaun Attwood for your lovely foreword, kind words and support.

To the amazing subscribers of my *YouTube* channel. Thank you all.

A very special mention to Terry Haley, who has changed my life and stood by me throughout. Your friendship means so much. Don't forget about that watch and the flat, mate...haha...

Also to Terry's mad kids Jade (and Ricky), Kerry (and Barron), Lauren, Sam (and Amy) Danny and Jason, and all the lovely grandchildren.

And finally, to Matt Trollope for your his hard work on this book. It was an emotional journey, but we got there in the end, mate. Let me know how much I owe you for all the chicken, eggs and milk...and apple turnovers.

Matt would like to thank...

Ray for digging deep into your past to provide the amazing content for this book, and for your access all areas approach. The journey and process was heart-wrenching, harrowing, horrific and hilarious in equal measures. It was a pleasure to be on this bit of work with you.

Terry Haley for all your support throughout this project. It really couldn't have happened without you. Many thanks for pulling everything together and to the pair of you for all the banter and laughs throughout.

Nicola Thatcher at Keystone Law for your legal report and clarifications.

And thank you to the finest Silk in town for your courtroom continuity and procedural advice.

Meghan Christie for your proofreading services. Derek Charles for the extra read-throughs and for all your help.

Ian Vaughan at MT Ink for your patience and for everything you do behind the scenes. Thanks so much.

Genna Gibson for your constant support...and all your inputs.

Ian Cordingley for facilitating initial meetings. Much appreciated.

Vaibhav Punia for your great work on the cover spread and creating the 'younger Ray' image.

Jaqi Loye-Brown for your ears and advice.

Alistair Morgan, Helena Duncan and everyone at Bell & Bain for all things printing. Always a joy to work with.

MCA DUTY MEMBER DIRECTIONS
Version (1.2)

LICENCE CONDITION VARIATION REQUEST

Date: 11/03/2024

Prisoner Name: Raymond Hill

Prison Number: TD4845

Prison: Not applicable

Referral Type: Post-release

Result: Licence Condition Revoked

Reasons:

The duty member considered a dossier of 235 pages. No representations were received.

This case has been referred to the Parole Board by the Secretary of State under sections 31A of the Crime (Sentences) Act 1997 to consider whether or not it would be appropriate to terminate the licence.

Should the Board not agree to termination of the licence then they are also asked under sections 31 and 32 of the Crime (Sentences) Act 1997 to consider whether or not it would be appropriate to suspend the supervisory elements of the licence or add/amend/vary any additional conditions contained within the licence.

Mr Hill received an IPP sentence I 2007 for robbery. He was released in 2012. Since then the licence has been complied with and there has been no further offending or warnings. He has engaged with interventions during his sentence and is currently publishing a book. Probation/the IPP panel are in support of the IPP Licence being terminated.

The panel concluded that there is good evidence of the development of internal controls to support desistance from future offending. In particular, Mr Hill has demonstrated the ability to avoid further offending over a sustained period, evidencing improved self-control, good motivation and the ability to build a pro-social life for himself.

The panel concludes that it is no longer necessary for the protection of the public for Mr Hill to be subject to licence conditions. The IPP Licence is therefore terminated.

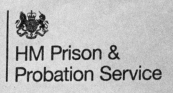

HM Prison &
Probation Service

HM Prison & Probation Service
Public Protection Group
Public Protection Casework Section

Raymond Roy Hill

14/05/2024   NOMS NO: A3255AL

Dear Raymond Hill

I am writing to you further to your application for your IPP licence to be terminated under section 31A of the Crime (Sentences) Act 1997.

The Parole Board agreed with your application and, as such, your licence is now terminated.

I therefore enclose a copy of the Parole Board's decision and the Licence Termination Order confirming this.

Therefore, your licence is cancelled, and all of your licence conditions cease to be in effect and may not be re-imposed.

Yours sincerely

Public Protection Casework Section

Enc.   Licence Termination Order

Parole Board decision

ALSO FROM MT.INK

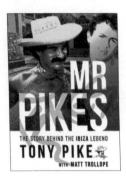

Mr Pikes: The Story Behind The Ibiza Legend — Tony Pike with Matt Trollope The playboy who built himself a playground reveals all in his hard-hitting memoir. The iconic hotelier reflects on a life of hedonism and the globe-trotting backstory that influenced his creation of pioneering Balearic boho bolthole, Pikes. Tony talks candidly about his relationships with hotel guests and friends including George Michael, Freddie Mercury, Julio Iglesias, lover Grace Jones and many more...and also goes exclusively behind the scenes at the legendary Wham! *Club Tropicana* video shoot.

The Life & Lines Of Brandon Block by Matt Trollope Brandon Block strips back his dramatic life as we chart the meteoric rise of a cocky schoolboy from Wembley who became an Ibiza legend along the way. A symbol for an acid house generation of excess, Brandon headlined a clubland era that changed the lives of millions. His spiralling drug habit peaked at an amazing ounce of cocaine a day but somehow he survived to tell the tale. This edition Includes extra chapters published in 2017 as Brandon entered the Celebrity Big Brother house.

Centreforce: House Music All Night Long by Matt Trollope The official biography and story of Centreforce, the first radio station to play house music 24-7 when it stormed London airwaves in 1989, and now a global digital success. Back to the past and into the future, via the music and scenes in between. Through the eyes and ears of Centreforce DJs, then and now, and producers behind the some of the station's biggest anthems. *'Watching the British people partying their minds out, all on the same pulse and rhythm, being touched by the music, was beautiful'* - Kevin Saunderson (Inner City).

DJ Wags: Housewives of House — Jaqi Loye-Brown (Portobello Novella Series 2) Some yummy mummies are not like the others. What lurks behind the domestic bliss of middle-aged party parents? Piper Blair and Dande Lyon's friendship comes to a head when their loyalties, love and lifestyle are tested under the spot-light of reality TV. Middle-aged, middle class and functioning...just! From Kensal Rise, Queens Park and Westbourne Grove to Ibiza and back again. From disco to discord...all the way.